Ethics and the Gulf War

Ethics and the Gulf War

Religion, Rhetoric, and Righteousness

Kenneth L. Vaux

Wipf and Stock Publishers
EUGENE, OREGON

Wipf and Stock Publishers
199 West 8th Avenue, Suite 3
Eugene, Oregon 97401

Ethics and the Gulf War
Religion, Rhetoric, and Righteousness
By Vaux, Kenneth L.
Copyright© January, 1992 Vaux, Kenneth L.
ISBN: 1-59244-146-7
Publication date: January, 2003
Previously published by Westview Press, January, 1992 .

Contents

Acknowledgments

The work of a moral philosopher takes on added verve when current events provide a moving backdrop for one's ethical reflections. The early months of 1991 and the war over Kuwait were such times of trouble, when issues of conscience were brought into sharp focus. Though Thornton Wilder's statement in *The Skin of Our Teeth* that "people are at their best in wartime" gives hollow justification for the risk and loss that war brings to so many people, conflict does force individuals and societies to declare their beliefs and values and take their stand for good or evil.

The winter and spring of 1991 were seasons of great moral wrestling and argumentation. For the benefit of the insight yielded by their passionate dialogue, I thank my fellow scholars in theology, history, and especially Judaic and Islamic studies at Oxford University. Regius Professors Oliver O'Donovan and Rowan Williams framed the debate with boldness and courage and stimulated a lively and respectful dialogue, not only in the university but also in the broader church and society. Their consultation regarding my own emerging convictions is gratefully acknowledged. I also thank the librarians at the Theological Faculty on St. Giles and my fellow kibitzers in numerous tea pauses, especially Alan, Simon, Chris, and Ted. Lindsey Hossack was swift and splendid in preparing the typescript. I thank the three women in my life, the two Saras and Catherine, for keeping body and soul together. My wife, Sara, as always, brings to my books not only any *baumherzigkeit* they may possess but any literary grace as well. Thanks to Bert Vaux for his preparation and editing of the bibliography and camera-ready manuscript and to Michael Blechner for preparing the final copy. I thank the Ben and Genevieve Wagner Ethics Bequest for support in the preparation of this book and my American connection, Bonnie Wilkie, for indispensable research assistance. Fay Dickerson graciously agreed to prepare the index. For permission to quote from Wilfred Owen's war poetry and to quote the "Jihad" article from the Encyclopedia of Religion I thank New Directions and Macmillan publishers.

This book contains many references to words and actions that remain uncited due to the rapidly unfolding events of this war. Although referencing these remarks noted from radio, television, newspapers, and magazines would overburden the general reader with an excessive apparatus, it regrettably shortchanges the scholar.

As I make the final revisions to this book our medical school has learned of the tragic death of our head, Dr. Abdul Waheed Sajid. To his gracious spirit, his ecumenical vision, and his legacy of excellence, I dedicate this book.

Kenneth L. Vaux

Preface

- On August 2, 1990, Iraq invaded and proceeded to occupy Kuwait. Iraq later said it had been assured that the United States would not interfere in this "border dispute."

- Iraq ignored ultimatums that it abandon Kuwait by January 15, 1991, and February 23, 1991, provoking the Allied air and ground assault.

- U.S. President George Bush prayerfully consulted the just war tradition.

- Iraqi President Saddam Hussein, taking to his prayer rug, invoked the rhetoric of holy war.

- The following forty days of air war and one hundred hours of ground war was one of the most one-sided campaigns in history.

- With cease-fire initiatives floundering in the UN, Iraq ordered its troops to withdraw from Kuwait.

- The Allies bombed a massive convoy of Iraqi military and civilian vehicles retreating on the Kuwait City–Basra highway, killing thousands.

- The Allies sustained 200, the Iraqis 200,000, casualties.

- The war's aftermath continues to unfold, with the infrastructure of Iraqi cities in ruins and civilians suffering from shortages of food, drinking water, shelter, and even rudimentary medical care.

Awe is the spiritual background of both shame and hope. At the dawn of the last decade of this shamefully war-filled century and tumultuous millennium, the world has witnessed geopolitical conflict in a tiny kingdom on the shore of the Persian Gulf named Kuwait. In certain prelude to wars that will one day be launched from the stars, this war transpired in electronic and laser wizardry in the skies over Kuwait and Iraq. In bitter irony, the great post-Christian powers, which unleashed this technological apocalypse, and the Islamic nation, which precipitated that display and then suffered the outcome, alike focused their imagination and conscience on those long-silent metaphors of "just" and "holy" war. Could such construal betray a contrition that might presage hope? The war would ring with an apocalyptic dread and expectancy.

In the wings back stage stood nation-Israel. That simmering cauldron of secularist and fundamentalist people, that noble and beleaguered people whom Matthew Arnold held knew where the world was going, chafed at the bit to enter center-stage after the bitter humiliation of Iraqi Scud missile attacks, yet was mercifully constrained by a more enlightened self-interest, or a more uncanny faith.

In the chaotic aftermath of this terrible conflict, the world has grown old and young again. The frigid necessity and irrevocability of war, which no one wanted, again haunted a world that seemed to lie so close to a springtime of renewal and freedom. A year that began with the ecstatic sounds of Beethoven's *Freude, Freude, Freiheit* at Berlin's Brandenburg Gate on the Kurfurstendamstrasse ended with the fiery massacre on the road to Basra. Yet even as the dark clouds of smoke from burning oil wells paint an ominous El Greco skyscape over Kuwait, a teenage girl decorates her room in Kuwait City, an Iraqi lad returns to school, and a twenty-year-old American POW named Melissa begins her long journey home to friends and family.

War, like birth and death--topics I customarily address--is sacramental in significance. It exudes damnation and liberation. Scenes of sacrament occasionally interrupted the patriotic, propaganda-laden media coverage of the war: a U.S. soldier kneels beside an Iraqi prisoner of war and in kindly fellowship shows him how to open the rations package that looks to be his first meal in some time. Their communion, against a background of explosion and flame, recalls the eschatological feast during World War I when French and German troops came together on Christmas Day 1914 in the no-man's land between their lines to share food, drink, and song in *koinonia* (fellowship).

In another scene, we who watched BBC during the conflict were allowed to see an Iraqi soldier, retired in weary fatigue from battle, crying bitterly as he carried the corpse of his seven-month-old baby from a Baghdad hospital. Oblivious to who caused the death of this child-- Saddam Hussein's aggression, the Allied embargo, or Norman Schwarzkopf's bombing--he and we could see only the tragedy of the slaughter of innocents. This *pietà*, this parent with dead child, evoked memories of Passover and of Herod's slaughter of the firstborn, deeper pictures of vicarious suffering and redemption that such poignant events must surely signify.

Reading religious, even moral, meaning into such traumatic events offends many people. The distinguished theologian and bishop of Durham, David Jenkins, argued that Prime Minister Major's proposed victory parade for homecoming British troops would be an obscenity. The director of the Muslim Institute in London, Kalim Siddiqui, decried the prospect that we would make "song and dance over a victory over a tiny dictator in the Middle East," adding, "It was hardly a war--there was no contest, in the air or on the land."[1] The call for sober and repentant commemoration rather than jubilant celebration was well-advised when recalling the fiasco after the London victory march at the end of the Falklands conflict in July 1982. The parade ended with a service at St. Paul's cathedral, led by the Archbishop of Canterbury. Prime Minister Margaret Thatcher was said to have been furious that the Archbishop avoided any note of triumph and instead led prayers for the bereaved on both sides.

A society imputes value or disvalue to any matter, including war, in imagery that identifies those things it finds to be true, good, and beautiful or false, evil, and offensive. Society's moral imagination about war can be traced in the history of ideas and in the history of battles. Names such as these punctuate a holy history (*Heilesgeschichte*) about war: Hammurabi, Moses, David, Cyrus the Persian, Judas Maccabaeus, Jesus, Paul, Augustine, Mohammed, Maimonides, St. Francis, Thomas Aquinas, Francisco Suarez, Hugo Grotius, Thomas Hobbes, John Locke, Pope Pius XII, Abraham Heschel, John Courtney Murray, Paul Ramsey, Fazlur Rahman, and John Howard Yoder. Ideas and cultural values about war and peace also come from writers like Shakespeare and Tolstoy and from composers like Shostakovich and Britten.

Events also contribute to our cache of normative ideas about warfare: the war over Kuwait, Panama, Grenada, Afghanistan, the Falklands, the Zulu War, the Six Day War, Vietnam, Suez, Korea, 1948-1949 wars over the plantation of Israel in Palestine, Hiroshima, World War II, wars of liberation against colonial oppression (for example, India versus the British presence), the Russian Revolution, World War I, the American Civil War, the Hungarian revolt of 1849, the French Revolution, the American Revolution, the war against the Native Americans, wars of the colonial period in Europe, the Thirty-Years War, the English Civil War, religious conflicts of the Reformation-counterreformation period, the Crusades, Medieval Islamic Jihad, Barbarian invasions, and Asian intrusions by the Huns, wars of the Roman and Greek conquests, wars against Israel and Judah, the Jewish wars to seize the land of Palestine.

From this residue of beliefs and events have emerged two tables of values, tables corresponding to the two Mosaic tablets of words, rules about what we can do and cannot do in war: *Jus ad bellum* and *Jus in bello* --the do's and don't's of war. This book will appropriate that evolving *logos*--that logic of just war--as an evaluative tableau to assess the good and evil of the war over Kuwait.

Just as a nation imbues meaning with its words about war, so any individual reflects his or her own biases and values in any interpretation. My own conscience is shaped by many forces and experiences, including the Christian pacifist tradition and the lasting imprint of the folly of the Vietnam War impressed on me as a young pastor; a healthy ecumenical respect for other world faiths and cultures, including Islam; a commitment to Israel; and a political advocacy of deterrence leading to disarmament. Finally, I view God as a warrior-savior effecting justice and peace in world history consummating in a kingdom of *shalom* here and now as well as there and then; a justice-building and peacemaking God who may at times make us make war. My conviction is shaped most intensely by the personal and pastoral tragedy of war as it leaves widows and orphans, kills innocents and combatants--the flowers of a generation--and usually leaves the conniving politicians unscathed.

The foregoing assumptions will shape the case I will set before the reader as well as the way in which I will structure the argument. In substance and style I hope to model the incisive thought of my mentors, Paul Ramsey and Oliver O'Donovan, whose thought opposes some facets of my own. Their careful commentary on the morality of warfare and their deep reservation about both the pacifism of the Church (as expressed by United Methodist and Church of England bishops) and the bellicism (O'Donovan's word) of the politicos and industrialists must be taken seriously by any Anglo-American ethicist.

The thesis I wish to propound is this: All rationalistic and certainly all theistic ethics abhor war and extol peace. Even the glorious commander, President Bush, still basking in the glory of the Kuwait campaign, had to agree with Independence Day protestors in Michigan that war was not a great and glorious thing. A religious worldview, aware of people's aggressive and malevolent inclinations, works forcefully for the peaceful reconciliation of differences and the robust establishment and maintenance of peace, under the mandate of the *shalom* of God for all creation and humankind. Yet hope keeps us realistic against the backdrop of sin. Conflict will erupt; and our task when prevention fails is to pursue justice, even the justice of punishment with force measured to the offense, careful safeguarding of the immunity of the innocents, and strong healing dispositions of mercy, forgiveness, and restoration as conflicts cease. When the Zumwalts[2] and our commanders in this campaign declare that the objectives of war are to hastily achieve your mission with minimal loss of life to your side, they cut away the broader fabric of defensible and righteous war and leave us with only tattered shreds.

The war over Kuwait not only challenges us to reaffirm traditional war ethics but also moves to a new level our understanding of what makes a war just. Intensified prohibition of chemical, biological, and nuclear warfare has been achieved. As in the conflicts in the Falklands, Afghanistan, Hungary, the Six Day War, Grenada, and Panama, it becomes clear that new conventions are needed where gross asymmetry of power exists. New guidelines are required for the high-tech laser and electronic war technology that has added an element of precision (the "surgical strike") but has also deprived war of any spontaneity and unpredictability, rendering war strategically obsolete. Just as a missile guided down to target on a laser beam cannot miss, the new warfare can involve no sport or honor. A war in this age or the age of Star Wars can be decided before it begins; it therefore need not begin. Rapprochement between pacifist theological ethics and realistic political ethics promises today to yield a richer and more relevant just war theory. Judaic, Christian, and Islamic responses to the war show a theological renewal that both tempers the aggressive tendencies inherent in modern tribalism, nationalism, and economic opportunism and offers a more ecumenical vision for a future world order where popular justice and liberty is served.

In this book I will ask whether the moral rhetoric employed by both sides was borne out in responsible action and search out the possibility of hope arising from the ashes of such a "wonder-full" war with its legacy of grievous waste. I will ask whether the unexpected resort during the conflict to traditions of justice and pacifism might offer hope for a newer and better world order in years to come and reflect on the causes, motives, actions, and sequelae of this war in light of the holy war, just war, and pacifist traditions. Examining this war as a particular case study yields a test of those time-honored precepts in light of new geopolitical, technological, and theological realities. I believe we will find that the stipulations of just war, chastened by the polar antinomies of pacifism and holy war, are not anachronistic but indispensable for sound politics and viable peace in our time.

This book will explore the sacramental and symbolic significance of war in general and this war in particular. By sacrament I mean earthly manifestation of the spiritual, and by symbol I refer to the way that we construe meaning with imagination and words. A long tradition of thought about what justifies the inception and execution of a war exists in Western Christian civilization. Just war theory in Western culture is enriched and challenged by three other religious ethics concerning war--Judaic war ethics, jihad (Islamic Holy War), and pacifism. These sometimes convergent, sometimes divergent traditions, active in the ideological and ethical impulses of that conflict, will also be explored in an attempt to comprehend and draw resolve from the war over Kuwait. This is a study of what might be called righteous rhetoric. Was the religious and moral rhetoric feigned or sincere? Did it lead to ethical action? Did it finally produce morally worthy ends?

In the first chapter I will delineate in a preliminary way the principal themes of just war theory and how these themes might have pertained to the unfolding events in the war over Kuwait. I will offer a chronicle of the war with initial commentary intended not to settle matters, but to offer suggestive leads into the deeper reflections to follow. I will then proceed to a revised rendition of a moral axiology of warfare by looking at war ethics in Biblical and modern Israel, in Iraqi Islam, and in Christian tradition. As particular moral themes about war and peace in these traditions surface, I will relate these to circumstances in the war over Kuwait, reviewing the secular lineage of just war tradition, again applying its norms to the war over Kuwait, and noting the moral lessons of that war in particular. Finally, I will project concrete moral implications for war and peace in the society that will emerge from that war and examine the prospects for a much touted "new world order." I will also ponder the ethical and eschatologic vision that should shape such an order. The reader will find a multi-dimensional ethical theory unfolding in which ecology, biology, psychology, philosophy, history, theology, and eschatology are bound together in the suffering, judgment, death, and transfiguration of all nature and history. Ethical positivism that comes from philosophy, law, or religion is tedious and uninteresting. Though the ethical yield of this more expansive system is wide-ranging and elusive, in the end it is more satisfying than arid speculation.

K. L. V.

Notes

1. "Bishop Attacks Victory Plans," *Independent*, March 4, 1991, p. 9.
2. E. R. Zumwalt and J. G. Zumwalt, "Bombing was justified to rein in rogue Iraq," *USA Today*, July 1, 1991, p. 11A.

1

An Introduction
to Just War Ethics

In antiquity we find both bellicist and pacifist traditions of war. The Greeks and Romans both justified and extolled war. Cicero's apologia for the Roman Empire is the classic example of this approach. Other literary texts and dramas resisted this patriotic and legal corpus. Homer, for example, laments the rude necessity and bitter human waste of war. Yet despite this somber realism, on the whole we find classical authors exulting in power, conquest, and victory.

Primitive Christianity brought to the world the plaintive cry of love and peace. "Who lives by the sword will die by the sword" (Matthew 26:52).[1] "I say to you, love your enemies and pray for those who persecute you" (Matthew 5:44). "Vengeance is mine, I will repay saith the Lord" (Romans 12:19). Encouraging passive endurance of persecution while awaiting the Lord's imminent return, the early Church held to a serene detachment from and disdain for the world in all its ways, including warfare. But withdrawal eventually gave way to participation, and the expectation of the end of time yielded to an accommodation for the time being. A theory of just war emerged from the pens of the two great scholars of the first millennium of the Christian era: Augustine and Aquinas. Blending scriptural and secular values, they formulated a tradition which might be summarized as follows:

Augustinian/Thomistic Tradition of Just War

A. There is a greater merit in preventing war by peaceful negotiation and conciliation than in vindicating rights by bloodshed.

B.   Peace attained by conciliation is better than peace attained by victory.

C.   There is a natural society of mankind which gives rise to certain rights and duties relevant to the morality of war.

D.   The absence of a superior tribunal before which a prince can seek redress can alone justify him in making war, except when he resists actual attack.

E.   Saving the direct intervention of God, the following conditions must in addition be fulfilled before a war can be just:

1.   It must have a *just cause*: this can only be a grave injury received (e.g., actual invasion; unlawful annexation of territory; grave harm to citizens or their property; denial of peaceful trade and travel) or a great injustice perpetrated upon others whom it is a duty to help (e.g., the same injuries as above, violation of religious rights).

2.   It must be *necessary*: that is, the only available means of restoring justice or preventing the continued violation of justice.

3.   It must be consequence of a *formal warning* to the offending state and must be formally *declared*.

4.   It must be declared and waged only by the *sovereign authority* in the state (i.e., one who has no political superior) and, if the defense of religious rights is involved, with the *consent of the Church*.

5.   The good to be attained by war must be reasonably supposed to be *greater than the certain evils*, material and spiritual, which war entails.

6.   A *right intention* must actuate . . . the declaration, conduct, and conclusion of war. That intention can only be the restoration or attainment of true peace.

7.   *Only so much violence* may be used *as is necessary*: in the case of defense, only so much as is necessary to repel the violence of the aggressor.

F.   The *moral responsibility* for war lies upon the *sovereign authority*, not upon the individual soldier or citizen: his duty is to obey, except in a war which he is certainly convinced is wrong.

G.   Priests may not fight, even in just war.

H.   The duty of *repelling injury inflicted upon another* is the common obligation of all rulers and peoples.[2]

Now that the war over Kuwait has apparently smoldered to an ignominious close and we watch the ghastly sequelae like the exodus of Kurdish refugees and the deaths of children from cholera and malnutrition, we may ask how the entire event measures up to these general moral criteria.

Commentary on Sections A – D. Lively debate continues as to whether, in Pete Seeger's words, we really did "give peace a chance." The sanctions policy was given five months to work with little evidence of repentant effect on Saddam Hussein and his lieutenants, even if severe deprivation was being felt in the community. Even the circle of "commanders"--Colin Powell, Norman Schwarzkopf, Richard Cheney, James Baker, and others--felt that sanctions should be given time to work.[3] In all human relations belligerence as a passion always hardens into deluding and destructive force, especially when superiority or inferiority is certain. Numerous warnings and ultimata were issued by the Allied powers, but most efforts at genuine concession and negotiations were rebuffed by those same powers. The United Nations proved to be a superb forum for the development of an international coalition opposed to Iraqi aggression against Kuwait, but when it came to peacemaking efforts at crucial junctures, as when the deadlines approached and when Soviet initiatives were offered near the war's end, the UN proved again to be an agency crippled by Third World rhetoric and first world manipulation as it has always been throughout its brief history.

UN Secretary-General Pérez de Cuéllar was not given sufficient authority by the United States, Great Britain, and Israel to act as a powerful conciliator, and in the end he could only accede to the inevitable violence. Perhaps in retrospect we can be grateful and hopeful that the United Nations was taken seriously even with these reservations and impediments. The coordination of commitment (and restraint) from nation-states as diverse as the Unites States, Britain, France, Saudi Arabia, Syria, Egypt, Iran, Israel, and the USSR may portend a future with more international reciprocity and resolve than we have known in the past.

Commentary on Section E-1. The certainty of "just cause" actually appears ambivalent. On the one hand, a situation of clear aggression, unlawful annexation of territory, and acts of brutality, even atrocity, against the people of Kuwait did exist. On this one point the war was clearly justified. On the other hand, the background causes are less clear. Was the situation between Iraq and Kuwait a "border dispute," in which case just war theory counsels noninvolvement? Was the "superior tribunal" of the United Nations given mediating authority, or was it strong-armed into belligerent action? Iraq claimed that unhindered passage into the Gulf was at stake and sovereignty over the islands of Bubiyan and Warba was disputed. Limiting access to the sea was accepted by the Western nations as a just cause for Israel's action in the

Suez conflict (1956) and the United States' intervention in Panama (1989). Were not Iraq's concerns the same? Then there was the matter of the Rumaila oilfield. If this reservoir of oil extends beneath both countries, and if Kuwait insisted on siphoning off the reserve extravagantly for low prices, was Kuwait committing a life-threatening aggression against Iraq? If, as some documents suggest, the United States had been consulted about whether it would intervene in this border dispute and assured Iraq that it would offer only verbal protest, as it had in the annexations by Israel (the West Bank, the Gaza Strip), Turkey (Cyprus), and China (Tibet), was there not a violation of good faith with Iraq?

Then there was the issue of Saddam Hussein's claimed messianic mission as advocate of the oppressed Islamic and Arabic peoples, including the Palestinians. Not only had the rights of these people been violated by Israel, they were severely oppressed under the Kuwaitis. Hundreds of thousands of Palestinians and other foreign workers in Kuwait did all of the dirty and servile work of the ruling al-Sabah family which ran the country. Was there an existing injustice in Kuwait directly and occupied Palestine indirectly that justified or at least created extenuating circumstances to Iraq's aggression? Did high-level U.S. and British interests in Kuwaiti Inc., Gulf Oil, Chevron, Zapata, even Beckwith Engineering, force the West into silence over this injustice? [4]

The modern political history of Kuwait is as ethically questionable as the dismemberment of the Ottoman and Arabic empire which gave it birth decades ago. Ruled over by the al–Sabah family, none of the thousand members of the Emir's ruling family appeared to perform socially useful work. The work of the society (except perhaps playing the stock market) was carried out primarily by Palestinians, Philippinos, and other aliens, none of whom had any legal rights. Today only 10–15 percent of the population--males who can trace their lineage to the 1920s --have the right to vote. Even after the establishment of a constitution and parliament in 1962, all MPs were from the royal family. The maids and man-servants were often beaten and kept in hideous conditions. The oil speculation of the Kuwait Corporation (in cooperation with British and United States Gulf interests) eventually brought about a crash much like the savings and loan debacle in the United States. When democratic opposition emerged in the late 1980s, parliament was dissolved and secret police reportedly killed, bombed, gassed, and otherwise silenced the opposition. With its approximately U.S. $100 billion investment fund, the ruling family escaped from Kuwait to Saudi Arabia on the first day of the Iraqi invasion. Was there a situation of popular democratic uprising in the face of severe injustice that should long since have prompted the Allies to take serious steps towards assuring human rights rather than resorting to war? Regrettably, the Western nations have not seen fit to intervene in such cases of tyranny beyond, for example, under-the-table support for the Afghan and Philippine freedom fighters against the Soviet hegemony and the Marcos corruption, offering only rhetoric and minimal economic and diplomatic sanctions in China (Tienanmen), Ethiopia, and most similar popular uprisings. In Kuwait the charred country has already been turned over to the Crown Prince for a three-month period of martial law.

Commentary on Section E–7. Was proportionate force employed? Here there was notable equivocation in the Allied purpose. The UN resolutions demanded the unconditional withdrawal of Iraqi presence from Kuwait. The Allied purpose quickly moved beyond that aim to the dismantling of Iraq's military capacity, then of its social infrastructure. The destruction of communications and supply systems, water, electricity, bridges, roads, and in general the whole society probably was overkill. From U.S. General Colin Powell's initial threat of megawar to the final blitzkrieg of fleeing vehicles on the Basra road, we probably killed far more soldiers and civilians than was necessary. As in the nuclear bombing of Nagasaki and Hiroshima, the full human toll will take years to work out.

It must be acknowledged that from the outset the Allies sought to limit civilian destruction and thus in part honored just war conventions. Pinpointing military targets with the awesome capacities of "smart weapons" could restrict collateral damage. But by the end of the war, resolve to end it swiftly replaced reserve and resulted in the bombing of the Amilaya bomb shelter, killing 500 civilian women and children; probable damage to some hospitals (some of which Saddam had cruelly doubled as military sites); and divisions of hunkered down, weaponless thousands, in the cool, impersonal rhetoric of war, eliminated by unresisted air assault.

Further analysis of the propriety of this war, viewed against the canons of just war theory, will punctuate the examination of the theological and secular sources for the just war. In the next chapter, the unfolding saga of the war over Kuwait with reference to that ethical typology will be reviewed. For the moment, I have sought only to outline just war ethics and show how specific developments in this particular war could be evaluated in that light.

The Mennonite pacifist theologian John Howard Yoder has said that four options are possible when we reflect on the meaning and morality of war.[5] Between the poles of war as an inherently amoral venture ("realism") and "holy war" are the options of "just war" and "pacifism." In the following pages, I will argue that the present state of moral and military affairs, and a casuistic moral analysis of this war, requires a just war theory that borrows important elements from the other three approaches. Yoder says that we must chose which ideology we will serve. I contend rather that the new conditions of warfare exemplified in the war over Kuwait call for a new just war theory which borrows from all approaches.

Notes

1. All Biblical quotations are my own translation or paraphrase unless otherwise noted.

2. John Epstein, *The Catholic Tradition of the Law of Nations,* Washington, D.C.: Catholic Assn. for International Peace, 1935, p. 92-93.

3. T. Woodward, *The Commanders,* New York: Simon and Schuster, 1991.

4. For a discussion of the "oil factor" see D. Yergin, "Oil: The Strategic Prize" in *The Gulf War Reader: History, Documents, Opinions,* ed. M. L. Sifry and C. Cerf, New York: Random House, 1991.

5. John Howard Yoder, *When War Is Unjust,* Minneapolis: Augsburg, 1984.

2

War Chronicle:
The Ethics of the War over Kuwait

The chronicles of the judges and kings in the Bible record in a special way the martial and political history of the Hebrew people. Authors like Thucydides or Josephus did not merely record a chain of events but rather a narrative that captured the meaning of those events. In this chapter I will attempt such a chronicle of the events in the war over Kuwait. While trying to be true and unbiased to the actual causes and events of the war as they unfolded, I will also place them in a context of ethical and spiritual meaning. The reader will ascertain my attempt to hold a tableau of just and holy war values as a backdrop to the unfolding saga of that war. These values will be described in subsequent chapters. However, my bias will be evident. On the one hand, I am limited to the reporting of the Western and English-language press and news media. On the other hand, the reader will sense a critical perspective, because as a theologian and moralist I seek to respond more to universal and transcendent values than a purely nationalistic and secular perspective might allow. Finally, I write this chronicle with a particular normative historiography in mind. Events, I will contend, are enfolded within a divine purpose: *Heilsgeschichte*. Holy, humane, and just patterns of meaning can be discerned in historical events as they prompt us to approve or disdain those actions on the basis of some ethical purview. I see redemptive movement in events as goodness and innocence call down and endure suffering and death in order to effect transfiguration and renewal.

This chapter is divided according to the major phases of the war from prelude to aftermath and through the central active episodes from

August 1990 through April 1991. This window of history necessarily brackets the phenomenon and regrettably ignores the larger patterns of prologue and sequellae. Commentary and interpretation will be offered to each descriptive section.

Prelude

A U.S. official told the press on April 10, 1991, that an undersecretary of commerce, Dennis E. Kloske, was told to vacate his desk by June 1 because he had testified to a House subcommittee that the government had ignored warnings in early 1990 to limit shipments of U.S. technology to Iraq.[1] This incident and others like it form the starting point for evaluating whether the war over Kuwait was just in its conception and inception.

I have noted how the United States, and the West more generally, supported Saddam Hussein and the Ba'ath government during the 1980s because of our fear of the Shiah government in Iran, following the revolution that ousted our favored regime of the Shah. Western arms supplied to Iraq supplemented the enormous provisions of the Soviet Union. Saddam Hussein's administration was schooled in the techniques of chemical and biological warfare in the United States and was supplied with materials by Germany and other Western powers.

For a war to be fully justified there must be an unmitigated aggression committed against an innocent party. If an aggressor is lured or pushed into that action by deception, or if bad actions encourage the aggression, the guilt is complicated and the rightness of counterjudgment is called into question. Granted, no vicious act is ever pure and unaided, and no distance from malevolence is ever pure and complete. Yet the history of inaction by the Western powers--even complicity in a long series of aggression--and the character, however well intentioned, of their cooperative preparation of Iraq for what might erupt in violence in the region from the outset invites our skepticism about the righteousness of the eventual onset of war.

Perhaps the most pronounced economic injustice in the world is found in the disparity between rich and poor in the Arabic world. As the prophet Mohammed found in his day, a millennium after a similar judgment by Amos and the prophets of Israel in early Semitic culture, the discrepancy of wealth between nations and individuals within nations had become unconscionable. The emirates--Kuwait, Saudi Arabia, and the United Arab Emirates--enjoy unparalleled wealth even as the poor nations--Egypt, Jordan, Syria, Iraq, and especially diaspora Palestine--grovel in abject poverty. Iraq sought to position itself as champion of the Palestinians in particular and of "the common people" of the Arabic world in general. Adding to this sense of manifest destiny, Iraq felt bitter against Kuwait for its noninvolvement in the war against Iran (even though it had provided U. S. $10 billion in aid).

Release from oppression in holy war and just war conviction is one of the objectives which justifies judgment and militancy. To fight oppression is justification for war. Although modern examples have usually arisen in internal revolutions or rebellions (e.g., American Revolution, Russian Revolution, the Philippine rebellion against Ferdinand Marcos), there have also been interstate conflicts (e.g., Namibia vs. South Africa, North vs. South Vietnam, Nicaragua vs. El Salvador). Usually mighty powers aid other mighty and oppressing powers in subjugating the poor and squelching neighbors who seek liberation. In the case of the war over Kuwait the pervasive injustice of the Kuwaiti state should long since have precipitated vigorous preventive action by advocates of human rights and humanitarian justice. The threat of war should have led to vigorous attempts to find peaceful solution to grievances. The hundreds of billions of dollars spent on the war could have been redirected to meet the basic needs of people for food, clothing, shelter, health care, education, employment, and a homeland.

Another element that complicated the etiology of the war was *oil*. On August 15, 1990, a high-placed adviser to President Bush said, "In terms of directional clarity [moral legitimacy?], this has all been an easy call. Even a dolt understands the principle. We need the oil. It's nice to talk about standing up for freedom, but Kuwait and Saudi Arabia are not exactly democracies . . . there's nothing to waiver about here . . . If Kuwait's export was oranges . . . there would be no issue."[2] In addition to seeing himself as a liberating Saladin or Nebuchadnezzar, Hussein saw himself as the OPEC quota buster. Kuwait and Saudi Arabia had sought to limit the flow and price of oil to accommodate investment interests. When Iraq invaded Kuwait, 20 percent of the world's known oil reserves were in Iraqi hands and by annexing Saudi Arabia, Iraq would increase that to 40 percent. That prospect was intolerable to the West. Since 1973 the Western economies have been constantly threatened by oil prices--which have risen from U.S. $3 to near U.S. $30 per barrel--and if the affluent economies of the West were threatened, those of Eastern Europe would have their fragile currencies devastated by additional manipulation. When Bush, in unguarded comments right after the occupation said that this crisis was about oil and the American way of life, he spoke a real but unsavory truth.

The acquisition or retention of resources does not justify beginning a war against another country. At best the insatiable Western demand for cheap oil could only be a secondary reason to declare war against Iraq in occupied Kuwait and in its homeland. If one could construe the crisis as one of national security and national defense, a case might be made for a war to be justly waged over oil. But as the matter stands, the West is extravagantly consuming not only oil but all the other natural resources of the earth at an alarming rate. No war justification can be found here.

In the weeks before the August 2 occupation, the U.S. Congress debated sanctions against Iraq for its threats against Kuwait. The Bush administration told Congress sanctions were unnecessary. On July 25, when reconnaissance pictures showed Iraqi military buildup on the northern border of Kuwait, U.S. Ambassador April Glaspie told Saddam Hussein that Bush wanted the United States to "expand and deepen its relationship with Iraq," implying to Iraq's leaders that the United States would not come to the support of Kuwait in this "border dispute."

War is often preceded by conciliatory gestures and optimistic words. Indeed, because a cause of initiating war is often to camouflage a grievous domestic crisis, economic or otherwise, the crisis is often clouded over by euphemistic and misleading rhetoric. One of the criteria of just war, which the British honor much more scrupulously than do the Americans, is the requirement of honesty and good faith. When British planes inadvertently bombed civilian sites in Iraq, they admitted it and apologized. When the American's bombed the shelter at Amilaya, they denied that it happened, then claimed the site was a command post, and when reporters examined the ruins as 500 dead women's and children's bodies were removed and found no command post, the rhetoric turned to flawed intelligence rather than confessing fault. When misleading rhetoric has led an adversary into a dangerous position, it is the responsibility of that misleading party to do everything possible to back away from an impending confrontation because one's own hands are bloodied with the provocative cause.

The final preliminary matter that a war chronicle must mention is the actual and imputed character of the adversary. Too much has been made of this being the war of Saddam Hussein or George Bush. If those individuals alone and not their nations and spheres of interest were involved, why not have the two strong men joust as representative warriors, as did David and Goliath, or medieval kings like England's Henry V? It is reported that Charles V volunteered to arm wrestle Francis rather than drag their entire peoples into the quagmire of war.

Much of the justification reasoning during the months before the air war focused on the character of Saddam Hussein. His violence in the Iran-Iraq war, his gassing of the Kurds, his stern discipline, even execution, of insubordinate generals were all woven into the caricature of a grotesque, Hitler-like dictator who needed to be liquidated before anyone in the world could sleep peacefully. Certainly there is much that is reprehensible in his character and his actions; these character flaws wove into a *causus belli* because of the threat this madman posed to Israel and the rest of the world if allowed to continue to expand his chemical and biological warfare capacity and even make Iraq a nuclear power. At one point in October or November the Western news media already had his finger on the nuclear trigger.

The actual and imagined violence of Saddam Hussein seemed to play a large part in the moral, almost Manichean, imagination of George Bush as he contemplated the justice of impending war. Later in the chronicle I will note Bush's grave concern over the atrocities against the Kuwaitis and the abuse he feared against the U.S. embassy staff and Western hostages. In his fierce difference of opinion with the majority of U.S. religious leaders (including his own Presiding Bishop) on the justice of the cause, he felt that he could not stand idly by while a madman was brutalizing innocent people. The analogy to Hitler was not original to the President, but surely his mind swept back to the Axis powers of Hitler, Mussolini, and Tojo and to his own miraculous Moses-like rescue from the waves of the Pacific Ocean during World War II. Was he spared for this personal Batman encounter with the Joker?

This kind of caricaturing, demonizing, and myth making is one of the most serious threats to world peace. It seems so natural to satanize the other and divinize our own cause. The just war criterion it violates is that which requires us to respect the adversary and the people who are the enemy: We must recognize the basic humanity of our fellows even when they fight opposite us. Evil is possible in the enemy as it is possible in us. When such a horrendous picture of Satan is applied to one's adversary, it is often the projection of something we see and fear in ourselves and in the end the exaggeration of Hussein's Draculan character, like the West's estimate of his political might, was just that--exaggeration.

Waiting and Warning

In the middle of the night of August 2, 1990, T-72 tanks of the Republican Guard churned toward Kuwait City as the Iraqi army occupied Kuwait. The several thousand members of the ruling al-Sabah family had already fled to Saudi Arabia. Claiming the necessity for access to the Gulf through the delta of the Tigris and Euphrates rivers at the uninhabited islands of Bubiyan and Warba and condemning the injustice of the Kuwaiti exploitation of the Rumaila oil field, Saddam Hussein restated the historic Iraqi claim to Kuwait as the nineteenth Iraqi province.

Though the claim to uninhabited land is justified in the just war thought of Grotius, Hobbes, and Locke, it has no relevance today. If such territories were necessary for the defense and well-being of Iraq, that country should have gone to the World Court in The Hague. Because that court is firmly within the ideological grip of the Western nations, the appeal would have had no effect. The only way to ensure that needed access would have been for Iraq to present the justice of the cause to the Arab League and then to subsequently mount an international appeal. Insecure access to the world's seas has been a legitimate just war cause since Grotius's *Mare Liberum,* but the occupation was an unjustified aggression, a clear violation of the central premise of just and holy war and a fatal political blunder that in the end could cost up to half a million lives.

On the days immediately following the occupation, Saudi Arabia, no doubt encouraged by the United States, appealed for protection against further Iraqi incursion into its own territory. The United States immediately initiated a ship embargo, subsequently extended by the UN. Meeting on August 7 and 8, the Arab League voted to condemn Iraq's actions by a vote of 14 to 7 (Iraq, Jordan, Libya, Sudan, Yemen, Mauritania, and the PLO dissenting); the league also approved the embargo against Iraq (only Iraq, Libya, and the PLO dissented). Saddam Hussein declared jihad (later to be seconded by Iran) saying "Oh Arabs! This is your day to rise up and defend Mecca [get Saudi Arabia?] which is captured by the spears of the Americans and Zionists." In September Iran's Ayatollah Khomeini echoed the holy war call saying "anyone who fights American aggression has engaged in jihad in the cause of Allah and anyone killed on that path is a martyr" (BBC).

The Islamic fabric of the Arabic world is hopelessly torn asunder and disparate, and all vestiges of the noble ethics of Islamic jihad have been lost in the cacophony of confused voices. Shi'ite and Sunni, Kurdish and Ba'athist versions of Islam are all colored by parochial and political ambitions. These make the call for jihad an uncertain trumpet which no one follows. The Arabic and Islamic world has very legitimate causes for jihad against the United States and the West. The atrocity of the Palestinian exile is perhaps the most grievous injustice of our time, and jihad might appropriately be called for to liberate these peoples from U.S.-encouraged oppression. This cry must be made to those who believe in Israeli prophetic justice, in the Christian conscience of love and concern for the weak and poor, and in secular-humanist values of fundamental human rights, good will, and peace on earth.

During September a series of promising peace initiatives began, all flawed by the common psychological error of presenting a belligerent ultimatum. President Bush met Mikhail Gorbachev at the Helsinki summit. UN Secretary-General Pérez de Cuéllar and French President

François Mitterrand began diplomatic efforts to secure peace. Regrettably, all efforts focused single-mindedly on Iraq leaving Kuwait with no acknowledgment of the underlying grievances and sense of injustice that precipitated Iraq's action. On October 1, Saddam Hussein sent a rambling 90-minute videotape to the West to outline his cause. It fell on deaf ears.

Very few Americans or Britons have lived among Arab peoples or learned to appreciate their unique values and beliefs, their styles of culture and speech, their grace and hospitality, or their fearful response when threatened. The number of Arabic-speaking consultants to the U.S. or British governments during this phase of watching and waiting was negligible. The most certain moral voice in the United States, familiar with the Arabic soul through years of interchurch contact and missionary activity, was that of the religious leadership. That voice was systematically ignored by the government and the press. The necessity of hearing plaintive cry (the Hebrew Bible's word for *grace* is an onomatopoetic word mimicking the cry of a mother camel searching the desert for her lost calf), of bargaining and bartering in the bazaar, of breaking bread together to work out differences--all were ignored by the West, which could only issue implacable and impossible ultimatums. Holy war and just war first and foremost desire the peace and truce of God. When U.S. officials fearfully asked, "What will we do if Saddam actually pulls out?" it was clear that this pacific goal was far from official minds. The unfolding events that showed our impatience to "get the thing over with" and rebuffs of all efforts at negotiation, settlement, even withdrawal proved the U. S. intention to be inimical to just war.

The first months of Western response to Iraqi occupation of Kuwait concentrated judgment into an act of siege and embargo. It began with great promise. All members of the UN Security Council, even Yemen, concurred in the decision. Iraq received 95 percent of its foreign earnings from the export of oil and 80 percent of its food was imported. Iraq imposed rationing, calling on its "great women" to exceed the austerity measures Great Britain practiced in World War II, and though UN sanctions made exception for foodstuffs and medicaments, the pinch was felt early. It soon became clear, even to a CIA study, that six to eight months of embargo would bring Iraq to its knees. But a siege is primitive and at best medieval; with F-111 fighters, Cruise missiles, and laser homing devices, why resort to a technique as old as Joshua? Impatience and skepticism as to efficacy won out only a few weeks after the embargo began.

Siege, the oldest form of total war, involving the entire community, is more and less brutal. Hitler's two-plus years' siege of Leningrad wrought on that civilian population what a nuclear bomb would have done instantaneously. Siege is indiscriminate warfare, with civilians being the principal target. Collective starvation, whether.in the Roman siege of Jerusalem in A.D. 72, Hitler's siege of Leningrad in 1941, or the beleaguered Kurds dying in the mountain passes leading into Iran and Turkey, is bitter agony. Moral law and war ethics have always insisted on a means of escape. The Talmudic law of sieges formulated by Maimonides in the twelfth century and affirmed by Grotius in the seventeenth, required that people be enabled to flee for their lives: The enemy could surround them only on three sides. The boycott of an entire nation does not permit this grace. In the Deuteronomic code and in Quranic teaching influenced by Judaism, trees, especially trees used for food, are not to be destroyed in a siege (Deuteronomy 20:20).

The embargo on Iraq should have been allowed at least nine months or a year to work. Siege is an ancient and traditional language of judgment that the people of a country like Iraq and a leader like Saddam Hussein could understand. The ambivalence, impatience, even cruelty of joining the confrontation on those terms and then immediately changing the rules of the game from a defensive to an offensive strategy was an unfortunate turning onto a path that eventually ended in hundreds of thousands of deaths. The lesson of patience would have been important to learn and practice, as the only just war that can be fought in a nuclear age will be one of severe limitation of combat to conventional means, difficult political bargaining, conflict forswearing recourse to other weapons--poison or nuclear--that could end it quickly. The contrary idea in just war thought (to end matters swiftly even if maximal force is required, so that in the end fewer people are harmed--the rationale of Hiroshima), runs the danger of causing vastly multiplied mortality. This idea that war is hell, most forcefully expressed in the nineteenth century by generals Karl von Clausewitz and William Tecumseh Sherman, creates a dangerous justification and is therefore obsolete in our time.

In the final days of the war in spring 1991, the final 300 Jews in Albania emigrated to Israel. This development ominously symbolized a world growing tragically more parochial in the epoch punctuated by the Gulf War. We are creating a world where there may be no Christians in Israel or Arabia, no Jews in Europe and the Soviet Union, and perhaps no Muslims in Christendom. Consider the data: With the imposition of Sharia law in Pakistan and potentially in Algeria and Libya, we are witnessing the gradual depluralization of the Muslim world. The Chaldean Christians in Iraq may soon be a lost community. Today only 6 percent of Arabia is Christian. In the Jerusalem of 1940 there were 30,000 Christians--today there are 11,000. A recent study by the City University of New York shows that United States is a much stauncher Christian stronghold than was thought, with only 1.8 percent of the population Jewish and .5 percent Muslim.[3] To its spiritual impoverishment the world is becoming homogeneously tripartite or pentapartite.

The rapid tribalization of the world confirms a moral, ethical, and spiritual distress that may signify the deepest meaning of a time in which George Bush can declare just war as Saddam Hussein declares jihad. In September 1990, King Fahd, protector of the holy shrines of Mecca and Medina, convened an Islamic conference of the World Muslim League in Mecca. The central question before the religious leaders was whether Christian (U.S., British and French) soldiers could enter and make war on the Holy Land of Saudi Arabia. Deciding the question in the affirmative more on the basis of expediency than theology, the conference again showed that something very wrong was going on in our world. The vehemence of Iraqi, Iranian, and pan-Islamic hatred of the United States, Great Britain, and Christians generally is profoundly disturbing and out of keeping with the noblest heritage of Islam. One of the saddest aftermaths of the Gulf War could be the consolidation of all Arab peoples under one *umma* ruled not by Islamic law but by hatred of Israel and the West. The Jewish-Islamic mutual-disgust covenant, reflected in the injustice of Palestinian plight, the terror of *Intifada* and the continuing violation of UN resolutions 242 and 348 (requiring Israel to leave the occupied territories), remains the hottest flashpoint that ignited the Gulf War and poses the greatest continuing danger to world peace. The deep-seated ethnic and religious animosity angrily expressed at the 1991 Madrid Conference and subsequent follow-up talks in Washington bodes ill for the world's future and confounds the confidence that the United States, victorious in the Gulf War, could cajole regional peace.

On October 8 a massacre occurred on the holy site known to Jews as Temple Mount and to Muslims as the Noble Sanctuary. On this site of Herod's temple, Jews worship at the Wailing Wall below the mosque where Muhammed "leapt to heaven." Close by, at the edge of Herod's city, was Golgotha, where Jesus was crucified. As old pious Jewish men rocked in prayer below that afternoon, from above Palestinian youths, agitated by a threatened march by Jewish extremists, hurled stones. The police opened fire, and as dusk settled, nineteen Palestinians were dead, with more to follow. In Baghdad, Saddam Hussein declared three days of official mourning.

King Solomon reigned; Jesus, the strangely crowned king, was crucified; and Muhammad ascended to heaven from that one mountain. The father of them all, Abraham, was said to have been buried in a tomb just down the road. Where will it end? Temple Mount and the Holy City of Jerusalem; Palestine and, a bird's flight away, Mesopotamia are, from a space satellite, just a small dot on planet Earth. Yet from this harsh, sun-baked land flow issues of life and death for the whole world. The navel of the earth was thought to be around Baghdad or perhaps just south in the Tigris-Euphrates valley in the old temple city of Babylon. Now again at this epicenter of creation the sand is soaked with blood as it has been so often over four millennia, the span Bishop James Usher thought to be the full course of creation.

Why did Jesus, the rabbi, die on those cross-posts on that rocky garbage pit outside the wall? Why did four Kurdish boys hang on similar crosses in a back alley of Kirkuk? Why did twenty U.S. boys from the small town of Greensburg, Pennsylvania, where I was born, die in the rubble of the barracks in Riyadh after a Scud missile attack? Why did thousands of charred bodies of Iraqi youth lie strewn along the Basra road? Why the *Intifada*, the holocaust, the Armenian genocide? I have no answer. I do believe it is all the same question. In Elie Wiesel's book *Night*, the old rabbi looks up at the young Jewish lad hanging in the Auschwitz gallows. "Where is God?" he is asked. "There, hanging on the cross," he answers.

The question of war ethics is a question of political or social ethics. Society exerts judgment on the basis of its moral sense. Persons are fined or imprisoned, are crucified or bombed or shot dead in acts of judgment or punishment. Human judgment is fragile and capricious. Each act of judgment assumes the redress of a previous wrong. Each judgment is thought to right a wrong. Instead, each punishment merely sets up a new wrong for tomorrow's redress. In human history there has never been an act of pure initiation or pure retaliation. All human judgment and violence belong to that unending chain of events, the first link or primal event of which can never be determined. The shape of history is cruciform. Suffering and death bring birth and new life. Life goes on, not in some monotonous merry-go-round, but in a simultaneous spiral upward and downward. Evil and good intensify together in time and space. Is the human saga on earth progress or regress? No one can be sure. We can only be sure of the crescendo.

As Thanksgiving neared, that U.S. holiday celebrating an occupation legitimated by the war ethics of Hugo Grotius and John Locke, two issues of just war import interrupted the dull and boring waiting. Soviet President Gorbachev began his efforts to secure a peaceful solution to the Gulf crisis; and the problem of embassies, foreign nationals, and hostages became more acute. Detecting conciliating tones from Iraq, Gorbachev sought to warm up to his old friend and ally and try to convince him to have the good sense to quit Kuwait and perhaps secure some concessions to redress his grievances. Although this moment marked the beginning of Saddam Hussein's search to find a way out, the bear hug from Gorby proved instead a kiss of death. U.S. and British politicians and public opinion quickly reverted to the old cold war suspicion of Soviet maneuvers and became even more resolute to prosecute a war. Glimmerings of peace became for Bush in this crucial hour the moment of inevitability for war. In those weeks, the United States doubled its military presence to upward of 400,000. It was the second concern that triggered this resolve: The U.S. and British diplomats were starving in their surrounded embassies. No provocation angered Bush more than the threat to ambassadors. Having served in China in such a post, Bush knew the sacred traditions of maintaining safety and safe passage for the representatives of nations. Saddam Hussein mistakenly allowed diplomats to leave, but would not allow the continued sustenance of their embassy. At the same time, violations of international law occurred in the treatment of 10,000 Western "guests" and the more than 1 million foreign workers in Iraq and occupied Kuwait.

The Geneva Conventions of 1949 on the protection of civilians in war clearly stipulate that foreign nationals must be protected (Article 4); that they may not be used to protect any place (e.g., as shields) (Article 28); that they must not be treated as hostages, and that the International Red Cross must be allowed to monitor their treatment (Article 3). Saddam Hussein disregarded (at least verbally) all of these conventions. The Thanksgiving holiday was a time of reflection and growing resolve. Strong reservations arose in the U.S. Senate as the declaration of war was debated. Senator Daniel Patrick Moynihan from New York predicted that whatever the outcome, the United States would lose. Normally hawkish Georgia Senator Sam Nunn, perhaps overinfluenced by inflated and fallacious Pentagon statistics, spoke of body bags. Senator John Kerry of Massachusetts asked if President Bush had really thought this thing through. Bush had, and with half a million U.S. military in the Gulf, another million in backup operations, and another 100 million of their family and friends committed out of love and sympathy, his course was set. To the situation was added the almost ludicrous notion that by April, when Ramadan would arrive, sand would disable the machinery and the horrid summer heat would prohibit fighting. The war had to be over by April. It was at this point, only after the decision had been settled, that intense reflection about just war and holy war began in France, Great Britain, and the United States.

The children of darkness are more cunning and quicker to the draw than the children of light. People finally paused to reflect on the *why* of warfare in mid-November when war seemed inevitable. They reflected on the *how* in February 1991 as the air war was destroying Iraq. The meditation on *jus ad bellum* and *causus belli* was lively in the universities, seminaries, churches, and political haunts of all the Western nations. The

French bishops, meeting through the fall, expressed the fear that an inexorable course was being set in motion, one that could not be interrupted. Commenting on what the bishops called "the logic of war," the Episcopal Archbishop of Los Angeles, the Most Reverend Roger Mahoney, wrote Secretary of State James Baker, "We understand that a strong military presence can give credibility to a vigorous pursuit of non-violent solutions to the crisis. My concern is that the pressure to use military force may grow as the pursuit of non-violent options almost inevitably becomes difficult, complex and slow."[4]

In November, when pressed by Congress to state the moral rationale, George Bush said "it was for our jobs, our way of life, our freedom and the freedom of friendly countries around the world." Perhaps one should not ask these protagonists delegated to enact judgments to explain what they do. Bush and Major, Baker and Schwarzkopf are better at doing than explaining. The best Baker could offer on November 13 was "the cause, in one word, is jobs." A bit more candid and circumspect, the *Spectator* in England argued that oil in the modern ages ought to be considered as necessary as food to both the Third World and the West, and war to safeguard it should be ipso facto just.[5]

I don't remember discussion about "just war" during the conflicts in my lifetime. My earliest memory is from December 1941 when Japan attacked Pearl Harbor. There may have been some philosophical tête-à-tête, but I doubt it. Nor was there reflection over the Korean, Vietnam, Grenada, or Panama conflicts, making one ask whether we only allow ourselves to ponder the question, "Is this war just?" when we're quite sure it is not.

By the first week of December 1990 the die was cast. Prompted by the United States and the USSR, the UN set a deadline of January 15 for Iraq to quit Kuwait or face the use of force. It was at the insistence of the Soviets that Iraq was given a warning period. Immediately after the ultimatum, Saddam Hussein ordered the release of all foreign guests "with our apologies for all harm and forgiveness from God Almighty." One of the three Western demands had been met; it remained for Iraq to leave Kuwait and restore the al-Sabah government. Meanwhile the sanctions were exacting their bitter toll: On December 3, the Iraqi health minister, Abdul Salem Mohammed Saleh, claimed that more than 1,400 Iraqi children had died because of a shortage of medicine and milk. The West shrugged this off as a lie. Only in retrospect when the UN reports upward of 70,000 deaths from the sanctions does it begin to seem credible.

When do you decide to be affected by the death of children? The world was struck with horror at the deaths of Kurdish children on the mountain passes between Iraq and Turkey. Why not then on December third? Was this a repeat of Prime Minister Margaret Thatcher's insistence that no prayers be offered at the memorial service for the losses suffered by the Argentinians in the Falklands War?

The war in the Gulf, says General Schwarzkopf, was a jubilant victory: so few casualties and deaths. Generals, like surgeons, may have to blot reality from consciousness and memory ; the people must not. In retrospect the Allies should have amplified the ultimatum with intense diplomatic efforts. Iraq was on the run, and desperately wanted a way out. The Western nations should have used the cunning of U.S. President John Kennedy in the Cuban missile crisis, offering Iraq a few concessions under the table, not to be announced for several months, accepting in principle their claim to an open pathway to the sea, with shared authority or an agreed-on open status for the uninhabited islands, and agreeing to support a regional conference and to work for a solution to the Palestinian question. Instead, the rhetoric turned in a direction completely out of keeping with the spirit of just war: The enemy must be humiliated. Saddam Hussein must be disgraced before his people and the world. A fateful decision must already have been made by that point, changing the Allied policy goals from Iraq's exit from Kuwait to the demolition of the Iraqi infrastructure, the destruction of its military power, and the deposition, if possible, of Saddam Hussein. Senator Moynihan's words would prove correct: We were on a course toward winning the war and losing the peace.

The significant moral decision that confronted the Western powers at year's end was whether to grant any credibility to or compromise on the moral demands put forward by the Iraqi government and its supporters, especially Jordan and the Palestinians. If any just cause could be found, it might have provided reason for some negotiated settlement short of war. The principal issues were (1) whether Iraqi access to the Gulf was threatened by Kuwaiti control of Bubiyan and Warba, the uninhabited islands jutting out into the Gulf at the Tigris-Euphrates delta; (2) whether Iraq's territorial integrity and national security were threatened by Kuwait's rapid draining of the shared resource of the Rumaila oil field; (3) whether Israeli occupation of the West Bank and the Gaza Strip in defiance of UN resolutions was grounds for an oblique attack on Kuwait which also contributed to exploitation of Palestinian people; and (4) whether demands for impossible reparations payments by Iraq could be dropped and Iraqi withdrawal and freedom from subsequent attack be guaranteed. In December 1990 all of these issues were explored among U.S., British, and other envoys. An attempt to arrange a high-level meeting in the four weeks remaining before the war deadline was sought. Iraqi Foreign Minister Tariq Aziz sought to meet with his U.S. counterpart, Secretary James Baker, on January 12. The United States

deemed that date to be too close to the UN deadline. The two did meet
in Geneva on January 3, but neither showed any flexibility. On January
12 the U.S. Congress gave the President authority to launch war, and on
13 UN Secretary-General Pérez de Cuéllar met with President Hussein in
Baghdad and acknowledged the failure of diplomacy to avert war.

Just war requires that the armed confrontation be a matter of last resort.
This principle seems to have been only a marginally important value to
the Western powers, as they were confident of their military superiority
and believed that time spent searching for alternative courses of action
would be interpreted by Saddam Hussein, the American people, and the
rest of the world as signs of weakness. A new post-Vietnam war ethic
had entered the American consciousness with fear above all, of
wavering, wobbling, negotiating, and compromising. Resolute, all-out,
decisive and victorious war was beginning to be announced as the
proper course for Allied war policy. UN Resolution 678 allowed any
country the right to forcefully expel Iraq from Kuwait with the latitude
necessary to strategically accomplish that military feat, giving the Allies
license to conduct air and ground war not only over Kuwait but over
Iraq. Word was leaked to the press in December that Bush was resolved
on war and no subsequent developments could now stay his course.

A final judgment of justice of cause for the war over Kuwait now
rests on three affirmative and four negative factors. In favor of the war's
just cause are the elements of an unjust aggression of Iraq on Kuwait, a
legitimating authority (the UN), and the high probability of success. The
charge against the Allied campaign meeting just cause criteria is
supported by the presence of ulterior motives (exploitation of oil
supplies), the lack of a desire for peace and reconciliation,
disproportionality of power, and the failure to exhaust all means to avert
war and use force only as a last resort. A problem that becomes evident
in the practical application of just war theory to actual conflicts is the
complexity of the doctrine. What if only five of fifteen justifying causes
are present? Is it still licit for a nation to resort to war? Here, war
properly becomes a national and international political act. Is *consensus
populorum* present? Is a general assent forthcoming from the religious
and moral leadership of the country? Do the common people sense a
rightness and justice in the endeavor? Can the matter be submitted to
God in prayer and to the deliberation of religious counsel? Like the vote
for support in the U.S. Senate, on all of these questions we come up with
a division of opinion.

A modern purpose of war, especially evident in both World Wars
and the U.S. invasions of Grenada and Panama, is to discredit an
unacceptable government, dismember its consolidated power, disarm
the military strength that maintained its power, and free its opposition

forces to overthrow existing leaders or at least assume participatory power in affairs of state. By December 1990 it was clear that this purpose had displaced the simple purpose of repelling Iraqi aggression and reestablishing the previous government of Kuwait. With Western support, Iraq's splintered opposition in exile met over New Year's in Beirut with twenty-one groups participating. They were encouraged to call for the overthrow of Saddam Hussein's regime and the political reconstitution of the state of Iraq. The coalition of twenty-one groups included radical opponents such as Kurds, Shiah Muslims, and deposed former generals. It also included pro-Syrian Ba'athists and representatives of other religious movements. The groups reported undertaking three unsuccessful assassination attempts against Saddam Hussein and listed a history of thwarted appeals to diversify and democratize the republic.

About this time and during the early weeks of the air war, an important moment of ethical reflection occurred in the West. If the purpose of national and international action had now become a swift knockout blow to Saddam Hussein, could one or more of three ethically controversial measures be used: the assassination of Saddam Hussein, nuclear weapons, or carpet bombing? The Princeton University social scientist and just war theorist Michael Walzer commented at this point, "Military professionals have a very strong sense of what distinguishes the work they do from butchering. It is a moral sense, even though it's entangled with professional pride and a sense of what works and what doesn't."[6] By this time Western leaders had made it clear that they hoped Saddam Hussein would be removed from power, but they stopped short of calling for or authorizing any agent to carry out assassination. As a general of combat forces, Hussein was a legitimate target, and early efforts were made to bomb his palace, suspected bunkers, and other "leadership targets." He successfully avoided both internal and external threats by purging suspected conspirators among his lieutenants and moving continually between bunkers and various civilian quarters. But is authorizing assassination a legitimate act in just war?

In the July 20th movement in Nazi Germany, a group of pastors, laymen, and disenchanted military leaders sought to assassinate Hitler by planting a bomb under his desk. The moral reflection leading to this desperate act, especially on the part of the Christian leaders, merits study. Did utilitarian grounds justify this breach of the commandment against murder? Would not thousands of lives be saved by Hitler's death? Hans Von Dohnanyi, Dietrich Bonhoeffer, and other theologians who conspired in the July 20th movement followed this moral rationale along with the ethic that found profound embodiment of evil in Adolf Hitler; they came to believe, at what proved to be the cost of their lives, that his assassination would prevent the furtherance of his ghastly acts of aggression and murder.

In the end, pragmatic considerations weighed against the use of this option in Iraq. The higher echelons of leadership had coalesced around Saddam Hussein. Militant Iraqi sympathizers might launch counterassassination attempts against Western leaders. During the course of the war a missile was launched against the London building where Prime Minister John Major was meeting with his cabinet. Although this turned out to be an IRA instead of an Iraqi affair, it showed the world the possibility for such retaliatory action.

The use of nuclear force was also ruled out from the beginning, as was the deterrence strategy of merely threatening a nuclear event to force capitulation. Again, the rule of the game and the maintenance of moral legitimacy in the eyes of the world precluded this action, as also in the more intractable conflict in Vietnam. The major just war criterion here was the deliberate, indiscriminate killing of civilians.

The more conflicted moral choice, focusing on the same moral point of endangering civilians, arose over the carpet bombing that eventually was undertaken of Republican Guard positions. Was carpet bombing, even of predominantly military zones, an indiscriminate act similar to bombing civilians? Was it a legitimate military action or was it an act of double effect, where the legitimate military purpose excused the unintended collateral and civilian effect? The U.S. carpet bombing of Dresden and Tokyo at the end of World War II had come to be widely discredited as unethical. The destructive air war over Iraq raises similar ethical questions.

The Air War

The "mother of all battles" began on January 16 about nineteen hours after the UN deadline had come and gone. The U.S., British, French, Saudi, and Kuwaiti air forces began with some trepidation the most massive air assault since World War II. This blitzkrieg was rained not on Japan and its vast island empire or on expansive Germany and its residual *Lebensraum* but on the tiny nation of Iraq, with its Third World economy and pieced-together obsolete military machine. Thousands of sorties were flown each day and night. The trepidation turned to exhilaration after several days when it became clear that Iraq could not mount any significant antiaircraft resistance or get its few hundred truly modern aircraft off the ground. To this observer the issue of proportionality and asymmetry of power constituted from the outset a grave issue. A bully pushes his or her way around with a weaker opponent. A just person recognizes the inherent injustice of such strife and either levels the playing field or seeks resolution of the conflict without recourse to force.

Reflection on the Announced Air Blitzkrieg

When the first bombs started tearing apart buildings and bunkers, tanks and planes, homes and human bodies, the question of just war in late-twentieth-century aerial warfare had to be confronted for the first time.

> The wise man, they say, will wage just wars. If
> he remembers his humanity, he will deplore his
> being compelled to engage even in just wars.[7]

The war would be swift and horrible. General Colin Powell, chairman of the U.S. Joint Chiefs of Staff, and Secretary of State James Baker, would make that point clear that week to Iraq and the world. In blitzkrieg that would make the attacks on Dresden and Hamburg look like child's play, every advanced U.S. weapon would be used: F-117 stealth fighters would zoom through at low altitude raining laser-guided bombs on command bunkers and missile control sites; F-46 Wild Weasels in concert with F-16 and F-15 fighters would attack anti-aircraft installations with HARM radar-seeking missiles; FB-111 and F-15E bombers would smash air defense installations, severing contact between the Iraqi central command and field commanders. EF-111 and other electronic craft would jam and disrupt all Iraqi communications; Cruise missiles launched from the Gulf, the Indian Ocean, and the Red Sea would home in on Iraq's concentrated installations on the Kuwaiti border and governmental and military centers in Baghdad. Hundreds of B-52s would drop thousands of 900-kilogram bombs on Iraq's 500,000-strong army. Thousands of tons of ordnance would obliterate every important Iraqi center of military, industrial, and governmental activity. And when the first wave of attacks was completed, a second would begin, and then a third, and a fourth. And a fifth. After two weeks this would be followed by a multipronged ground and amphibious assault. And then what?

This announcement of the exact nature of the attack was not the announcement to the enemy called for in just war theory; it was anticipatory gloating. The sad aftermath of that assault caused Westerners to reflect on the justice of this war as holy zeal had prevented at the moment. Two hundred casualties on the Allied side, 200,000 in Iraq, should surely give the victors pause and raise the question, Why?

Although, as Baker and Bush warned Iraq, many lust for and relish war, and although even prudent and thoughtful persons hoped that the wrong of Iraq's occupation would end and regional peace would be achieved, that was not to happen. Any justice and peace that will eventually be achieved will be proximate, fragile, and unsatisfying. Pope John Paul II prayed in his 1990 Christmas message that we be spared from war from which there is no return. To paraphrase Augustine, architect of our just war theory, there is no glory or victory in war. Take away the screens of a morbid fascination and let the naked deeds be examined.

The sacred oaths of victory and glory in the United States and Israel these days ring as hollow as the immortality promises of jihad in Iraq and among the Palestinians. In the end we will hear only war poets like Wilfred Owen sounding the true liturgy in *Anthem for Doomed Youth.* [8]

> What passing-bells for these who die as cattle?
>
> Only the monstrous anger of the guns
> Only the stuttering rifles' rapid rattle
> Can patter out their hasty orisons.
> No mockeries for them from prayers or bells,
> Nor any voice of mourning save the choirs -
> The shrill, demented choirs of wailing shells;
>
> And bugles calling for them from sad shires.
> What candles may be held to speed them all?
> Not in the hand of boys, but in their eyes
>
> Shall shine the holy-glimmers of good-byes.

The bitter paradox, ambiguity, and mystery of war make it imperative that we examine the Gulf conflict in light of the best our past has to offer determine what makes a war just, necessary, and right, if not good and holy. Let us examine the naked deeds. The only philosophical and theological justifications of killing and war are self defense, repelling aggression, and restoring peace. Strange as it may have sounded in a world of *Realpolitik* caught in the alluring frenzy of mortal conflict, our Western just war tradition allows war only for purposes of love, as General Schwarzkopf surprisingly acknowledged in one of his press conferences. The criteria of just cause, rightful authority, and benevolent intention have to be met. Were they?

For eight months the West struggled to elucidate those just causes that would legitimate the war against Saddam Hussein. Perhaps the U.S.

ire was uniquely intense because of a sense of guilt over the mixed signals given this ally of the days of the Iran-Iraq conflict regarding the Iraqi border dispute with Kuwait. Perhaps Great Britain concurred because of its role in creating, just decades ago, the unjust and non-populist emirates in the Middle East. The following causes have been enumerated:

1. *Iraq had invaded an innocent neighbor:* This was the strongest justification for sanctions and war, if it comes to that. One only wonders why previous occupations--Israel of the territories, China of Tibet, the United States of Panama and Grenada--were acceptable.

2. *Western vital interests were at stake:* Stability in the region, continued affordable oil prices, protection of the American way of life. These purposes, though laudable, sound strangely at odds with Augustine's preconditions for *iustum bellum.*

3. *Now or later:* Only daydreamers were not frightened by what Saddam Hussein might do with his incipient nuclear capacity and the chemical and biological warfare he learned in the United States, for which West Germany had provided him the means. But destroying him now for what he might do later was, like deterrence, an unworthy cause. If universalized as a Kantian imperative, the rule would apply to a few countries, including South Africa, India, and Japan.

4. *The United Nations resolutions:* There was a nobility in putting confidence in the UN at long last. That the United States had ignored a long series of resolutions on Palestine and failed for years to pay its dues should not prevent a commitment to a new world order established through the UN. Whether the United States will henceforth honor all UN resolutions with the full force of its military power remains a serious question.

Rightful authority was sought in the remarkable consensus building by Secretary Baker, through the United Nations, among the European allies, and among the concerned neighbors in the Gulf region, such as Egypt and Saudi Arabia. But at the same time Augustine's appeal (in Romans 13:1 "There is no power but of God") and the equivocation of Western purposes should have made its leaders humble and skeptical of the authority by which they proceeded.

Finally, just war must be carried out with right intention. What Augustine called the grace of right love and the good heart should be present. We need not attack the satanic forces hiding in every crack, though these fanatics and "living missiles" were threatened to be unleashed at any moment. Our purposes ought to have been the liberation of the oppressed--in this case, removing the occupation and atrocities from Kuwait and making a commitment to seek free determination and justice throughout the region. Our approach should have been proportionate--in sanctions, and retaliations if necessary, but not the Apocalypse Now envisioned by Powell. As in the case of the Cuban missile crisis, the Allies should have agreed upon Iraqi withdrawal from Kuwait to deal with the manifest injustices and the situation, potentially strangling to Iraq, of the Rumaila oil field and the islands of Bubiyan and Warba. The Allies should have sought as much as possible to safeguard noncombatant immunity and insure, in Augustine's words, that all "military initiatives be modest and limited." A United States still stunned by the tragedy of the Vietnam War found this pill hard to swallow. Above all the West should now be prepared to seek new understanding and reciprocity with the Arab and Muslim world. Western children and statesmen alike need to learn the Arab language (spoken by more people in the world than any language other than Chinese) and culture. As former President Jimmy Carter desired, the United States should strive for a kind of shalom, *salam*, peace among all the Abrahamic peoples on earth together with the whole human family. Then perhaps we will find ourselves closer to the haunting utopian vision about this land received from the Lexicon reading in my college Evensong that week: "Violence shall no more be heard in thy land, wasting nor destruction within thy borders; but thou shalt call thy walls Salvation and thy gates Praise" (Isaiah 60:18).

The Allied strategy in the war was twofold. According to Chief of Staff General Colin Powell: "We're going to cut off the Iraqi army--then kill it." The high tech blitzkrieg undertaken for this purpose pounded military encampments in southern Iraq and bombed the major cities, especially Baghdad, with the view of severing all supply centers, food and equipment supply lines, communication and command centers, and essentially all the sustenance network of the Iraqi government and military system until it was completely incapacitated. After this initial effort, the bombing continued in order to liquidate Iraq's military capability by eliminating divisions--a euphemism for killing tens of thousands of Iraqi soldiers in the process of disarming them by destroying all their equipment. After one week of bombing, sixty out of sixty-six airfields were totally incapacitated and the chemical weapons stockpile was obliterated. The two nuclear reactors were destroyed and ninety percent of the Scud missile launchers were taken out, although a few remained active until the very end of the air war. On January 28, a defiant Saddam Hussein gave an interview to CNN in Baghdad. He continued to claim that he could win the war by using his nuclear, biological, and chemical warheads. Why he made this fantastic threat when it would only intensify the fear-driven obliteration strategy of the Allies, no one knows. Did Saddam Hussein not only disregard disregard his people but himself as well? This suicide thesis received support when, on January 30, Iraqi tanks and supportive troops moved across the border into the Saudi Arabian town of Kafji. It was a military disaster for Saddam Hussein, with Iraq losing dozens of tanks and hundreds of soldiers, against only eleven Allied dead. Significantly, Saudi and Qatari troops retook Kafji.

Iraq responded with another destructive action by releasing three massive oil spills into the Gulf. A small spill was caused by Iraqi shelling of a Saudi storage facility. A massive flow followed from Kuwait's sea island terminal, caused by U.S. bombing and Iraqi action. Soon the Mina al Bakr refinery in Iraq was also releasing a massive slick, caused again by U.S. bombing and Iraqi sabotage. The worst fears of those who had opposed the war from the outset of threats eight months earlier now came true. An ecological catastrophe was underway and would intensify when Iraq ignited Kuwaiti oil wells during its frantic retreat at the war's end. These stigmata of the war will haunt the world like a mark of Cain for years to come.

The revulsion against nuclear war and the successful exclusion of that unspeakable violence from the active war armamentarium since 1945 has been based on the fear that it would devastate the creation itself. Indeed, it would indiscriminately maim, blind, and kill hundreds of thousands of persons, mostly innocents. But the opprobrium goes deeper. Nuclear attack would release toxic clouds that would contaminate earth's fragile life support envelope for decades. The poison would float around the globe, damaging everyone in that circle of duty Kant described that eventually comes around to you, yourself. It would invade and degrade the genetic and biological substance of life, harming future generations. Releasing oil, and petrochemical and chemical oxidation damage, onto sea and sky around Kuwait is the same kind of rage against the earth and also the natural world itself. The reason that most ethics, including just war theory, have taken a pacifist turn in recent decades is that it has become clear that not only people and cities are now targets, but also the natural world itself. Just war asks if the near-range and long-range costs of a war authorize its execution. When not only cormorants and hawksbill turtles but a whole ecosystem and the chain of life, including humans, that it supports are exterminated, a new ethical purview has appeared.

Morbid and gallows humor during the air war began to speak of the confrontation as a vast video game—electronic wizardry worked out with laser devices guiding smart bombs precisely to their targets. Early news photos showed a laser-guided bomb dropped out and guided right down the smokestack of a targeted factory. The smug confidence that this pinpoint bombing would end the Iraqi threat with hardly any casualties (on either side) was violently disabused with the inadvertent bombing of the bomb shelter/bunker in Baghdad at the height of the air war on February 13. Five hundred persons, mostly women and children, were killed.

The new age of electronic warfare does indeed create new challenges for just war theory. Theoretically we could identify on field vision computers every stationary target that needed to be liquidated. We could then guide destruction to that very point by just throwing it out and letting guided lasers take it "home." In the future we might be able to tag any object in the environment, even any human being, and send out sensors with destructive warheads as search and destroy devices. The new moral requirements for an age of Star Wars and smart weapons will be one of the tasks for moralists and military strategists to develop in the aftermath of the war over Kuwait. For now, the cleanliness of the surgical attack has proved to be more like obstetrical care before Semmelweis in the late nineteenth century, featuring dirty hands and contaminated instruments.

Reflection on the Bombing of the Baghdad Air Raid Shelter

The U.S. missile bombing of the Amilaya air raid shelter in Baghdad and the death of hundreds of women and children brought both combatants and the world at large to the somber realization that the war had to end. That the bombing was a mistake we can be sure. Yet the inhumanity, as in Iraq's rape of Kuwait and earlier gassing of the Kurds, made it clear that neither side fully possessed righteousness or wickedness. Through the obscuring clouds of hyperpatriotism, propaganda, and understandable devotion to one's country's soldiers, all could see some sunlight shining through, light that would help all parties to find a way through the dark storm to peace and home. The following peace symbols rose during the bombing campaign:

Birds. How strange it was to watch on television the carpet bombing of the Republican Guard and the Scud missiles arching toward Tel Aviv and in the next story witness the long hours of care with which volunteers, who had also traveled to the Gulf, cleaned a few of the millions of birds caught in the incoming oil tide. Allied bombing caused the first slick, and Iraq opened the valves to release the second. Now in graceful repudiation of both ecocidal cruelties, a single heron was saved from the sacrifice to be a symbol of hope.

Hostages. Hussein's release of the thousands of hostage "guests" from many nations was surely a crack in his armor. Pulling them back from shield sacrifice to return to London or Munich showed that he was no more the Hitler or Satan of Western caricature than George Bush was of that by Iraqi propagandists. Given the ideology of jihad and his sociopathic personality, Saddam Hussein showed remarkable willingness to compromise and find solutions.

Three Little Pigs. Also inexplicable was the fact that Saddam Hussein wouldn't come out to fight. The harder the Allies huffed and puffed, the more he curled up and hunkered down. He let his air force go to Iran and refrained from use of chemical weapons. Granted he launched Scud missiles into Israel and Saudi Arabia, ordered the suicidal incursion into Kafji, and filled the Baghdad night sky with ineffectual antiaircraft flak. But his absorption of immense military and civilian loss without more retaliation was either shrewd military strategy, utter contempt for himself and his own people, or desire for peace.

Peace in Zion. The extraordinary and exemplary patience of Israel despite being hit by dozens of missiles also showed that the world could realistically hope for a more lasting peace and justice in the region when the war was over. An inadvertent side effect of the war may be to bring Israel, Egypt, Syria, and the Palestinians to the table of accommodation, if not reconciliation.

Surgical Attack. Despite the frightful disaster in the air raid shelter and the significant collateral damage with civilian casualties, both sides exhibited generally careful attacks on military targets, supporting infrastructure, and lines of supply and communication. The embargo and first month of war will go down in military history as the cleanest and least harmful engagement of adversary and enemy the modern violent world has seen. Only the gruesome conclusion and aftermath of war shocked us back to the horrendous reality of modern conflict.

Solution. Moral reflection on the air war should confirm our resolve that a new world order will proceed from this inaugural event. All must confirm that we will in the future take international disputes to the UN and heed its resolutions. We will pay our dues, support its work, and bring our influence to bear on all nations to do the same. We will never again allow one country to invade or occupy another. No nation will subjugate or exploit another with impunity. No constellation of nations will refuse any other the right to exist. With this done, we can then get down to dealing with the real danger threatening this world and its peoples—the global economic and ecologic calamity.

By mid-February the air war had dealt near lethal damage to Iraq's air force, navy, tanks, and artillery. It was clear at this point that a subsequent ground war, supported by unresisted helicopters and bombers, would be swift and relatively easy. As the extent of the devastation became clear, Pope John Paul II, deeply disturbed by Bush's distortion of his communique, issued the statement, *inutile strag* (a useless struggle). A furtive effort also began at this point to negotiate an end to the war. Soviet Foreign Minister Alexander Bessmertnykh met on February 18 in Moscow with Tariq Aziz, Iraq's foreign minister. If Iraq would now withdraw unconditionally from Kuwait, as required by UN Resolution 660, Moscow would support the integrity of Iraq's borders; veto UN Security Council penalties, including any war crimes trials, of Saddam Hussein; and help with the adjudication of regional issues. Though politely thanking the USSR for this initiative, the United States dismissed it out of hand. The USSR--indeed the United Nations--was now impotent to curtail the war.

One of the failures of the jus in bello *tradition is that it has focused on procedural minutiae, addressed superficial issues of moral conduct of war, and, tithing mint and cummin, has evaded the weightier issues of the law.* Like medical etiquette, which emphasizes discussions of fee splitting, alcohol and tobacco on the physician's breath, or bedside manner and evades the profound life-and-death questions of justice and mercy, war conduct ethics has focused on uniforms, Red Cross privileges, and other technical questions much to the neglect of the weighty questions like when and how to end a war, what limits there should be to violence, and how to maintain the dignity and humanity of the enemy. The war over Kuwait, at first glance, looked like a nobly conceived and immaculately conducted war. But as the millions of Kurdish refugees suffered and died on the mountains of the Turkish and Iranian borders, it became clear that none had asked the most searching questions about justice and humanity until after the ends and the means of this war had been decided. War is only good, in holy or just perspective, when the evil it unleashes is far less than the evil sought to be remedied. The Iraqi occupation and brutalization of the Kuwaiti people (provoked or not) was a grave and serious wrong. The devastation of Iraq by the Allies and the residual tragedy of human death, ecological destruction, and refugee trauma may in the end prove to be the far greater evil.

As the air war gave way to the ground war several goals were articulated by the Allied political and military leadership that deserve comment from the just war perspective. Bombing and artillery action came to be seen as a "softening-up" measure. Leaders in the U.S. Congress asked that the bombing continue, even the carpet and saturation bombing, in order to insure that only minimal Allied casualties would be incurred once the ground war, or "mopping up" operation, began. A second goal articulated was to "get it over with fast." This desire was based in the West on the hope to minimize casualties and bring the troops home quickly. Among the Arab coalition members, especially Egypt and Morocco, sentiment arose to "end it rapidly" before internal protest could mount and Saddam Hussein's cause turn into a righteous and popular crusade. A third goal articulated at this juncture of the war was to encourage the Iraqi opposition to rise up and overthrow Saddam Hussein's Ba'athist government. The West seemed not to believe, despite all informed counsel, that stripping Iraq of economic power, security capability, and life sustaining infrastructure--water, medicines, and the like--would leave Saddam Hussein with only brute force to exert his authority over the people.

The demand that bombing serve a political purpose in minimizing subsequent ground casualties converges on the military aim of surgical strikes that avoid civilian casualties and the just war value of discriminate and proportionate methods. To compound destruction in a war zone, especially with fuel-air and percussion weapons, approaches *herem,* or holocaust, with all of the ethical fault of those tactics. Getting it over with fast also runs the risk of haphazard and indiscriminate actions. When the mood and mode is desperation, not deliberation, the great danger of excessive harm is present. The just war tradition requires that "just enough" or proportionate force alone should be employed. Human aggression, though certainly not honor, tends to vent rage and outrage in the display of strength. In boxing, the referee stops the fight when one fighter is defeated. In war new rules are needed to discern the moment of victory and call a halt to further, superfluous, violence and wastage.

Remembering the cowardly and ignoble evacuation of Vietnam, U.S. leaders wanted to be sure that this war ended decisively. But the political strategy vis-à-vis postwar Iraq was ill conceived and not carefully thought through. Before the war began, all knowledgeable commentators pointed to the danger of dismembering Iraq, compromising central sovereignty, and inciting rebellion or flight by Kurds and Shiah Muslims. But it is difficult to fight a limited or measured war, and it is even more difficult to wage a war and leave your opponent in a politically viable state. Much easier, perhaps, would have been a more ambitious goal of totally ending the existing government and replacing it with a new democratic government. This course would have violated the rule of noninterference in the internal affairs of another government and would have required a long range presence to safeguard the imposed new government. Western governments, fed up with the cost and destruction that the Middle East was causing the rest of the world as it sought to get on with urgent problems, wanted only to get out fast. But in May 1991, news stories decried Saddam Hussein's repression of Kurdistan, not only of rebellious fighters but of civilians as well. The ambivalence of Allied goals in the war helped create the most agonizing and genocidal refugee crisis the world has yet known.

The Ground War

The ground war began on February 24 despite signs that the Iraqi army wished only to surrender after the devastating loss of life and military capacity in the air war. Saddam Hussein had agreed by that point to withdraw from Kuwait, as indeed some of his troops already had done, but the Allies dismissed this promise as yet another cruel hoax from a man who could not be trusted to keep his word. One can only wonder what made Western leaders think their words so trustworthy, when they repeatedly said that all that was required for the war to end was an Iraqi pledge to leave Kuwait--but when that pledge came it was not accepted. The jubilation in Baghdad triggered by the announcement of war's end was short-lived when the people realized that the Allies intended to exact a final measure of punishment and were not prepared to offer mercy or magnanimity.

On February 20, the Allies had delayed for twenty-four hours their scheduled inception of the ground war to give at least apparent and respectful acknowledgment of a final Soviet peace initiative. The Bush administration went through the motions of suggesting revisions in the draft of Moscow's peace proposal. At the same time it was feared in Washington that Saddam Hussein would actually accept the proposal, as he eventually did. Thus the United States intensified the demand that there be no "linkage," "qualification," "conditions," "negotiation," or "questions." Bush had issued, in other words, not only an ultimatum, but an ultimatum impossible to accept. On Friday, February 22, 1991, Bush gave Saddam Hussein the final order to begin withdrawing Iraqi troops from Kuwait by noon Saturday. Confident in the Pentagon estimates that it would take a minimum of two to four weeks for Iraq to receive and communicate such an order and implement it in visible signs of withdrawal, Bush had already ordered the ground war to begin. After only one hundred hours, on Wednesday, February 27, the Allied troops had liberated Kuwait City.

The initial Allied thrusts were marked by massive Iraqi surrenders, which proved to be a merciful sparing of lives. Upward of 100,000 of the ragged, cannon-fodder Iraqi front lines came across offering no resistance. Helicopters and tank forces moved across central Iraq in a flanking maneuver, directly from Saudi Arabia across the western edge of Kuwait while others came directly from Kuwait's southern border. Almost before it began it was over. Again massive Iraqi casualties and meager Allied casualties proved the one-sidedness of the war. Two final events bore out General Sherman's warning that war is never glory, but only hell.

On the evening of Monday, February 25, just hours before the end, an Iraqi Scud missile hurtled undetected into Dharan, Saudi Arabia, and killed twenty-two U.S. servicemen as they slept in their living quarters. The dead were mostly members of a National Guard Unit from Pittsburgh, Pennsylvania. It brought the total Allied ground war casualties to twenty-six. The event symbolized the irony and unpredictability of war. Like the death of the infantryman from Detroit who returned home from Kuwait only to be killed in front of his home in a drug shooting, this tragedy showed the way war escapes human control and is displaced by the inscrutable uncertainties and mysteries of a deeper fatality, judgment, and providence.

On Tuesday, February 26, Iraqi central headquarters, decimated by heavy Allied bombing, issued orders for its troops to withdraw and return home. What occured as they fled north along the Basra road in their trucks and buses, mini vans, motorcycles, and co-opted civilian vehicles with no air or ground cover whatsoever, can only be called a massacre. The Allied strafing and bombing of thousands of retreating soldiers, leaving a miles-long line of charred bodies, will burden the conscience of the world as the war's lasting disgrace.

Evil has a strange ubiquity and virulence. It takes on force and magnitude far greater than the precipitant and participant human actions. The moral genius of holy war ethics was to relegate war and its spoils to God rather than leave its awe-filled and awful power in human hands. The moral genius of just war constraints, for all of their limitations, was to place a check on vengeance and violence, which inevitably grow to demonic proportions. Perhaps one day persons will not have their chests blown open and their heads blown off in war. In the days of SDI (Star Wars) we are told that bullets will hit bullets in the vast stellar regions and no child or creature of God will be hurt. On that day there may no longer be heard crying or tears "in all my holy mountain" (Isaiah 65). A strange outcome, bitter, not sweet. For now, war can only be a call to repentance and prayer as we attend the widow and the orphan.

On what basis have I offered these moral judgments? As in the chronicles of the judges and kings in Hebrew scripture, events of the war over Kuwait have been looked at here *sub specie aeternitatis* with a particular ethical historiography. I will now attempt to explain the roots of war seen as an ethical responsibility before God and the human community as this is expounded in Jewish, Islamic, Christian, and secular-humanist war ethics.

Notes

1. "U.S. Aid Dismissed Iraq," *International Herald Tribune*, April 11, 1991, p. 3.

2. *Time*, August 20, 1990, p. 11.

3. "Broad New Study of America Confirms It: In God We Trust," *International Herald Tribune*, April 11, 1991, p. 1.

4. Quoted in *The Economist*, November 17, 1990, p. 97.

5. Ibid.

6. Lisa Beyer, "Three Ethical Dilemmas," *Time*, February 4, 1991, p. 36.

7. Augustine, *City of God*, 19:7.

8. Wilfred Owen, *Collected Poems of Wilfred Owen*, Ed. Edmund Blunden, London: Chatto and Windus, 1972, p. 27. Reprinted by permission of New Directions Publishing Corp.

3

War Ethics in Israel: Biblical and Modern Perspectives

Holy War and Harsh World

The strange world of the Bible squares poorly with our troubled world. Even the primitive and naturalistic strains of tribal holy war catch us by surprise. Even more do the serene higher reaches of the prophetic and apocalyptic rendition of that same tradition strike us as coming from another world. The juxtaposition of that sacred and eternal world with our sordid and mundane experience became clear to me one day in morning matins. As I cycled down to the cathedral of my college, Christ Church, one particular dull and rainy morning, a service of song and sermon promised to be as discontinuous with our rough world as the biblical depiction of Israeli holy war was from the harsh diary we were closing that week in Kuwait and Iraq. Yet, Word and world met this morning in that ever-surprising mysterious admixture. The preacher was my associate in sabbatical-learning, Regius Professor of Morals, Oliver O'Donovan. The text was Psalm 137; the music, Palestrina and Stravinsky.

The mood of the worshipping community, perhaps more in my troubled spirit than in the stiff-upper-lipped back-to-business British congregation, seemed to be one where exultation in the victory of war mingled with disgust and sadness for the destruction it took to end it. It reminded me of the repentant response of the ancient Germanic tribes who, when they had finished their invading and marauding ways, ravaging and raping in *herem* worse than holy war, sat down and wept at what they had done.

The words of the psalm had stark power as the clouds of war still hung over a modern Babylon which lay in ruins:

> By the waters of Babylon we sat down
> and wept: when
> we remembered thee, O Zion.
>
> As for our harps, we hanged them upon
> the willow trees . . .
> For they that led us away captive
> required of us a song . . .
>
> . . . Remember the children of Edom O
> Lord in the day of Jerusalem:
> How they said Down with it, down with
> it, even to the ground.
>
> . . . O daughter of Babylon, wasted with
> misery . . .
> blessed shall he be that taketh thy
> children
> and throweth them against the stones.

There it was--benediction and brutality wrapped up in one moving poem of captivity.

The other scriptures of the morning expressed a haunting counterpoint with this poem, together striking to the hearts of our worshipping community which had gathered with a sense of relief and remorse for the turbulent days just ended:

> Exodus 24--Moses went up to "inquire"
> from Yahweh in the cloud of smoke atop
> Mt. Sinai. He fasted for 40 days in the
> smoke listening for some word. He
> received the command of justice . . .
> "thou shalt not kill . . ."
>
> Luke 23--The prisoner Jesus, on the eve
> of his execution was bounced to Herod
> for a second opinion--then back to Pilate.
> Neither could find fault worthy of
> death--but the howling, vengeful mob

> insisted–and his life was exchanged for one who deserved the death sentence– the murderer, terrorist-Barrabas. This contradiction of warrior-messiah dies vicariously for that thug and all the rest of us like him who have ever or will ever live.

> Psalm 51 . . . cleanse me from blood guilt–David had just sent Bathsheba's soldier-husband Uriah the Hittite to his death in battle while he himself broke with her both holy war law of continence and the law of adultery.

> . . . The sacrifice thou desirest is a contrite and broken spirit (not the cultic soldier's sacrifice, burnt offerings or holocaust).

The liturgy from the *Book of Common Prayer* also had an eerie currency:

> . . . Preserve thy inheritance, O Lord (remember Jerusalem). Give peace in our time, O God.

As the preacher mounted the pulpit, Thatcher's words in the White House the night before crossed my mind. She, too, captured some of the wretched genius of holy war when, receiving the U.S. Medal of Freedom, she replied: "Mr. President, like you I hate violence. But there is one thing I hate more--giving in to violence." De-selected by her own Tory party in favor of John Major and thus robbed of a victorious glory such as she enjoyed in the Falklands campaign, she now knew what losing out meant, a vital moral lesson for any "Christian soldier."

The psalmist also knew such humiliation. Being brought low, down to earth, is the theme of the Magnificat, another text in the liturgy: "He has put down the mighty from their seats and sent the rich away empty. . . . He has exalted those of low degree" (Luke 2). These convictions speak to the side of that archaic holy war tradition which gives all glory to God. It also gives substance to the prophetic holy war theme of disavowing any human triumphalism.

The preacher commented on this dramatic Hebrew poem that begins in such tranquility and ends in such cruelty, "It is like throwing a hand grenade into a prayer meeting." Again my thought wandered to instances when this contradictory action was employed in warfare. I thought of the bomb thrown into a black Baptist church in Mississippi, killing four little girls. I remembered the Jews herded into a Ukraine synagogue and burned to death. Holocaust and *herem* have a twisted history. We want to eliminate those not like us. But the text also recalled the age-old war convention of not destroying a place of worship.

Psalm 137 reflects the cross-generational mood of vengeance as the Jew in bitter memory remembers that ancient Saddam Hussein, Nebuchadnezzar, and the destruction of Jerusalem in 586 B.C. by the fiery Scud-like missiles of his arsenals. "Let my right hand fall paralyzed if I forget thee, O Jerusalem," the preacher went on, " . . . our dislocated memory, hell-bent on victory, self-vindication and vengeance is transformed only in God's grace and peace—our furious memory is overcome only by God's serene memory . . . Remember O Lord. Forgiveness and renewal are afforded in the gentle lamb of God who submitted to the violence of the sin of the world, an innocent and pure sacrifice . . . " (*Agnus Dei*). As in all English cathedral schools, the word of worship is set to heart in the music. On this day the boy's choir sang Palestrina's Psalm and Stravinsky's Mass. The message continued to build with the Benedictus, "preserve us from our enemies. . . . Guide us in the ways of peace." Stravinsky's alien harmonies seemed like music of chaos, *Agnus Dei* a plaintive pastoral wail in which I heard a lost and sacrificial lamb. The *Sanctus* is violent yet serene, reminiscent of the fiery Russian war history that refined the composer's soul. The final hymn resembled the apocalyptic transmutation of Judaic holy war. In Charles Wesley's words we found a glorious subjective, transcendent, and perfect kingdom far removed from all worldly cares: "more and more thyself display shining to the perfect day." It seemed to me a fitting conclusion, particularly as both Charles and his brother John once sat as Christ Church students in these very stalls. A meditative and reflective understanding of the war now transpiring in ancient Babylon reminded me of the people of the Bible.

In considering the right and wrong of the war over Kuwait, we turn to Hebrew ethics of war and peace. These ethics form the moral basis of Jewish, Christian, Islamic, and, in part, secular-humanist values; these are the ethical systems of the major players in the Kuwait conflict. Any modern rational inquiry into political or social ethics must begin with these origins.

Though they never lifted a gun, flew an aircraft, or launched a boat in this war, Nation Israel was at the heart of the meaning of the war over Kuwait. Desperately scrambling to justify his misguided occupation of

Kuwait, Saddam Hussein contended that his action showed that someone was willing to stand against the U.S./Israeli axis. He argued disingenuously that his moral purpose was to redress the unjust oppression of the Palestinians by Israel. Israel was center stage in the geopolitical drama surrounding the war over Kuwait.

Winston Churchill pondered gassing the Iraqis to subdue the embittered Arabs after the Paris conferences in 1919 and 1920 had betrayed Lawrence of Arabia's promises for a self-determining Palestinian homeland; Martin Buber presented his provocative 1946 lectures in Jerusalem on "Zion" in which Arabs were viewed as central to any Jewish state in the region; since those times, the destiny of Israel has been a central theme in Middle Eastern politics.

Israel is at the center of our inquiry for another reason: From Israel the world has received two powerful ethical ideas about war and peace, ideas enshrined in the ethical and legal documents of most modern nations. Phrased in the theocentric and theocratic language of Hebrew faith, these convictions are, first, that God's image and will create life in persons. Therefore we do not kill another person. Only in extreme and exceptional circumstances are we permitted to kill others. In the text on which John Donne based his last sermon, "Death's Duell," "unto God the Lord belong the issues of death" (Psalm 68:20).

Second, God is the author and finisher of human life and therefore "by whom man's blood is shed shall his blood be shed" (Genesis 9:6). Although justifications of homicide have tempered these forthright ethics and modern secular states often repudiate the requirements of justice and mercy that lie behind them, these concepts retain compelling power.

The ethics of warfare in Israel fall into two epochs: those of the ancient and those of the modern people. The war ethics of the Bible reveal several strands, all of which eventually influenced rabbinic or Talmudic war ethics. Until recently, this composite theological heritage had little influence on the war ethics of the modern state of Israel. Recently, though, the ascendency of more relevant orthodox beliefs and ethics, and the reawakened currency of holy war ethics, require that we revisit the classical and contemporary ethos about war making. The institution and retention of nationhood are fundamental ethical values that Jewish history has preserved for global society.

In Hebrew history and scripture we find war ethics evolving through three distinct phases: the holy war tradition, which reflects the historical period of the Palestinian conquest; the settlement in the "promised land"; and the consolidation of rule over native and neighboring peoples. Second, there is the autonomous war ethic of the monarchy severed from the theonomous and theocratic understandings extant in the period of the judges. In some ways the war ethics of the monarchy presaged the modern secular ethic of the state of Israel. A sub-theme emerges under this second strand, namely the political critique of the prophets regarding war making as they both sought to recall the people to a theocratic faithfulness and looked forward to an eschatological reign of peace. The final phase of biblical war ethics builds on this apocalyptic and eschatologic mood as a people devoid of political power, subjugated by Persian, Greek, and Roman occupation, reconceived and apotheosized the moral nature of conflict and warfare. When we examine the levels of Judaic war ethics, we discover they relate to questions of morality surrounding the present conflict in the Gulf.

Many moralists and political scientists consider the religious ethics found in Judaism, Christianity, and Islam obsolete in our time of secular rationality and political expediency. Yet there are reasons that make it imperative that we listen to the war ethics, even the foundational holy war ethics, of the faith communities party to this conflict. A sizable population within those nations—Orthodox Jews, conservative Christians and fundamentalist Muslims—believe in some fashion in the stipulates of "enthusiastic" (God-filled) war.

The idea of war as activity to vindicate the deity, as resistance to enemies who would harm God's children, as the divine judgment of God, as an enterprise in which He is for or against you, in which a divine plan guides the events and outcomes of war down to the exposure or protection of each particular soldier and civilian—even today these are patterns of primal and popular belief, with a religious dimension. Such *sensus fidei* are an important source of normative morality. Further, even the most modern and secular states seem to label their own cause divine and the enemy's demonic. Saddam Hussein and George Bush were each caricatured in archsatanic colors in the United States and Iraq respectively. More commonly, we elevate some idol through apotheosis —the American way of life, the preservation of freedom, the restoration of Arabia—in effect making some penultimate ambition our god. The war then becomes a crusade or holy cause. Familiarity with religious war ethics can alert us to this dangerous idolatry. Finally, these traditions deserve attention because they are founded on a kernel of truth. God is active in history. In ways far removed from our projected schemes, the divine will, plan, and presence is available, perhaps even as precipitating, undergirding, and consummating cause, in all crisis and conflict, even war.

The extreme danger of this rationalization is to project our petty anger into divine wrath. The essence of the war ethics of ancient Israel is that the people are not to subsume violence to themselves. God is judge and warrior, but foremost "He makes wars to cease" and "breaks the bow and shatters the spear" (Psalm 46:9). The perennial human propensity for violence and war is most odious when couched in divine rhetoric. The divine name is not to be lightly invoked, nor the divine power usurped. When Bush and Hussein began using the rhetoric of attacking the demonic Hitleresque rapist and pillager or fighting Holy War against the great infidel, we should have remembered the words of George Orwell, quite in keeping with Hebrew iconoclasm: "Saints should always be judged guilty until they are proved innocent."[1]

Holistic Ethics and Sacred War

For Israel as for most ancient peoples, war was a sacral undertaking with accompanying religious rituals. The exodus from Egypt and the conquest of Canaan were ritualized campaigns of nomadic tribes--Judah, Simeon, and Joseph in the south; Reuben, Gad, and Manasseh in the east --seeking to ward off the counter attacks of the Canaanites whose land they had usurped. Alliances and pacts such as the pact of Schechem (Joshua 24) and Gideon's coalition (Judges 6–8) were conceived to hold on to conquered territory and fend off counter-assault. Only when Saul called all Israel to arms against the Ammonites and Amalakites (I Samuel 11, 15) was there a consolidation of forces and some articulation of common understandings and purposes. The judges became liberator warriors and the kings anointed charismatic saviors in the holy purposes of claiming, cleansing (*qadosh*) and controlling the territory as a divine allotment. Methods of war varied from annihilating massacres (vs. the Amalakites) to the representative warfare in the custom of second millennium B.C. Egyptian and Canaanite nomads, with one combatant sent forward against the champion of the adversary (I Samuel 17: David and Goliath). In all of these campaigns Israel not only defended its own interests but forwarded the purposes of Yahweh against the competitors' less-potent deities.

Throughout antiquity generally and particularly in ancient Israel, war was begun at the command of the gods and conducted with divine help (health) that ensured victory. The Greeks gave the phrase holy war (*Ieros Polemos*), to campaigns against those who defamed and contaminated Apollo. In jihad the holy purpose was to spread the faith that was to decontaminate heathen presence. Holy war was literally an act of saving (cleansing) a place or people by clearing away abomination and establishing sanctity and sanctuary. Combatants had to be in a state of ritual cleanliness and continence if God was to tent down (make sanctuary) in their midst (Joshua 3:5, I Samuel 21:6, Deuteronomy 23:10– 15). Now tethered in sacred bond, Yahweh fought for Israel (Judges

20:35), unleashed forces of nature in the cause (Judges 5:20), tricked the enemy (Judges 4:15), and planted terror in the enemy's heart (I Samuel 14:15). Combat concluded in the wiping-up operation of *herem* (anathema), in which all living things were put to death and all belongings burned (Joshua 6:18-24). The acts of war were so thoroughly attributed to a divine imperative that human agency was rendered somewhat incidental. Only in the monarchy was this mythology abandoned and a more blatant secular purpose acknowledged.

After the conquest, as in the modern state, Israel's wars can be said to be purely defensive actions, warding off aggressive neighbors and seeking only to defend their existence as a people rather than to spread the faith. To this day the Suez campaign, the Six Days War, the occupation of the West Bank, Gaza Strip, and Golan Heights, even the incursions into the Palestinian refugee camps and counter violence and preemptive violence against the Intifada have been rationalized as defensive action concerned only with survival and preservation of the state.

The mythologies and rituals of holy war in early Israel, Islam, and the Christian Crusades served exactly the same purpose and had the same "truth value" and ethical import as rational theory in seventeenth-century Europe and modern jurisprudential theory about the law of war. Each asked: Why shall we go to war and how shall war be fought? It could be further argued that for all its exaggeration and fantasy, holy war theory is even more adequate to truth than the just war or "secular realist" ethical theory, in that it responds in however distorted a fashion to a feature of truth ignored by those perspectives, namely the nature and activity of God.

What is the connection of the themes of holy war and just war in the early war ethics of Israel? Why may one conduct war? For one reason alone: divine call and purpose. Establishing a homeland, relieving a situation of oppression, even vindicating the divine name and presence in the sense of removing falsehood and injustice from a domain (e.g., the U.S. invasion of Panama to extirpate Noriega or the attempt of German pastors to assassinate Hitler), remain the only reasons to wage a war. Holy war conviction claims that the only justification for war is divine purpose, which is righteous purpose.

At this point it is important to relate another theme of holiness ethics to the holy war morality of why and how war can be waged. The theme of sanctity of life and the anathema of spilling human blood is another powerful consideration in "holiness" morality, indeed it is the root of taboos behind Kosher customs, even *herem* removal and fire and the levitical prohibition of spilling and mixing life blood.

A parallel example emerges from contemporary bioethics. This year the equivalent of a Nobel prize for theology, the Templeton Award, was given to Great Britain's Chief Rabbi Emeritus, Emmanuel Jakobovitz. This great scholar, who has so carefully traced the bioethical traditions of biblical and rabbinic Jewish medicine, has shown that Orthodox Jewish ethics prohibit us from robbing a human being even of a few precious minutes at life's end. Each moment of human life contains an eternity, each particular person embodies the whole human race. The implications of this ethic for imperiled newborns and dying persons is evident. But it was not for reason of this work alone that Rabbi Jakobovitz was honored. He was also cited for his gentle moderation in dealing with the Arab-Israeli crisis. Life affirming and death aversion ethics obviously are the essence of contemporary Jewish ethics of medicine, civil affairs, or war and peace. We can now summarize this foundational block of Jewish war ethics:

"Holy War" in Review:

- Through consultation with the deity, war is declared
- War may only begin with divine sanction
- Yahweh, the warrior god, has the power to gain victories
- Holy war is acquisition, defense and establishment of land, establishment in covenant
- The commander leads by inspiration; (charisma; divine gift)
- Soldiers are chosen by virtue of strength and become sacrifical leaders (priests)
- War therefore becomes a cultic act
- Yahweh delivers the victory by empowering his people and weakening the foe
- Conquered cities are offered peace and citizens are not killed except within Holy Land where *herem*, total eradication and cleansing, is required
- All war looks forward to conclusion in penultimate peace and ultimate peace: "*shalom.*"

The current war in the Gulf was preceded by earnest and vigorous attempts to avert armed conflict. It was a last resort (a criterion we will review under the secular legacy of just war). Constant consultation took place between the United States and its allies, Saudi Arabia, Egypt, Syria, Israel, Turkey, the Soviet Union, Japan, Great Britain, and other nations. As much as is possible with moderns who no longer hear the direct voice of God, George Bush, John Major, Yitzhak Shamir, Saddam

Hussein, and the others (we may believe) inquired of the divine will "Come let us reason together, saith the Lord" (Isaiah 1:18).

In the United States, President Bush sought to lift the matter to God in his own Episcopal congregation; with his closest advisers in services of worship and prayer; with Billy Graham, an overnight guest in the White House; and in his personal meditation. In a speech given at a prayer breakfast with religious broadcasters, he made it clear that he had come to the conviction that the war was right, having consulted, it appears, both the holy war heritage in the Bible and the just war heritage (he cited Augustine).

Cynics claim with some justification that otherwise-secular leaders evoke religious symbols when popular support is required for political actions, recalling Machiavelli's advice to the prince. Prayer breakfasts and prayer rugs became more prominent in Washington and Baghdad, to be sure. It must surely be the case, as well, that the leaders came to realize the awe-filled responsibility that rested on their shoulders and the terrible burden for which they were now accountable in any sacral or secular rendition of ethics. Like Moses before the burning bush, political leaders were facing decisions that brought them trembling before "the Holy." And rather than boasting in divine command or self-righteousness at the outset or gloating in divine victory or impressive strategy at the end, they struck a more appropriate posture of humility, thanksgiving, and magnanimity. There was work to be done in the service of that peace that is the end purpose of the holy war. This response, we may assume, was not only adherence to George Bush's mother's good advice and appropriate reaction to the horrific violence and tragic loss of life that the war involved, especially for the small and poor nation of Iraq; it was also in keeping with the holy war ethical tradition of committing the spoils and the glory to God.

Following the Marshall Plan to rebuild post war Germany and the generous assistance that lifted Japan from the ashes of Hiroshima, Nagasaki, and Tokyo into the major world power it is today, the commitment to long range and lasting peace (shalom, *salaam*) will need to be strong in the aftermath of war. This is ethical response in the spirit of holy war. Within days after the cease-fire , the Allies were concerned to strengthen Saddam Hussein's political authority, albeit for the political reasons of undercutting the Shiah leadership emerging from Basra and the Islamic fundamentalist uprising in the south. Communistic influence in some cities and Kurdish separatism in the north were also feared. The Allies will certainly offer massive humanitarian aid to rebuild Kuwait and Iraq and will press firmly, as George Bush promised in his victory speech, for an immediate process to settle the perpetually destabilizing tensions of the Arab-Israeli problem in the Middle East.

In ancient Israel, holy war ethics formed the foundation of the war morality that shaped the subsequent monarchic, prophetic, and apocalyptic phases of Hebraic ethical culture. It shaped the great traditions of rabbinic and Talmudic thought that influenced all forms of modern casuistry. It provided the foundation of Christian and Islamic warfare ethics, and turgor and grace to the war ethics of the modern secular state of Israel. To these later mutations we now turn.

Monarchic War Ethics and Realpolitik

The inauguration of the monarchy was an important turning point in Israel's spiritual, ethical, and political history. The pious purist would say that it was an unequivocal decline into faithlessness, a turn away from chosenness and uniqueness, to become like all other nations--to become security conscious, economically exploitative, self-aggrandizing, belligerent.

Once the disparate tribes that would become Israel were confederated, a new ethic of warfare emerged. The Canaanites and Philistines had standing armies, cavaliers, and charioteers; Israel to survive had to have the same. The innocence and exuberance of holy warfare under Yahweh's command faded into distant memory. King Saul had household troops, mercenaries, runners (I Samuel 22:17), and David created an elaborate professional army. He captured Jerusalem with his mercenaries (II Samuel 5:6) and defeated the Philistines (5:21). His retinue included bodyguards, household troops, republican guards (II Samuel 11, 14-17), cadets, commissioned officers, charioteers, and professional soldiers. Nomadic and tribal patterns of livelihood and hit-and-run combat also yielded to the prevalent Canaanite pattern of living in fortified cities. As soon as David captured Jerusalem, he proceeded to fortify it. One of the remarkable feats of modern archaeology has been the uncovering of the Davidic south wall of Jerusalem. In 1962 in a memorable summer in my own education I had the privilege of working with the French Jesuit Roland DeVaux and British archaeologist Kathleen Kenyon on their joint project of the British School and the École Biblique.

Community life, even national life in this mode, began to be seen as a process of fortification, self-sustenance, and defense of Israel's interests against other powers who would assume aggressive or land-grabbing initiatives such as those that had established Israel's foothold in the land of Palestine. The securing of these strongholds was short-lived, as Jeremiah warned (5:17) and the Chaldeans realized (II Kings 25:10) when they razed the walls of Jerusalem. The monarchy retained many strains of the holy war heritage such as "inquiring of the Lord" and the "victory prayer" even as a new age of international treaties, war cabinets, and war making as an instrument of national policy superseded the ethic of desert sanctuary. God was no longer the "man of war" (Exodus 15:3) on the move via the Ark before the migrating people. He was now settled down at home and soon to be enshrined in Solomon's temple. In this period a theological counsel was still found in the king's court; prophets still prophesied, although they often became "yes men." The king was now seen as representing Yahweh. He was called God's son (II Samuel 7:14-17, Psalm 2) and was expected to exact the divine will, which was sustenance of the divine name and presence, the survival and flourishing of the people, the execution of justice, and the establishment of peace. Although some of the sacral rituals were compromised by kings like David, who broke cultic ritual by treachery and lechery in going down into Uriah's household, Uriah himself, a common soldier, remained chaste (II Samuel 11:6-13).

The main yield of monarchic ethics to a modern theory of just war was the code of conduct presented in Deuteronomy 20, 21:10-14, 23:10-14, 24:5, 25:17-19. This ethical code, it is believed by scholars such as Thomas Driver, Gerhard Von Rad, and George Ernest Wright, is part of covenantal tradition preserved in the Schechem sanctuary in northern Israel, going back to the final teaching of Moses before his death.[2] It preserved the theological themes of gratitude for deliverance; covenantal duty to God and neighbor; ethnically and universally conceived; and the overarching judgment of God on human worship and ethical life, conferring blessing and curse. A people who were no people were chosen to bear the divine presence into history; their destiny was not self-adulation but humanitarian justice and service in humble obedience to the law of righteousness and life. To summarize the war ethics of early monarchy:

Davidic War Code in Review :

- Those with pressing and distracting domestic concerns should not fight but return home (Deuteronomy 20:6,7).
- The purpose of a campaign against a people is to declare peace, preferably without combat. Only if the enemy refuses peaceful negotiation shall siege, sanctions, or blockade be undertaken (20:10-13).

- In a besieged city that will not capitulate after defeat, the males shall be slain (military and populational future undermined) and the women, children, and animal herds expropriated (20:14).
- Obliteration and extermination must occur for the lands to become holy (20:15-18).
- Trees shall not be cut down (20:20).
- The woman taken in battle shall remain in your house untouched for a month to grieve for her family but then she may become your wife (21:10-14).
- The unclean soldier (soiled and contaminated in any way) shall be placed in quarantine, cleansed, then offered reentry (23:10-14).
- The newly married (within the year) shall not be sent to war (24:5).
- Godless ambushes like the Amalakites, (Exodus 17:8-15) deserve holocaust (Deuteronomy 5:17-19).

The code betrays a strange nobility and a now-outmoded violence and intolerance. Except for such separatists as the right-wing Rabbi Kahane, who would expel Palestinians from the territories, these sentiments have yielded to a more humanistic and universalistic ethos, one more in keeping with the underlying theology of covenant. Just as Arab Muslims cannot desire the eradication or extermination of Israel without destroying something of their own hearts and heritage, so modern Israelis must accommodate Arabs and Muslims who share a common habitat as their neighbors. Nobility is found in the pacifism that should go before any violence, the holy regard for marriage and family, and ecologic respect. Each of these moral guides was severely violated by both sides in the Gulf War. The wildlife destroyed by U.S. bombing and the combined destruction of Iraqi sabotage and scorched-earth tactics will long disgrace any virtue that may come from the war. On the Allied side, soldiers were taken from their new wives and unborn children, and in frightful legalism about equity and against humanity, both moms and dads were taken from some children. Then there was the frantic rush to get on with the war and get it over with, which violated even these rather primitive canons of Hebrew monarchical ethics by their insistence that vigorous campaigns for peace precede any resort to bloodshed. Starting the air war while French peace overture was pending, starting the ground war while a Soviet and UN peace proposals were being initiated disgraced the Allies just as much as the Basra road massacre that, like fiery holy war holocaust, will render this war more a tribute to human impatience and violence than to justice in the eyes of God and to history.

The monarchic phase of Judaic war ethics struggled with the tension of sacred and secular norms. The period represented a moral advance in that a distance was now placed between the human perception of divine will and the more mundane function of human rational judgment. When moral right is unmediated, moral freedom and humility disappear. A skepticism about self-righteousness and the rightness of one's nation's cause allows for more thoughtful national assessment of the pros and cons of potential confrontation. It also encourages a sympathy for the adversary that fosters a sense of justice, prudence, and proportion. With the prophetic phase of Hebrew ethics, deeper sense of judgment and mystery entered to sharpen the conscience .

Prophetic Ethics and Universal Conscience

> Day of wrath and Doom impending,
> Day of wrath when all creation wakes . . .
> Rest eternal grant them . . .
> Dies Irae, G. Fauré, *Requiem*

A new voice in Hebrew war history was heard with the prophets. A new vision of everlasting peace and transcending moral conscience brought divine judgment against particular political and economic moves, including war making. The subject of prophesy and war is rich and complicated and can only be summarized here. As a theological genre, prophesy could be called a symbol of eternal warfare in the midst of temporal warfare. The early prophets (*nabim*) like Amos and his predecessors were troubling figures who upset official policy and the status quo, unlike the court and house prophets, who were schooled to tout the official line and prophesy "smooth things," (Isaiah 30:10) although on occasion they also turned the tables. The noble high prophets bestowed a new vision of justice and peace into human affairs.

War, all the prophets agreed, was the judgment of God. Initially it was judgment against Yahweh's enemy in holy war, but in later prophesy the judgment could turn on Israel itself (Cyrus the Persian, Isaiah 45) or become universal. War always becomes a judgment on the world for its failure to establish and sustain justice and peace. After World War II Benjamin Britten composed his *War Requiem* for the rededication of the bombed Coventry Cathedral and arranged the central passage of the wrath of God *(Dies Irae)* to resonate with the great Christ in Last Judgement tapestry at the front of the restored cathedral. Sir William Walton and Patrick Doyle's musical score for the film version of Shakespeare's *Henry V* repeats the theme in the context of Agincourt. In All Souls College, Oxford, founded by King Henry VI in 1438 in memory of the souls departed at Agincourt, one sees an original sculpture depicting the Rising of the Dead. The scourge of war enacted divine wrath and judgment.

The ethical essence of prophesy in all of its moods of ecstatic was to affirm the authority and integrity of holy war obedience. In this phase of war ethics two themes, still vital today, predominated. In the first, Israel was called as a people with special vocation to trust in God, not in its own military power, wealth, or alliances with other nations (Isaiah 30:1-5, Jeremiah 9:23, Amos 2:13-16). Isaiah's oracle has a contemporary ring:

> Woe to those who go down to Egypt for
> help and rely on horses,
> who trust in chariots because they are many
> and in horsemen because they are very
> strong,
> but do not look to the Holy One of Israel or
> consult the Lord (31:1).

We find here a pragmatic and proleptic message. In practical terms, tanks fail or can be overwhelmed, as the Iraq's formidable force quickly showed. Wealth is such an interdependent phenomenon that it can dissipate with a collapse on the New York Stock Exchange or a precipitous rise in the price of oil. As for alliances--if history has any lesson, it is the fragility of diplomatic agreements as today's ally becomes tomorrow's enemy. The only trustworthy security is in the Lord. But that comfort is hard to grasp. The prophetic truth is that God's will, which is His intentional future, is really all that matters even in politicals.

The second moral theme the prophets introduced into war counsel is that God's righteous will is set on judgment against injustice, brutality, and inhumanity (Jeremiah 51:25,26; Amos 1:13,14; Nahum 3:5-13). The inference of this truth for the rightness of war over Kuwait when it comes to unbridled use of power, adulation and protection of wealth and oppression of the poor has moral lessons for the U.S., Kuwait, Saudi alliance. The bitter brutality, even the forbidden Arab against Arab barbarism, undercuts the claim of jihad by Iraq.

Apocalyptic War Ethics

The elusive character of the Word, will, and presence of Yahweh, together with the need on earth to take sides, declare wars, exert pressures, advocate self-interests, and generally survive, eventually dissipates holy war convictions. This denouement and the haunting realization that we might be instruments of judgment or indicted by that same judgment led to a transcendental construal of warfare and righteousness in the period in which Israel itself was taken captive, occupied, and stripped of national power.

Prophets like Joel, Habakkuk, and Daniel, along with many intertestamental writers during the period of Greek invasions and Roman occupation of the ancient Near East, made these metaphysical assumptions about what was going on in the world: The nations and kingdoms of this world were under the control of demonic powers, and the present world order was coming to an end, which would take the form of a great holy war preceding an era of divine rule and global peace.[3] The powers of evil that had turned against God now sought to destroy the creation by stirring violent ambition and thirst for power in the minds of the world's godless rulers. Just as Cain and Abel wrought havoc in their rebellion, so these "fallen angels" or "Sons of Noah" (Enoch 69:6-7, Jubilees 15:2) provoked and taught warfare. Human history on earth was seen as a process of mounting violence and destruction that would eventually culminate in some final conflagration or Armageddon, erupting in the fertile crescent east of Eden, where Adam first turned his back on the garden.

The wars at the end of time would become ever more harsh and brutal. They would be unleashed with great tribulation, particularly against the people of God (Daniel 7:24-25, 8:23). But these penultimate wars would not be decisive; they rather portended that final war of the ultimate enactment of ancient Israel's holy war. Would God act through his Davidic Messiah to bring the world back under His control (Daniel 5:10-12)? Ezekiel's prophecy (38-39) depicted a final battle in which the antigod (Gog) would be torched by Yahweh's flamethrower like an Iraqi tank, and the great messianic sacrifice (39:17-20) would yield victory for the "sons of light" over the "sons of darkness" (Qumran), inaugurating an age of peace. This expectation of cosmic conflict in which human peoples and armies merely enact divine will set the stage for primitive New Testament pacifism which, as the ultimate transfiguration of Israel's holy war, became the foundation of war ethics in the Christian era.

The Jewish mind and ethical sense became dissatisfied with this post exilic, apocalyptic thought. The strong worldly affirmation and secular mood of the faith disavows this dualistic literature as either a pathetic lamentation of helplessness or, more often, an heterodox import of non-Hebraic mentality under Hellenic or Persian influence. Jewish ethical reflection remains profoundly of this world, practical and humanistic in thrust, evidenced in just war ethics through the Talmudic and rabbinic age and into the modern era.

War Ethics in Rabbinic Tradition

The paradoxical Israeli tradition of war ethics honoring not only the God-fearing warrior but also the peacemaker is reflected in the unexpected event whereby David was forbidden to build the temple, the home for Yahweh's presence, because "You have been a fighting man and have shed blood" (I Chronicles 28:2-3). Was the soldier by the nature of the work cultically unclean or was this the ancient notion of blood guilt? When Jehu, supported by Elisha, massacred the heretical house of Ahab and the Baal-worshippers, Hosea the prophet condemned the bloodshed as a crime. "I will punish the line of Jehu for the bloodshed in Jezreel and put an end to the kingdom of Israel" (Hosea 1:4). Yahweh, it seems, was not so much a god of conquest, subjugation, and war as he was God of grace, forgiveness, and compassion (Exodus 34:6). Yahweh, indeed, was one who puts an end to war. "From end to end of the earth he stamps out war: he breaks the bow, he snaps the spear and burns the shield in the fire" (Psalm 46:9). The "prince of peace" became something of an oxymoron; in post exile Judaism the image of a suffering, empathetic Messiah was added to the picture of a warrior-conqueror. The strange parody of a military parade Christians call Palm Sunday became the final caricature of the holy warrior. In the Maccabean period, furious violence seemed only to fuel even greater retaliatory violence from the occupying Romans. Barrabas may have been such an insurrectionist in the hammering (quick-hit) tradition of Judas Maccabaeus; and were it not for the ironic twist of his fate, he would surely have been crucified like all the other hit-and-run guerrillas.

Rabbinic and Talmudic ethics are ethics of diaspora. During the Hellenistic era, Judeans moved into Asia Minor, Egypt, North Africa, even Eastern Europe. Following the Roman destruction of Jerusalem, the Jewish people commenced their dispersal throughout the world. Ironically for the present study, the most important cultural site of the Hebrew people was in ancient Iraq. The authority for normative practice during that period was the Babylonian Talmud, which took shape from 100 B.C. to A.D. 640, the time of the appearance of Islam. After the Bar Kokhba revolt in Palestine against Rome in A.D. 132-135, the Palestinian

Jewish rabbinate fled to Babylonia and Mesopotamia, where for 400 years Jewish learning and ethical instruction continued to develop. In cities--many now demolished by Allied bombing--from Basra south of the confluence of the Tigris and Euphrates, north over the Mesopotamian plateau to places like Babylonia and Baghdad, the people of Israel survived, even flourished under Iranian, Parthian, Sassanian, and eventually Iraqi rule. Finally, in 1948 the community of Iraqi Jewry was received back into Palestine.

In the cosmopolitan culture of the late Roman period, religious differences were accommodated and the feverish passions of holy war and rebellion abated into the hope for a secure pluralistic and secular peace. In this society Jewish power resided in an exilarch, who served as an ethnic ruler over the Jewish community and liaison to the Iranian court. The rabbis who articulated the ongoing religious and theological story of the people then developed ethical instruction to guide the people's decisions. Rabbinic interpretation in the unfolding Talmud became the prism through which Hebrew scriptures *(Tanakh)* were predicated. Convictions like the Torah law that "whoever sheds blood diminishes God's presence in the world" (Gen. Rabbah 34:14) now became central to Israel's sense of its destiny to live at peace with its neighbors and its host societies.

Reflecting back on the war history we have rehearsed, we find the rabbis held that there were three kinds of war: *Milchemer chovah* was obligatory war, of which the conquest of Canaan was the single instance (although some modern rabbis saw the war against Hitler as obligatory, especially when its outcome portended the very survival of the Jewish people). *Milchemer reshut*, optional war, was the more ethically ambivalent action of extending one's borders, as with David's expansion of his kingdom. The modern occupation of territories can be seen similarly as political, less easily justified pursuits. *Milchemer mitzvah*, what we have called holy war or "commanded war," is like the war against the Amalakites or in the Warsaw ghetto, where struggle to death and extermination was necessary because holocaust desire animated the enemy. In the present conflict, if Iraq had used chemical warheads in its Scud attacks on Tel Aviv and other areas of Israel or if it had developed or utilized nuclear arms, this holy war fury might have flamed up again. Modern Israeli war ethics justify, for example, a preemptive strike against an enemy's nascent nuclear or chemical/biological capacity. These ethics also explain Israel's complete support for the Allied cause even as it held that most difficult kind of aggressive posture of complete restraint.

Maimonides, the Jewish physician-theologian serving in the Muslim court in the twelfth century, reworked the Deuteronomic war ethic (ch. 20-25). It is not surprising that a physician-pastor emphasized themes of restraint, proportion, peace, and the restoration of well-being. Furious and vengeful destruction of the land was forbidden:

> It is forbidden to cut down fruit-bearing trees outside a city, nor may a water channel be deflected from them so that they wither. Whoever cuts down a fruit-bearing tree is flogged. The penalty is imposed not only for cutting it down during a siege; whenever a fruit yielding tree is cut down with destructive intent, flogging is incurred.

> Not only one who cuts down trees, but one who smashes household goods, tears clothes, demolishes a building, stops a spring, or destroys articles of food with destructive intent, transgresses the command 'thou shalt not destroy.

> Maimonides, *Mishneh Torah*: Hilchot Mehchim (5:1, 6:8,10).

Against this standard, certainly Saddam Hussein's war and probably George Bush's war violated Jewish war ethics. That itself may be of little matter, but as Jewish ethics contribute elements that are true and universal to global ethics, those who commit prohibited acts are culpable before an objective world court. Saddam's actions and furious jihad abandoned the conservationist preservative ethos that holds that "the earth is the Lord's." Allied bombing of food supply routes, the demolition of noncombatant buildings and bridges, the disruption of urban water supplies, and harming of medical care systems clearly violate the spirit of Mishnah elaboration of Torah.

The tension between rabbinic ethics and an emerging secular tradition of war ethics is seen in the question of a backdoor escape policy for sieges. In leaving the fourth flank open to spare civilians from danger and death, Maimonides went beyond Deuteronomy:

> When siege is laid to a city for the purpose of capture, it may not be surrounded on all four sides but only on three in order to give an

> opportunity for escape to those who would flee
> to save their lives, as it is said: 'And they warred
> against Midian, as the Lord commanded Moses'
> (Num. 31:7). It has been learned by tradition
> that that was the instruction given to Moses
> (6,7).

Walzer finds this teaching "hopelessly naive."[4] Only a refugee people, he argues, people who have lost a militant perspective, could dream up such a policy: When we think of the major incidents of siege throughout history, the Jews on Mount Masada besieged by the Roman legions or the German siege of Leningrad, for example, we realize that combatants will mix with civilians and then turn again to harm those who have them circled. Soldiers, who always receive preferential treatment such as access to scarce food in a siege, will exploit civilians, disguise themselves as innocents, and do everything they can to exploit this convention. But Walzer misses the point. Yahwistic reasoning is not consequentialist. The genius of Judaic casuistry is to open a situation to the surprise of grace, where life may be spared even in the midst of the fine calculations of closed-door military strategy. Like trial by water or Solomon's verdict with the contending and pretending mothers, divine justice requires that, despite the risk, a door must be kept open to protect the innocent. God's exodus nature always requires a way out. The theological origin of this notion, that none is killed, or for that matter given life, apart from the divine will, returns to the essence of the Israeli moral tradition of war and peace. God's will is life and shalom for his creation. War is always human foolishness and malevolence. Against great evil or a threat to the people's heritage that can only be checked and cleansed by war, then as a last resort, war may be undertaken, but must be carried out honestly, swiftly, and with maximal protection of life and land. Maimonides stressed these points:

> No war is declared against any nation before
> peace offers are made to it. This obtains both in
> an optional war and a religious war (6,1).

> Once they make peace and take upon
> themselves the seven commandments, it is
> forbidden to deceive them and prove false to the
> covenant made with them (6,3).

The universal Noachite law must be offered to the foe (as with the universal laws of humanity imposed at Nuremberg), and when those humanitarian stipulates are received and murder, theft, adultery, and cruelty are disowned and justice is established, then the adversary must be treated with civility and honor. The meaning of human life in the world is to "do justice, love mercy and walk humbly with God" (Micah 6:8). All human purpose is gathered into the ethical imperative of fighting injustice and establishing peace and love in the world. To love is to give life, to harm is to kill. In a memorable passage, Maimonides focused on this intensification of ethics as the resistance to evil and positive introduction of good into the world:

> Whoever is able to protest against the transgressions of his own family and does not do so is punished for the transgressions of his family. Whoever is able to protest against the transgressions of the people of his community and does not do so is punished for the transgressions of his community. Whoever is able to protest against the transgressions of the entire world and does not do so is punished for the transgressions of the entire world. (Sanhedrin 54b)

That mercy and compassion are at the moral heart of life's meaning and obligation is the profound enigma at the heart of Israel's history: the mystery of suffering. Love in its deepest divine reaches entails faithfulness (Psalms), heartbreak (Hosea), fellow suffering, and ultimately sacrificial love for another. As understood in Yahwistic faith, the underlying drama of life on earth is one of suffering, sacrifice, judgment, death, and transfiguration. Crucifixion, which Paul the Apostle thought was the deepest ethical offense to Hebrew consciousness, was actually the essence of its moral view.

Israel has assumed a vocation of redemptive suffering in world history. Rabbi Joshua ben Levi said, "He who gladly accepts the sufferings of this world brings salvation to the world" (*Baba Kamma* 93a). God's self-disclosure to His created and alienated human family requires loss not only in the chosen vessel but in God himself. The implications of the doctrine that the shalom of God requires sacrifice for the ethics of resistance and aggression are complex. Perhaps only the primitive Christian notion of martyrdom, the Augustinian doctrine of nonresistance even to lethal assault, and the military doctrine of

surrender approximate this theological insight. To these themes we will
return as our argument unfolds.

"Israel," wrote Matthew Arnold, is the one people on earth who
know "where the world is going." Time and space, nature and history
are suffused with redemption--holy warfare yielding shalom. The *Alenu*
prayer of Rabbi R. G. Hirsch captures this vision of what remains after
warfare is accomplished:

> May the time not be distant, O God, when thy
> name shall be worshipped in all the earth, when
> unbelief shall disappear and error be no more.
> Fervently we pray that the day may come when
> all men shall invoke thy name,when corruption
> and evil shall give way to purity and goodness,
> when superstition shall no longer enslave the
> mind, nor idolatry blind the eye, when all who
> dwell on earth shall know that to thee alone
> every knee must bend and every tongue give
> homage. O may all, created in thine image,
> recognize that they are brethren, so that, one in
> spirit and one in fellowship, they may be forever
> united before thee. Then shall thy kingdom be
> established on earth and the world of thine
> ancient seer be fulfilled. The Lord will reign for
> ever and ever.[5]

War, Peace, and Holocaust in Israeli Moral History

The Nazi holocaust, inflicted on the passive and peaceable
population of European Jewry by the Third Reich under the last caesar,
Adolf Hitler, forever mutes religion, even wartime faith, fires the
righteous flames of indignation and self-protection, and makes possible
the ultimate meaning of that faith. Not only was God not present as
aggressive conqueror, He was absent also as defender. He was not there
at all. Auschwitz spelled the death of God and the birth of Israel as a
people of self-definition, maker of its own aggression, its own defense.

"Why did the heavens not darken?" Princeton political historian
Arno Mayer asked in his study of the holocaust. Drawing from the
Chronicles of Solomon Bar Simson in the massacre of the Jews of Mainz by
crusaders during the First Crusade, A.D. 1096,[6] Mayer asked, "Where
was God?"

> Let the ears hearing this and its like be seared,
> for who has heard or seen the likes of it? . . .
> Why did the heavens not darken and the stars
> not withhold their radiance; why did not the
> sun and moon turn dark?[7]

As in present-day Kuwait, war like holocaust blotted out the sun. Saddam Hussein's ecoterrorism aside, war eclipses God as did the holocaust. The immediacy of divine command and fellowship has vanished. It is as if God withdraws His breath *(nephesh)* when we resort to taking life. The vibrant sense of Yahweh's presence, as when the Ark was carried out front in tribal wandering and warfare, is now more hidden.

The expectation of apocalyptic resonance in nature to historical human righteousness or dissonance to injustice is not merely poetic or metaphoric imagination but a legitimate demand that space and time reflect the judgments of their creator. When Joshua besieges Jericho the skies *ought* to darken without igniting oil wells and the walls *ought* to come "tumbling down." But on occasion natural law prevails and divine intervention and revelation are not forthcoming. What did the climactic event in Israel's history--the holocaust--do to its war ethics? Certainly it paved the way for the modern secular state that now engages the community of twentieth-century nation-states with the same assumptions of power and defense that all others exhibit. As a state, Israel has fully succumbed to the prophet's indictment that it has become like all other peoples. Israel's modern history, shaped by the 1948 implantation in Palestine, the immediate wars of resistance, the Suez crisis of 1956, the Six Day War of 1967, the surprise attack of 1973, the perennial *Intifada* of the Palestinians and the recent conflict with Iraq, all have fashioned a political and military ethos perhaps best described by what Army Colonel Yakov Hasdai, a resident philosopher, might call "doing what is right in your own eyes and hoping Yahweh sees it that way as well."

The new post holocaust political reality is genocide, or what Mayer called "Judeocide." In ancient *herem*, Israel was commanded to eradicate a people when they were overcome within the bounds of holy land. But genocide is a new phenomenon. When an entire nation is threatened or when apocalyptic taunts to wash Israel into the sea are made, a new ethic of survival and defense comes into play. Modern Israeli policy is animated by the reality, or perceived reality, of such threats. This mutant war ethic, far removed from its biblical or rabbinic precursors, may lie behind one strain of Anglo-American Middle East policy, which seems to say that any Arab power or collectivity of power that comes near to equalizing that of Israel (e.g., nuclear capacity) must be put down preemptively.

Mayer argued that it was the failure of the Nazi all-or-nothing campaign against the USSR that provoked the compensatory policy of genocide or the "final solution." We might go further to argue that the earlier humiliation of the German nation in the settlements following World War I necessitated that a domestic, nonmilitary scapegoat to restore the semblance of pride and dignity to a disgraced people. The old ethical principle of refraining from humiliating another lest the natural pecking-order phenomenon be unleashed might have been at work in this instance. One can only wonder in the frightful aftermath of the war over Kuwait as the tattered remnant of Iraq's Republican Guard unleashed terrible fury against the Shiah, Kurdish and Communist uprisings in various provinces, whether the announced Allied policy of humiliating Hussein, forcing him to lose face before his own people, was psychologically wise.

If homicide becomes obviously unjustifiable under conditions of modern war, genocide must just as obviously be outlawed, especially in this day when secular nation-states cut from the "fascist" mold of early twentieth-century politics fulminate against "dirty niggers," "conniving Jews," "greasy Arabs," and other racial, religious, and ethnic groups. The impulse to exterminate a people--be it Muslim Palestinians, Jewish Israelis, Irish Protestants, or Irish Catholics--must be obliterated from the modern mind. This would be the preeminent convention of any truly modern just war ethics.

What is the connection of holocaust with holy war? We have noted that in the most primitive version of Jewish holy war, the conquest of Canaan, holocaust was a means of executing holy war. In the Christian Crusades and in the counter Crusade of Islamic jihad, decimation of a people and holy incineration of heretical faith was often a motive. Even in the early twentieth century, in the events of World War I, as Rabbi Richard Rubenstein and to a lesser degree Arno Mayer argued, holocaust and holy war passions were present. Rubenstein, in his numerous writings on the First World War and the holocaust of 1938-1945, showed that all of the elements of evangelization, extermination, and immolation in Hitler's holocaust were fully present in 1914-1918. From the trench warfare near the towns of Vaux and Verdun to Auschwitz, Mayer notes that "this immense blood-letting (a phrase from Jewish cultic sacrifice). . . . was not due primarily to the deadliness of modern weapons such as automatic machine-guns but must be attributed to the zeal with which swarms of officers and men kept going over the top in the face of impossible odds. This dutiful self-immolation was a measure of the extent to which the war of 1914-1918 was a secularized 'Holy War.'"[8]

Part of the resolve of the people of Israel after two World Wars and the Nazi holocaust is never again to lie down in passive sacrificial surrender to enemies with incendiary holy war ambitions. "Lambs led to slaughter" may have been an epithet directed at the unresisting pacifist resignation in death camp victims that enabled handfuls of Nazi guards to herd thousands into the gas chambers. The question must be raised, however, whether sporadic resistance would in any way have altered the outcome and, significant for my inquiry, whether a posture of "next time get them before they get you" really fosters peace or only perpetual simmering strife.

War Ethics and the Search for Peace in Haretz Israel

While Iraqi fires still smoldered in Kuwait, U.S. Secretary of State James Baker met with Israeli officials in Jerusalem, proposing a "land for peace" arrangement to settle the Palestinian question; he left affirming Israel's "dual-track" approach. Peace, which all reasonable persons assume requires both a secure Israel and a Palestinian homeland, could come either from Israel relinquishing occupied territories in exchange for an end to Intifada and the assurance of permanent security or from bilateral treaties carved out between Israel and individual Arab states (e.g., Egypt) as well as the Palestinians. In either case, the war ethics and the more fundamental political ethics of the state of Israel will come under intense scrutiny. The holy war and just war ruminations of biblical and Talmudic Israelite religion will also be dusted off and taken down from the shelves. What might be the shape of a contemporary appropriation or repudiation of those historic beliefs and values? Do Arab promises to lift the boycott on Israel and reciprocal Israeli commitments to remove settlements on the West Bank portend *shalom* ?

The contours of two more radical views and a middle view more sensitive to the nuance of Israel's moral history can be discerned: Calls for a more theocratic and belligerent state with a belligerent posture are heard in present-day Israel. Rabbi Shlomo Aviner wrote, "It was not Herzl or Ben-Gurion who established our state, not the political or practical Zionists that did it, but God Almighty."[9] The God on the march in Israel in the 1990s, at the close of this apocalyptic century and millennium, is again a man of war--a Messiah. Writing of Gush Emunim and his followers, even Yitzhak Shamir, holding both the military and prime ministerial portfolios in the Israeli cabinet, rejected this as "the myth of the strongman"--an allusion to Nietzschean and Nazi

Übermensch. Surely an approach will seek quickly to settle the occupied territory with Soviet, preferably Georgian, Jews and to expel the Palestinians, or at best keep them in a permanent noncitizen, servile *Fremdwerker* status. A linked political philosophy inflamed by holy war rhetoric will work for the foreseeable future to maintain an upper hand in a perpetual balance of terror.

Another view, drawing more on the justice and pacifist strains of Hebrew ethics, holds that the very concept of Judaism as a spiritual and moral phenomenon is incompatible with twentieth-century power politics and warfare: The idea of a Jewish state is a contradiction in terms. Gershon Weiler, one of the most powerful voices of this tradition, contended that theocracy is impossible in the light of the best Jewish philosophy and ethics in the tradition running through Josephus, Philo, Maimonides, Spinoza, *Tanaka* (Scripture) and *Halakha* (tradition). Using a theme that has been taken over in Christian and secular just war theory, Weiler unfolded an argument that for the Jew only *Halakha*, not the state, has legitimate authority. Can the state of Israel or even the United Nations command legitimate authority to declare just or holy war? No, wrote Weiler. That would be idolatry and blasphemy. *Halakha* cannot provide the justification, the religious rationale, or the *fundamentum* of the state. To preserve their separate integrities and purities, the state must go its way and religion its own, separate way. Quoting Amos Elon, Weiler concluded, "It seems clear that if Zionism was destined ultimately to merely bring about the establishment of another national theocracy, combining medieval orthodoxy with modern chauvinism, both Jews and Arabs will have paid too high a price for it."[10]

There is another option. Biblical and rabbinic ethics extol an age of justice, human community, and peace. The bellicist view is right in its contention that God is active in history and that messianic redemption is at work in the world. The foundation, defense, and sustenance of nation Israel is part of that "will" and "way." He will remember his heritage and we must "remember Jerusalem." But national aggrandizement and subjugation of Arabs--what the Israeli press calls peripheralization (continually repelling threatening power centrifugally to an outer rim of remote nonthreat)--is not Yahweh's will, for He is a God who gives liberation and habitation to all peoples to dwell on the earth in peace. The pietist option also holds a fragment of truth in its recognition of prophetic shalom as transcendent of any worldly structure. But permanent religious schizophrenia, with an inner, transcending eschatologic realm of piety and an outer, secular, political construct is not tenable, certainly not within Judaism, the faith of creation.

Beyond the "rejectionists" (Noam Chomsky) on both sides, those like Muammar Qaddafi, the Ayatollah Khomeini, and radical Islamic groups who deny Israel's right to exist, and M. P. Zev'eri, Sharon, Rabbi Kahane, and their ilk, who would inflict latter-day holocaust on Palestinians if they could, a new consensus of those who desire peace, understanding, and mutual respect would be in keeping with Judaic ethics. Keholeth, the preacher, claims there is "a time for war and a time for peace" (Ecclesiastes 3:8). Justice is the precondition for peace and peace is the confirmation of justice. Justice confirms Israel's right to exist both as modern settlers and as ancient heirs of the promise. Justice also requires that a permanent habitat be provided for the indigenous Palestinians. Because of the presence of God, this holy land and its holy city must forever be preserved as a sacred site for all Abrahamic peoples.

In reviewing the roots of holy war and just war in Judaic tradition, we have laid the foundation for a discussion of Islamic and Christian appropriation of that heritage. We now turn to Islamic tradition because of the literal way that jihad expresses holy war ethics and because of the resurgence of this tradition in Iraq's recent wars with Iran and the defenders of Kuwait.

Notes

1. Quoted in L. H. Lapham, "Onward Christian Soldiers," in Sifry and Cerf, *op. cit.*, p. 452ff.

2. See "Deuteronomy" Introduction, G. Ernest Wright *The Interpreters Bible*, Nashville: Abingdon, 1953, p. 323ff. Gerhard Von Rad *Deuteronomium Studien*, Göttingen; Van den Hoeck, 1947, and *Der Heilige Krieg*, 1951.

3. "War," *The Interpreter's Dictionary of the Bible*, Nashville: Abingdon, 1962, p. 800.

4. Michael Walzer, *Just and Unjust Wars*, New York: Basic Books, 1977, p. 168.

5. R. G. Hirsch, *The Most Precious Gift: Peace in Jewish Tradition*, New York: Hebrew Congregations, 1974. Quoted in John Ferguson, *War and Peace in the World's Religions*, London: Sheldon Press, 1977, p. 97-98. I have used Ferguson's excellent summary of the tradition(s) throughout this study.

6. Arno J. Mayer, *Why did the Heavens Not Darken? The Final Solution in History*, London: Verso, 1990.

7. Ibid., p. 1.

8. Ibid., p. 4.

9. Hanoch Bartor, "The New Messiah," *Ma'ariv* , 4 May 1984, p. 1.

10. Amos Elon, *The Israelis: Founders and Sons*, London: Weidenfeld and Nicholson, 1971, p. 436. Quoted in Gershon Weiler, *Jewish Theocracy*, Leiden: E. J. Brill, 1988, p. 329.

4

Islam, Jihad, and Iraq's Holy War

To continue the exploration of war ethics in the religious cultures that joined in battle during the war over Kuwait one might now turn to the Christian heritage of holy and just war. Two reasons prompt me to delay that consideration until the next chapter. First, Islamic jihad builds so directly on Judaic and Semitic martial theology that its treatment follows more logically from what I have explored thus far. Second, the Christian tradition of war ethics contributes most directly to the secular just war theory and therefore better serves as a bridge from the religious to the secular heritage. The reader will bear in mind that Islam emerged in the seventh century as the final major Abrahamic faith, though often in enmity with those precursor faiths. It has explicitly and self-consciously developed in continuity with Judaism and Christianity.

Scenes from the war over Kuwait flash before my mind when I consider the faith tradition of Islam. Most affirm the humanity and affinity of that sibling religious tradition with which Jews and Christians have found company at times and controversy at others. On the light side, many were delighted when the customarily demure British Foreign Secretary Douglas Hurd, in a moment of fury at the irascible Saddam Hussein, reached deep into his francophobia for the ultimate expletive, " that puffed up frog of a man." One night as I watched TV, I recognized an Iraqi infantryman who was a student at my university in Chicago. Captured in the bermuda shorts and basketball shoes which were now his uniform, he had apparently returned to his home in Iraq in the middle of the war. Two other scenes arose from the final days of conflict when Iraqi troops were surrendering rapidly: a U.S. soldier knelt beside an Iraqi POW showing him how to open his rations packet and joining him in a meal. Finally, who could forget the photo in the *Observer*, one of the few pictures of fellow humanity that the highly censored British

press was allowed to pass: the scorched, dead face of an Iraqi soldier
entombed in his tank on the Basra road.

As a faith seen within its enfolding culture, Islam's ethos is shaped
by scenes such as that tank pilot or the wreckage on the Basra road.
Writers have pointed to the role that defeat and surrender played in the
early history of Islam. Retreat, humiliation, and simmering revenge have
worked their way into the fabric of the Arabic-Islamic soul. Before the
oil boom, Islam had taken root in a poor and suffering-filled part of the
world. The rise of Islam must be understood in part as a judgment on
the paths of expansion and evangelization chosen by the universal faiths
of Judaism and Christianity. Judaism chose a narrow ethnocentric
destiny, despite its universal roots, and Christian mission history, leapt
over Arabia from its eastern origins and made its homeland in the
Western Roman Empire. Even today, as the Emir returns to Kuwait City,
the discrepancy is pronounced between rich emirates and poorer states
like Iraq and Egypt. Even within a country like Kuwait, the disparity
between rich and poor is stark. The thousands of rich fled with their
gold on the day of Iraq's invasion. The poor were left to suffer. The
Islamic life-journey, wrote the sympathetic observer V. S. Naipaul, is one
of "fear and reward--war and worldly grief."[1]

Five times each day, hundreds of millions of Muslims turn toward
Mecca, kneel, and pray to Allah, "the Merciful and Compassionate;
Master of the Day of Judgment." Despite U.S. and Western attempts to
retain power for kings, shahs, or secular presidents like Saddam
Hussein--despite attempts to discard the veil and *chador*, and displace
solemn shared meals with McDonaldses and wailing calls to prayer with
satellite dishes and porno films–a pervasive popular piety endures. This
faith and moral life-style not only permeate the solidly Islamic world
from Senegal in the west to the Philippines in the east, from Uzbekistan
in the north to Madagascar in the south, but are also making a marked
impression on Western Europe and North America. In my own
university hospital in Chicago, a majority of our medical residents stem
from these cultures and profess, however reservedly, this faith.

To answer the question of *why* and *how* war is made within the
culture of Islam--even in the highly secular and nationalist state of Iraq--
requires delving in the history of Islam in the Arabian desert, tracing the
contours of jihad in both its ancient and recent expressions, and finally
relating these notions to what has transpired in the war over Kuwait. As
noted in the discussion of war ethics in ancient and modern Israel,
enormous discontinuities exist between the classical religious society and
the modern secular state. As with Israel and later with Christianity, the
reader will have to ask whether the faith being explored, given its ethical

and eschatological character, is in any way compatible with war--or the very notion of statehood.

The Origins of Islam and Dispositions of War and Peace

The origins of Islam and Judaism ultimately coincide. Although Islam includes learning from Jewish communities in Arabian cities such as Khaybar and Medina and from Christians living in Mecca or travelling along the trade routes, the borrowed beliefs and values are not as important as the common heritage of the two peoples shaped in early Semitic and ancient Near Eastern moral culture. Sephardic, prophetic, and sacred monarchic traditions reach back to the dawn of conscience in ancient Egypt, Mesopotamia, and Arabia. Convictions about monotheism, the soul, divine judgment, and moral responsibility are a common heritage of Jew and Muslim. Both peoples are children of Abraham. For centuries, Bedouin tribes lived a pastoral and nomadic existence on the Arabian steppe and desert. On the move in search of pasture for flocks of sheep, goats, and camels, dependent on isolated water sources to sustain animals and people, herding, trading, and raiding became ways of life. As in the tribal life that presaged Israel, laws and rules of conflict and dispute were formulated and enforced by clan and tribe ethics and customs.

Tribal beliefs and mores always have a strong animistic flavor. Springs, trees, stones, and wells become sacred places, identified with deities. The exotic and ecologic stirrings of faith, that characterized early Islam were exploited and violated in both the Iran-Iraq war and in the Iraqi campaign against Kuwait. When Iraqi soldiers, like Iranian youths before them, marched into battle hoping for the instantaneous heavenly presence of God, beautiful women, and a bounty of pleasures, they may not have seen through Saddam Hussein's mirage. The ecoterrorism in which smoke destroyed monsoon harvests elsewhere on the planet and oil slicks decimated plankton and all in the food chain dependent on it seems strangely alien to this primitive pastoral ethic.

Muhammad was born about A.D. 570 and became a trader in Mecca in the tradition of his father. Troubled by the chicanery and exploitation of the market economy, he became a conscientious and contemplative young businessman. At age forty, on the Night of Power and Excellence, he received the first oracles that over the next twenty-two years (610-632) formed the Quran (recitation). It was the warrior-angel Gabriel who commanded its publication. Muhammad was reluctant, and like the disdained Hebrew prophets, he was ignored. His condemnation of child abuse, woman battering, usury, suppression of the poor, and manipulations of power led to his castigation and persecution. Finding that he was a prophet without honor in Mecca, he accepted an invitation to mediate a tribal dispute in the city of Medina. This flight *(hejira)* changed the fortunes of his fledgling movement and fostered the creation of the Islamic community/state. Once prophet-ruler of Medina, he extended his rule over all Arabia by diplomatic and military means. The victory over Mecca at Badr was an Allah-sanctioned holy war of monotheistic righteousness over polytheistic barbarity.

Badr is a sacred moment in Islamic history. In the final conquest of Mecca in 630, following the failure of diplomacy to gain "submission" (Islam), Muhammad granted amnesty and assimilation to the archadversaries. In the prophetic words of his last sermon, words that in the light of the Kuwait intrusion and the subsequent Kuwaiti persecution of Palestinians make us wonder whether the people who did these deeds are really Islamic peoples, he said: "Know ye that every Moslem is a brother to every other Moslem, and that ye are now one brotherhood. It is not legitimate for any one of you, therefore, to appropriate unto himself anything that belongs to his brother."[2]

Like the tribes before they settled in Israel and the Schechem confederation that had to fight syncretism and assimilation, in pristine Islam the world was divided between good and evil, believers and heathen. Following Zoroastrian martial imagery (which also rubbed off along the trade routes across Arabia), "The believers fight in the way of God, and the unbelievers fight in the idol's way. Fight you therefore against the friends of Satan" (Quran 4:76). Fight or flight (jihad or *hejira*) were the only actions open to a people with expansionist ambition and persecutionist fate. "So let them fight in the way of God who sell the present life for the world to come; and whosoever fights in the way of God and is slain, or conquers, we shall bring him a mighty wage" (4:74). Holy warriors *(mujahidin)* joined company with the army of angels sent to the battlefield to wage Allah's jihad. The reason that a quick and decisive victory of Christian crusaders over *mujahidin* is particularly satisfying was that, as for Elijah on Mount. Carmel, the event vindicated not only the army but also God. Conversely, as John Yoder noted, in holy war, "You don't need to win."[3] "Saddam won," an Iraqi recently told me, "by holding out against Uncle Sam for so long." Although forty days and one hundred hours did not seem to me to be that long, in terms of desert temptation it was an eternity.

Muhammad introduced a spiritual and moral reformation, even revolution, into human life that even today, after the Crusades and the Ottoman accommodation, secularism, and bizarre fundamentalism, remains a vital force in world history. One of the best modern studies of Islam concludes:

Muhammad introduced a new moral order in which the origin and end of all actions was not self or tribal interest but God's will. Belief in the Day of Judgment and resurrection of the body added a dimension of human responsibility and accountability that had been absent in Arabian religion. Tribal vengeance and retaliation were subordinated to a belief in a just and merciful creator and judge. A society based on tribal affiliation and man-made tribal law or custom was replaced by a religiously bonded community *(umma)* governed by God's law.[4]

Spreading the Faith by the Sword

In the seventh century of the Christian era two great kingdoms met in Arabia. The Byzantine Eastern Roman empire and the Sassanian Persian empire also divided the Christian and Zoroastrian faiths. A century later the Arabic language and the Muslim faith had, with the defeat of both empires, made Turkish and Persian the secondary languages of Islamic civilization. Turkish Islam, radiating from the city where Constantine founded the Christian empire, staved off Mongol invaders from the east and Christian crusaders from the west, and for a millennium consolidated and extended Muslim culture. At its apogee, Islamic culture extended across North Africa and into southern Italy, Spain, and France. The cross-fertilization of Christian, Islamic, and Jewish peoples from the tenth to thirteenth century produced brilliant intellectual achievement within each of those cultures, including the revival of Greek science and philosophy.

By this time Judaism had become purely a faith, ritual, and way of life with no political power or aspiration. Christianity, though often vested with political power by popes and rulers, had at its heart a tension between *regnum* and *sacerdotium*, the secular and spiritual realms, that could be traced to Augustine's two cities. Islam, however, was a political and militant faith, a fusion of the sublime and the secular. Under the caliphs, Allah's deputies on earth, Muslim Arabia was turned into a great conquering empire, the fires of which have only been banked in recent times in the back and fill of orthodox revival in states already nominally Islamic. For a millennium, that militant faith and faith-infused militancy fueled a war ethic that our generation has come to know through the *mujahidin* (holy warriors) of the Iranian revolution and in a somewhat anemic version in Iraq. What are the features of jihad or Islamic holy war?

Islamic and Arab Doctrines of Holy and Just War

In his important book *The Legal System of Iraq*, S. H. Amin reviewed the Iran-Iraq war in light of the legal and moral doctrines of Iraqi society.[5] Quoting Amin in the *Times Literary Supplement*, Charles Tripp wrote: "Iraq has an elaborate code of civil and commercial procedures . . . these provisions are strictly adhered to unless a case is somehow politically important to the Iraqi Government."[6] In similar fashion Islamic law outlaws all forms of war except jihad. Muslim jurists distinguish the word *harb* (war) from jihad (holy struggle). The Muslim historian Ibn Khaldun (1332–1406) held that all conflicts such as tribal feuds and raids (which Muhammad outlawed) were unjust wars and that only jihad against internal rebels or nonbelieving aggressors was justified. The first theme of Islamic political ethics is that all war except jihad is wrong. Quran (2:190, 9:5) laid down the foundational premise that only self-defensive war is permissible for Muslims. In a passage that supports Yoder's point that struggle against oppression is valid even if it fails, Quran states "Slay them whenever you come upon them because oppression is even worse than killing. But if they desist, behold God is forgiving, a dispenser of grace. Fight against them until there is no more oppression and religion belongs to God" (2:190-192). Jusi, the Shi'a jurist, believes that holy war is required against opponents of Islam, except Jews, Christians, and Zoroastrians, adherents of the parental faiths of Islam.

Lacking priests or any sacerdotal system, Islam is principally a way of behavior. Prescribed behavior in times of threat constitute the traditions of moral war or holy war in Islamic thought. The few primary texts have been assembled in the resourceful work by Bernard Lewis, *Islam: From the Prophet Muhammad to the Capture of Constantinople*, especially v.1, *Politics and War*.[7] The basic texts from the *Quran* are as follows:

> And when the sacred months are passed, kill those who join other gods with God wherever ye shall find them; and seize them, besiege them, and lay wait for them with every kind of ambush: but if they shall convert, and observe prayer, and pay the obligatory alms, then let them go their way, for God is Gracious,

Merciful. If any one of those who join gods with God as an asylum of thee, grant him an asylum, that he may hear the Word of God, and then let him reach his place of safety. This, for that they are people devoid of knowledge (9:5, 6).

Make war upon such of those to whom the Scriptures have been given as believe not in God, or in the last day, and who forbid not that which God and His Apostle have forbidden, and who profess not the profession of the truth, until they pay tribute *(jizyah)* out of hand, and they be humbled (9:29).

Let those then fight on the path of God, who exchange this present life for that which is to come; for whoever fighteth on God's path, whether he be slain or conquer, we will in the end give him a great reward. But what hath come to you that ye fight not on the path of God, and for the weak among men, women, and children, who say, 'O our Lord! bring us forth from this city whose inhabitants are oppressors; give us a champion from Thy presence; and give us from thy presence a defender.' They who believe, fight on the path of God; and they who believe not, fight on the path of Tagut: fight therefore against the friends of Satan. Verily the craft of Satan shall be powerless! Hast thou not marked those to whom it was said, 'Withhold your hands awhile *from war* ; and observe prayer, and pay the stated alms.' But when war is commanded them, lo! a portion of them fear men as with the fear of God, or with a yet greater fear, and say: 'O our Lord! why hast Thou commanded us war? Couldst thou not have given us respite till our not distant end?' SAY: Small the fruition of this world; but the next life is the *true* good for him who feareth God! and ye shall not be wronged so much as the skin of a date-stone (4:76-79).

They will ask thee concerning war in the Sacred
Month. SAY: To war therein is bad, but to turn
aside from the cause of God, and to have no
faith in him, and in the Sacred Temple, and to
drive out its people, is worse in the sight of God;
and civil strife is worse than bloodshed. They
will not cease to war against you until they turn
you from your religion, if they be able: but
whoever of you shall turn from his religion and
die an infidel, their works shall be fruitless in
this world, and in the next: they shall be
consigned to the fire; therein to abide for aye.
But they who believe, and who fly their country,
and fight in the cause of God may hope for
God's mercy: and God is Gracious, Merciful
(2:214, 215).

SAY to the infidels: If they desist *from their
unbelief*, what is now past shall be forgiven them;
but if they return *to it* , they have already before
them the doom of the ancients! Fight then
against them till strife be at an end and the
religion be all of it God's. If they desist, verily
God beholdeth what they do: but if they turn
their back, know ye that God is your protector:
Excellent protector! excellent helper! And know
ye, that when ye have taken any booty, a fifth
part belongeth to God and to the Apostle, and to
the near of kin, and to orphans, and to the poor,
and to the wayfarer (8:39-42).[8]

These Quranic verses are not in the initial revelation to Muhammad
but in the Surahs, given after political power over enemies had been
established. The later sayings attributed to the Prophet elaborate these
points:

God is sponsor for him who goeth forth to fight
on the road of God *(Sabilu 'llah)*. If he be not
killed, he shall return to his house with rewards
and booty, but if he be slain, he shall be taken to
Paradise.

> Guarding the frontiers of Islam for even one day
> is worth more than the whole world and all that
> is in it.
>
> He who dies and has not fought for the religion
> of Islam, nor has even said in his heart, 'Would
> to God I were a champion that could die in the
> road of God,' is even as a hypocrite.[9]

In these texts, warfare is seen to be the proper state of religious consciousness in Islam. Just as the Apostle Paul spoke of perpetual spiritual warfare against "principalities and powers" (Colossians), the Muslim is to believe and live with a constant attitude of striving. We may assume that this refers to the war against one's own temptations and spiritual enemies--*al Jihadu 'l Akbar* as well as the warfare against infidels--*al Jihadu 'l Asghar*.

The war against unbelievers takes on several characteristics that were present in the holy war speeches of Saddam Hussein during the war. The enemy is seen as one who seeks to destroy not only your lives and property but your way of life--values, beliefs, even places of worship. The Shi'a Iranians after the 1980 revolution charged the United States with seeking to destroy their puritan (holy) belief and practice with the introduction of materialistic beliefs and hedonistic values. Although rhetoric during the war over Kuwait was more muted, perhaps because of the presence of Muslims (Saudis, Egyptians, and others) in the Allied force, venom was expressed for the "Western satanic" forces.

It can be argued that Iraq sought to be faithful to Quranic teaching of "withholding your hand a little while from war." In this day of fierce and instantaneous war, they may have withheld their hand a bit too long. They did seek to hold back, buy time, stall, and try to find another way out. The Allies refused to let them back away and save face. Consider these actions: They released the thousands of foreign prisoners and refrained from using them as shields. Although they threatened to resort to global terrorism, they did not do so. If they had chemical weapons, they did not use them. They responded affirmatively to French and Soviet peace initiatives. When the land war broke out, they laid down arms, surrendered, and beat a retreat as rapidly as possible. Regrettably, in retrospect, they responded in rage and belligerence to the Allied demands, ultimata, and deadlines to get out of Kuwait.

Reward for holy war is expected more in the life beyond than in the here and now. The prospect of instant paradise is vivid. For young soldiers who were poor, out of work, away from wives and girlfriends,

separated from families, tired, and hungry, the Quran's promise must
have given hope.

> in gardens of bliss a multitude will be seated on
> couches set close together. Immortal youths will
> serve them with goblets, pitchers and cups filled
> with water from a spring which will not upset
> them or dull their senses; and they may choose
> fruit of any kind and whatever fowl they desire
> and chaste companions with eyes of a beauty
> like pearls hidden in shells . . . We formed them
> perfectly and made them spotless virgins,
> chastely amorous and of the same age (56:12-37).

Early Israeli holy war texts adopted a ferocious posture toward
highly threatening enemies. The Amalakites or the Meccans at Badr are
objects of holy wrath. Yet on closer look the deeper currents of Islam felt
even in the jihad texts are those of compassion and peace. In 1960 I spent
a summer in Jerusalem working on an archaeological project. I was
struck when visiting the Church of the Holy Sepulchre that an Arab was
the keeper of the keys to the church door. Every morning he opened the
holy place and at sunset he locked it up. I was told that the Christian
sects that had quarters within the church, Orthodox and Catholic, Greek,
Armenian, and others, fought so much with each other that only the old
Arab could keep peace. One historian argues that *Pax Islamica* had a
similar pacifying effect in the Christian centuries when Nestorians,
Monophysites, Jews, Jacobites, Copts, and others were persecuted as
schismatics by the Orthodox Christian empire. As one scholar put it,

> The [Islamic] conquests destroyed little: what
> they did suppress were imperial rivalries and
> sectarian bloodletting among the newly
> subjected population. The Muslims tolerated
> Christianity, but they disestablished it;
> henceforward Christian life and liturgy, its
> endowments, politics and theology, would be a
> private and not a public affair. By an exquisite
> irony, Islam reduced the status of Christians to
> that which the Christians had earlier thrust upon
> the Jews, with one difference. The reduction in
> Christian status was merely judicial; it was
> unaccompanied by either systematic persecution
> or a blood lust, and generally, though not

everywhere and at all times, unmarred by
vexatious behavior.[10]

When Arab armies took Jerusalem in A.D. 638, they left Christian
churches and shrines unmolested. They also restored Jewish access to
the holy sites of that faith and built a shrine, the Dome of the Rock
(where Muhammad ascended to heaven), and a mosque, the al-Aqsa,
near the site of Herod's temple, close to the Wailing Wall that is the last
remnant of Solomon's temple.

Christian Crusades and Islamic Counter-Jihad

A final chapter in Islamic holy war emerged in the lone Christian
undertaking of pure holy war, the Crusades. By the eleventh century,
Islamic rule prevailed from Anatolia to Spain, and well into Christian
Europe. Christendom's response took two forms: the *Reconquista* in
Spain (1000-1492), Italy and Sicily (1061), and the Crusades in the
Mediterranean (1095-1453). In 1099 crusading armies stormed Jerusalem
and massacred the Muslim residents who had been there for 400 years.
They desecrated the Muslim sanctuary, Haram al-Sharif, and made it the
residence for a Christian king--the temple of Solomon. Latin
principalities were established at Antioch, Edessa, Tripoli, and Tyre. In
1187 Saladin reestablished Muslim rule over Fatimid Egypt and after a
fierce battle recaptured Jerusalem. By the fifteenth century enthusiasm
for the Crusades had waned, and in 1453 Constantinople fell to the
Turkish Muslims. The capital of old Byzantium became the seat of the
Ottoman empire.

Jihad doctrine was revived during these centuries, with extreme
versions of jihad, much like those of the Kharijites of the eighth century,
resurfacing. These were to rise again periodically throughout Islamic
history (e.g., in the strife of Indian Muslims against Hindus in the
eighteenth and nineteenth centuries), but pacifist and latitudinarian
policies more often prevailed. Now in our own day the Islamic jihad has
arisen once again.

Modern Developments

Fazlur Rahman argued that the modern renaissance of Islam,
growing out of genuine self-criticism and desire for reform, has taken an
intellectual form in the reconstructionism in Sufism and a commitment of
moral reform in the reassertion of jihad.[11] The impact of modernity, the

rise of modern science, and the worldwide ascendency of Western culture has elicited this jihad. Some historians argue that the Crusades marked the beginning of the conflict between Europe and Islam, but the age of strife might more usefully be seen as beginning with Western exploration and colonization in the fifteenth century. When Vasco da Gama opened European trade routes to India in 1498, transoceanic navigation insured this new confrontation. By the seventeenth century widespread trade between the Ottoman empire and Europe was underway, largely in European ships. Western ways of life were initially welcomed. Their very influence led to desires for freedom and independence in the pattern of Western European nations and the English (1650) and French (1789) revolutions. For 400 years Arabia languished under the oppression of the Ottoman empire. When the World War I broke out in 1914, British and French interests, led by Lawrence of Arabia, an archeologist from Oxford, persuaded the Arabs to join the Allied coalition against the Turks, who had mistakenly allied with the Germans. The upsurge of secular freedom and the hope for independent Arabic states in the western anticlerical model was soon to be betrayed by the postwar imposition of imperial mandates and the deposition of Faisal in Syria, later enthroned as king in Iraq.

The new jihad slowly became a war for the mind and heart. New intellectual forces in Europe made claims on human devotion and commitment, striking to the very heart of theology and ethics. Thinkers like Descartes, Kant, and Hume paved new understandings of truth and duty. Following the Islamic intellectual renaissance of the eleventh and thirteenth centuries, spiritual and moral vitality waned in Muslim lands and frontiers of thought moved to Europe. The twentieth-century confrontation with modern thought and "the acids of modernity" has taken Islamic theology, politics, and ethics in two directions. The liberal attempt to recast Islam into a credible modern worldview and lifestyle has been led by the Pakistani Fazlur Rahman, who taught at the end of his career at the University of Chicago. The fundamentalist response under scholars such as those at the Khomeini school at Qom has sought to articulate a new orthodoxy and orthopraxy.

Rahman sought to return to the spiritual and moral roots of Islam in the Quran, in the spirit of modern evangelical biblical scholarship, which has searched for the abiding meanings of the whole of scripture. Calling for *Mujaddid* rather than *Mujahadid* (creative renewal rather than defensive warriors), Rahman and other progressive scholars of Islam have been deeply saddened by the fundamentalist resurgence exemplified by the Iranian revolution. In the early 1980s I convened a scholarly project which examined the contribution of faith traditions to one particular contemporary ethical concern, that of biomedicine;

Rahman wrote a book on Islamic ethics for that series.[12] Weaving historic themes and present problems into a living religiosity and ethics was the genius of Rahman's work on this and other projects.

On the side of conservative and reactionary response to modern civilization, many Muslims have resorted to an identification of faith with war. Beginning in the 1940s, militant fundamentalist groups undertook guerrilla and rearguard actions against modernity in the name of pure Islam. When Sayyid Qutb was condemned and executed in Egypt for terrorism, he contended that he was acting in defense of "a truly Islamic order" against the corruptions of the decadent "progressive" state. The prosecutor in the case contended that Sayyid Qutb had led his people to believe that they were a holy society at war with the rest of society. The mullahs held that their terrorist acts were jihadic acts of religious righteousness. The notion that there are two kingdoms in this world–the Islamicized realm *(Dar-al-Islam)* and the pagan and infidel world *(Dar-al-Harb,* "region of warmaking"), still awaiting submission through jihad, has had several disastrous consequences for peace in the modern world. First, it has positioned the Arabic-Islamic world against a satanic Christian technological world of Europe and North America. Second, it has led to a righteous fear so intense that traditional taboos of wars against other Muslims have been discarded and Iran engaged even sibling Iraq in holy war. The Iraqi campaign against Kuwait and the more general cause against the satanic West must be understood in part as an expression of these two impulses, in addition to Iraq's desire to become the single center of one Islamic world. And finally, a profound animosity toward Israel is fueled by this concept dividing the world into a region that has been pacified and a remaining region of warfare. Israel, in this new exegesis (quite out of keeping with the Quran and traditional Islam), becomes a people who have corrupted *(tahrif)* scripture and who are now, because of westernization, no longer a sibling faith tradition, but an archenemy. The Islamic demonization of the West is as theologically irresponsible as the West's demonization of Saddam Hussein, Iraq, or Arabs in general.

Iraq's foolish incursion into Kuwait was surely, on one level, a purely political and economic act. A disputed oil field, trade access to the Gulf, and other geopolitical matters were at stake. Yet, as the war unfolded and as rhetoric mounted on both sides, a deeper intellectual-spiritual-ethical animosity surfaced. In Saddam Hussein's rhetoric, this was a war of Islamic faithfulness against demonic materialism. In Western rhetoric it was struggle for freedom and our way of life against the tyrannical ways of a dictator. In the end, when Iraq opened the valves to let the oil flow into the sea and set the wells afire, Saddam Hussein showed clearly that his primary ambitions were not economic, but ideological. The West was the harbinger of a destructive intellectual faith constituted by higher textual criticism, cultural relativism, secularism, and anticlericalism. Bent on destroying the religious fabric of the Islamic way of life, it was demonic and called forth jihad. It was this impulse that led hundreds of thousands of Iraqi Muslims to lay down their lives in the war over Kuwait, not their devotion to Saddam Hussein.

As with ancient and modern Israel, Islam identifies faith and people with the land. Although strong voices such as Rahman's have argued for secular states that honor but do not embody the faith, fundamentalist voices have called for a theocratic polity. Most recently Pakistan has joined this circle of states governed by Islamic law. The religious state is a rare phenomenon in Islamic history, however. Caliphs reigned in the first centuries, but by 945 the Abbasid caliphs of Baghdad had lost all political power. After 1258 Egypt maintained only the semblance of a caliphate, and during the Ottoman empire caliphal power was purely ceremonial. With the founding of the Turkish Republic in 1924 along with the emergence of Reza Shah in Iran that same year, a modern pattern of secular states seemed to be set. In 1947 the Islamic Republic of Pakistan was established. Although this state, founded by Mohammed Ali Jinnah, was more secular than sacred, it paved the way for a recapitulation of the ancient theocratic pattern. Indeed, the ideological stage had been set by a reassertion of jihad doctrine by Mawdudi in 1932:

> *Jihad* is a part of this overall defence of Islam. *Jihad* means struggle to the utmost of one's capacity. A man who exerts himself physically or mentally or spends his wealth in the way of *Allah* is indeed engaged in *Jihad*. But in the language of *Shari'ah* this word is used particularly for the war that is waged solely in the name of Allah and against those who perpetrate oppression as enemies of Islam. This extreme sacrifice of lives devolves on all Muslims. If, however, a section of Muslims offer themselves for participating in *Jihad*, the whole community is absolved of her responsibility. But if none comes forward, everybody is guilty. This concession vanishes for the citizens of an Islamic State when it is attacked by a non-Muslim power. In that case everybody must come forward for *Jihad*. If the country attacked has not the strength to fight back then it is the religious duty of the neighboring Muslim

> countries to help her; if even they fail, then the
> Muslims of the whole world must fight the
> common enemy. In all these cases, *Jihad* is as
> much a primary duty of the Muslims concerned
> as the daily prayers or fasting are.[13]

In the 1950s the pattern of secular states resumed, often with official disdain for Islamic fundamentalism, as in Egypt, Syria, and Iraq. After the bitter defeat of Egypt in the 1967 war, a change of mood could be sensed. It was the old pattern of holy zeal being ignited and fueled by defeat. It was widely said by the Egyptian priesthood that the Virgin Mary appeared in Alexandria after the defeat to comfort the defeated Egyptian people. Although the Coptic church embraced this miracle, Muslim teachers held the defeat to be God's punishment--in other words, a call to jihad.

The rise of the Iraqi Ba'ath party and Hafiz al-Assad's takeover in Syria in 1970 were brief throwbacks to the secular approach. Elsewhere the state took a religious turn. In Egypt Anwar Sadat became the Believer President, and General Ehud Numairi was elected imam by the Islamic Front in Sudan as *Shar'ia* (Islamic legislation) was adopted in both nations. The climax of this religious reform and a decisive denouement to secular Arab statehood occurred in 1979 when the Shah of Iran was overthrown and Ayatollah Khomeini was recalled from Paris to become head of the Iranian Islamic Republic. His platform rested on suspicion of the secular West and his *modus operandi* was jihad.

> The United States is the number one enemy of
> the deprived and *'mustaz'af'* (oppressed) people
> of the world, and it does not refrain from any
> crime to extend its political, economic, cultural
> and military influence over the dominated
> world.
>
> We, who say that we intend to export our
> Revolution to all Islamic countries, and even to
> all countries where the *'mostakberin'* (arrogant)
> rule over the *'mustaz'afin'* (deprived), want to
> create a condition that no oppressive, cruel or
> murderous government can exist any more.[14]

More progressive Sunni Islam had sublimated jihad, the evangelical doctrine of winning the day for Islam, into an intellectual and cultural activity. The strife needed to save Islam was creative cultural response to the modern world. Now Shi'ism, the zealous doctrine of a minority (15 percent) of world Muslims, seized the initiative. In Iran 80 percent of the population were Shi'ites, in Iraq, 60 percent. Indeed, with just slight alterations in historical events, Iran and Iraq might have turned in a powerful partnership against the sacred emirates and secular states in the region: Saudi Arabia, Kuwait, the UAE, Syria, and Egypt. Having challenged those Islamic peoples who had compromised with the West, they could then turn in holy war against Israel. As it was, when Iran's revolution failed to gain pan-Arabic support because of its Persian and un-Arabic flavor, Baghdad, not Tehran, was now pitted against Riyadh. This new configuration of power made the eventual conflict over Kuwait, or something like it, inevitable.

The concept of holy war that evolved in Iran is twofold: It is a defensive jihad against injustice and defacement, against occidentosis, or the imposition of Western values on the Islamic way. Second, it is a renewed apologia and aggressive stance for Islamic orthodoxy and orthopraxy. It seeks liberation and higher devotion. Khomeini wrote: "Islam is the religion of militant individuals who are committed to truth and justice. It is the religion of those who desire independence. It is the school of those who struggle against imperialism."[15]

The quest for social justice and liberation of the oppressed places the Islamic jihad in a new light. It is no longer the restitution of oppressive subjugation of women, harsh reprisal for crime, and puritanical imposition of petty rules of behavior and piety; it now becomes the righteous cause of care for the poor of the world. As with the liberation movements in Latin America and Africa, the West finds itself defending regimes which oppress the poor, against the spirit of its own values. A U.S. anthropologist who lived in and studied an Iranian village summarized the new ethos of contending warriors that blends the themes of Persian dualism and Islamic jihad:

> Because he actively chose to face death and worldly defeat in order to become a *shahid* (meaning both martyr and witness) of Islam for all times, Husain and his martyrdom . . . have become the central paradigm of Shi'i Islam. In this view of Islam, all human history is pictured as a continuous struggle between the forces of evil and the forces of good. In every age, villagers told me, there is a Husain, a man who fights on the side of God, and a Yazid, who fights against God.[16]

Jihad, Iraq, and Holy Rhetoric

The battle you are waging today is the mother of
all battles (Saddam Hussein, radio broadcast,
January 7, 1991).

There is no path except the path we have chosen.
Any other course would lead to indignity and
darkness following which there will not be a
bright spot on the heaven or a ray of light on
earth (radio broadcast, February 21, 1991).

In Saddam Hussein's speeches to the Arab Summit in Baghdad in
early 1990, and in subsequent correspondence with Arab leaders, the
holy justice and destiny felt in Iraq were articulated. They had saved the
eastern gateway of the Arabic world by holding off Iran. The moral
leadership of the Arab world therefore belonged to Iraq, along with the
duty of deterring Israel. Iraq therefore needed economic buttressing
from its neighbors, including the consolidation with Kuwait.[17]

Before the Gulf War began, Saddam Hussein ordered his Ba'athist
party to change its slogan from "The Ba'athists stride forward" to "The
Believers stride forward." He next changed the flag to read *"Allahu
akbar"* (God is great). At the very early stages of the conflict over Kuwait,
two major conferences were held in the Gulf region. The theme of jihad
provided the backdrop for both meetings.

At a gathering of Islamic leaders in Baghdad, speakers addressed the
impending confrontation with the infidels. In Riyadh a similar
conference sought to make clear that Iraq's policies were clearly non-
Islamic. As the world watched Saddam Hussein bowing on his knees on
the prayer mat and placing all of his remarks within a religious
framework, George Bush listened intently to Billy Graham pleading that
the United States "fight for peace," and Bush laced his own speech to
religious broadcasters with just war themes from Augustine. It was
evident that a reversion to religious ideas, Machiavellian or genuine, was
at work.

As the war proceeded, fervent uprisings, jihadic to the heart, were
seen throughout the Islamic world: in Turkey, Jordan, and Yemen in the
Middle Eastern region, in Algeria and Egypt in Africa, and in Pakistan
and Indonesia in Asia. This ferment which was felt from the Soviet
republics to the North African states was in part a search for leadership
of the true Islam. Would it come from the Gulf emirates? Not unless
they were radically democratized and became governments of the

people. Could it come from more distant centers of Islamic wisdom--
Pakistan, Tunisia, Egypt, Iran? Perhaps. Who would champion the
cause of the homeless Palestinians? This question lies at the heart of
Islamic justice in the spirit of compassion for those who suffer and of
concern for the orphaned and dispossessed. It is the heart of the moral
issue of jihad as it is the global focal point of Islam under attack.
Although Anglo-U.S. efforts to assign him to the "dust bin of history" are
premature, it seems clear that Yassar Arafat may indeed soon yield
leadership of the exilic Palestinian government to some more convincing
leader. Could Syria emerge as a more satisfactorily Islamic people, yet
possessed of sufficient cunning to withstand, even woo Israel? Perhaps
some pan-Arabic association can emerge in the post war period which
will inspire a political and spiritual mandate.

Could the site of the ancient Baghdad caliphate--the spiritual and
political center of Islam under the Abbasidic rulers of the ninth and tenth
centuries--again be the champion of jihad in its defensive and assertive
dimension? Saddam Hussein, conjuring up images of Nebuchadnezzar
and the ancient caliphs, aspired to that leadership role, though surely he
lacks the moral credibility and statesmanship to become the spiritual and
political leader.

The biography of Saddam Hussein parallels the struggle that jihad
and Islamic faith more generally have endured in the modern world as
they have attempted to find religious authenticity and secular relevance.
As a youth in the 1940s he was schooled by his uncle, Khairullah Tulfah,
in anti-British, pro-German patriotism stressing the *Sturm und Drang*
unification of blood, race, faith, and soil. A writing by Saddam Hussein,
which reportedly came to light during the war but was quickly repressed
and repudiated as a myth of the Western tabloids, was entitled *"Unser
Kampf."* The traditional Ba'athism of the 1950s and 1960s, in which the
young Saddam Hussein was an ideologue, was fashioned under the
tutelage of the French and strongly influenced by socialism. Its
adherents believed that *Shari ah* (Islamic political philosophy) should be
modernized to meet contemporary problems, but they opposed such
military arrangements with the West as the Baghdad Pact (1955), which
sought primarily to resist Soviet activities in western Asia. When the
Ba'athists came to power through a military coup in 1968, they tried to
suppress the mostly Shi'ite Kurds who comprise 20 percent of Iraq's
population. Khomeini's fears that Saddam Hussein's vicious suppression
of Kurdish Shi'ism would lead to desecration of the holy places at Najaf,
Karbala, and Kazimayan in part fueled the Iran-Iraq war. Saddam
Hussein and the Ba'athists moved strongly against the Shi'ites, who had
demanded a separate Islamic state for eastern Iraq. Al-Sadr, one of the
world's most respected Shi'ite theologians, was tried and executed for

treason. Only in the strange and silent complicity of Iran with Iraq's intrusion into Kuwait and its neutrality in the war was a tacit signal given that Saddam Hussein might not be the "secular Satan" but in some sense an advocate of Islamic purpose.

Another historical force that has influenced the currency of Islam and jihad in the minds of Iraqi leaders, including Saddam Hussein, is Marxism. The French socialism of the 1950s was strongly influenced by Marxism, and many Iraqi leaders were schooled in this tradition. The decade of the 1980s saw not only enormous Soviet influence and arms supplies but also some strengthening of the influence of Marxist secularism, certainly in its anticlerical aspect, as Iraq's war with Iran ground on. In the Soviet Union beginning in the 1920s, official policy cracked down on the expression of Islamic faith as on Judaism and Christianity. The government confiscated sacred properties (*waqf*), closed Shari'ah courts and reorganized *madrasas* and religious schools. Stalin abolished Islamic marriage and pilgrimage, and mosques became museums. In the 1960s Leonid Brezhnev encouraged the resurgence of Islam after Nikita Kruschev's continued suppression. Gorbachev stepped lightly on the religion issue, allowing freer expression under his human rights and regional initiatives policies of *glasnost* and *perestroika*. He remained wary of Christian sectarianism in the Baltic states and Islamic revival in the southern Republics alike, as encouraging separatism and the dissolution of the Soviet Union.

The Iraqi exposure to Soviet influence, from the arms supplied in the 1980s to the fascinating trust that Foreign Minister Tariq Aziz inspired during the furtive Soviet-Iraqi negotiations during the Gulf War, remains for scholars to trace. Perhaps some new kind of Iraqi secular state will emerge in the aftermath of the current war, somewhat in the emerging Soviet pattern, in which iconoclastic regimes of terror against faith such as the Chinese against Tibet and Romanians against Protestantism are repudiated and a pluralistic yet vitally religious commonwealth is encouraged. One might imagine a new Soviet Union in which a U.S.-style republic neighbors a Lithuanian Catholic state and an Azerbaijani Islamic republic. Iraq may indeed become that new kind of state, if, for example, it could, in its present political weakness, allow the emergence of respected and self-sustaining Shi'ah and Chaldean Christian communities within its overarching government. As in the Soviet Union, the Western democracies, and Israel, however, it is unlikely that postwar Iraq will allow military, political, or even economic power to rest in jihad, *Shari'ah*, or in any other kind of religious authority. Communist influence will most likely mute further religious pretensions in Iraq.

The Future of Islamic Jihad and Politics in the Middle East

Several scenarios are emerging in the early 1990s concerning the future of the Middle East and the role of Islam and a debilitated Iraq in that future. The noted authority Falih 'Abd al-Jabbar believes that both Islamic fundamentalists and secular modernists will yield leadership to Arab intellectuals. He expects Saddam Hussein to be replaced or assassinated for losing the war, and Islam to gain new footholds in places like Tunisia, Jordan, and perhaps Syria.[18] Ultimately scholars will achieve a rapprochement between jihad and *Realpolitik* and the fundamentalist revolution will reach a new accommodation with culture.

Other analysts, myself included, feel that moral rectitude is deeply compromised at present both in the Jewish and Christian West and in Islamic Arabia and Iraq. But this situation could allow for a proper humiliation and humility in both worlds, giving rise to new mutual respect and appreciation. The West needs to have its rapacious materialism and oil-dependent luxury challenged. When the politics of the war over Kuwait are reviewed, it should become clear to U.S. leaders that they wrongly blocked the UN at every turn--when it sought to censure Iraq's attack on Iran, when Israel occupied the Palestinian territories, and when the United States altered Iraq's terrorist-sponsor status and renewed military aid. Most tragically, the United States remained silent, held the UN to silence, and opposed sanctions on Iraq for gassing 3,000 Kurds in July 1988.

On the other side, jihadic Islam, while reconstituting spiritual and cultural values and rightfully defending itself against the assault of Western materialism, has been brutally inhumane in its puritanical activities and backward in accepting intellectual and scientific gains that could enrich the lives of Arab peoples. A more careful study of the Jewish and Christian roots and affinities of Islam could open a more creative dialogue from that side.

The *Independent* correspondent Robert Fisk, one of the few British journalists to maintain integrity and credibility during the war, believes that holy war and holocaust lusts are evident on both sides, with the West intent on destroying Saddam Hussein, the Iraqi infrastructure, and any future Islamic force in the region. The West takes this unjust approach because of its insatiable thirst for inexpensive Middle Eastern oil. Iraq similarly holds ambitions of a none too holy jihad holocaust for the United States and Great Britain. The resulting mutual obliteration of not power, but moral respectability, will end, according to Fisk, with: "Iran [emerging] as the dominant Gulf power. Israel would be free to ignore Palestinian demands for autonomy for at least a decade, perhaps even find some excuse to deport the entire Arab population from the

West Bank (as is now proposed by at least one member of Mr. Shamir's cabinet)."[19] Fisk finds the holy war and just war rhetoric symptomatic of unreconciling will on both sides, which can, in the end, only harm both: "King Fahd, who calls himself the Custodian of the two Holy Places, demanded that Saddam Hussein return to God's order--a distinctly theological version of the 'New World order'--and added that 'we invoke God that he might register victory for His army.'" Echoing Saladin, his other mentor along with Nebuchadnezzar, Saddam Hussein intoned as the war began, "Satan must not win. Satan will be vanquished." Fisk concluded: "God heard the embattled nations shout. Good God, said God, I've got my work cut out."[20]

The best outcome of this war may well be tripartite self-examination: Israel reviewing its holy way theology; the United States, just war theory; and Iraq, jihad. Jihad has now become an internal intellectual and cultural struggle within Islam. This majestic faith, in its essence compatible with the law, prophets, and Gospel, is not some fossilized relic doomed to oblivion. In the mysterious providence of the one God, it has risen in the Arabian peninsula, a region in which diaspora Judaism found a home before its new homeland in Israel, and which Christianity leaped over in its rush to the western reaches of Europe. In its soul Islam possesses a sense of justice and mercy, of prayer and discipline that is God's will for His ecumenical people. Islam is an ethical and political faith. Its genius in world history will perhaps be to show civilizations the holy mode of social governance.

The grand saga of Islam, like the apostolic succession in the Roman Catholic church, has sought to trace the political lineage from prophet to caliph, to *mulik* or kingdom, to republic. Whereas David's kingdom and *Res Publica Christiana* were at least transient phenomena by divine dispensation if not historic reality, Islam by its archaic and theistic definition is physical and worldly in nature. Throughout the Abbasid and Ottoman empires, indeed, into the modern age, Islamic leaders are usually kings. The leader and king, according to Islam, is a popular figure; he rules under God through the will of the people. When military dictators depose rightful democratic leaders, they violate the justice of Islam; authority belongs to God and is given through the voice of the people. Any other rule is usurpation.

Several areas in which Islamic governance becomes problematic, however, and where jihad doctrine requires refinement include non-Muslim minorities, taxation, warmaking, and the punishment of crimes according to Quran. If Islam is more a way of life than a way of belief, methods of dealing with these matters within the structure of modern democratic and pluralistic states must be addressed. The Quran and tradition offer clear authorization for mutuality and plurality in sharing political power with non-Muslims. As for taxation, the justice and compassion theme in Islam leads to an interpretation of taxation and usury as victimization of the poor. Tax collectors are usually degraded in religious texts. But the imperative to give alms calls for some more generalized form of beneficence, if only to avoid the injustice of hit-and-miss charity. The Islamic state in a modern guise might well leave parochial education to religious authority and subsidize all schools from a general tax. With temporal Quranic punishment a more complicated situation arises. Although Shari'ah laws are well intentioned and certainly exert a deterrent effect on matters like slander, stealing, adultery, and exploitation of women, the potential for abuse is enormous. Innocent women can be exploited and accused of infidelity. Hatred can be turned into accusation and punishment. A constituency is building within Islamic society for national and international law that better reflects ethical convictions. Relating to the particular theme of this book, one of the creative frontiers where the religious law of Judaism, Christianity, and Islam could more adequately inform secular law would be in the realm of social justice, war, and peace. Secular law, influenced as it is by national interests of power and economics, could be transformed into care for the oppressed and honesty against injustice with some interplay with religious jurisprudence.

As the meanings of holy war, jihad, and just war continue to unfold in the Abrahamic faiths, more refined meanings will surface about the why and wherefore of war than can exist in secular law, even in its nobler recent expressions of international and UN law. When human impulses of vengeance and love of violence are checked by divine imperatives reflecting a Lord who has judgment and mercy toward all people, a more exquisite law, even law of war and peace is possible.

Summary

The 1989 *Encyclopedia of Religion*, edited by Mircea Eliade, contains an article on jihad by Rudolph Peters, noting the recent tendency in Islamic ethics to identify jihad doctrine with Islamic international law and *bellum justum*.[21] In an excellent bibliographic note, Peters summarizes the latest discussion in the field.[22]

Three concurrent developments give us cause to hope for peace: the revival of thoughtful attention to jihad doctrine in religious circles, the invocation of these themes in the cacophony of God talk/war talk while tragic and unnecessary war waged over Kuwait, and the sensible yearnings for freedom and peace throughout the world. These developments may now converge to make the poor Earth safer and more like the envisioned paradise of all religious hope.

Notes

1. V. S. Naipaul, *Among the Believers: An Islamic Journey*, London: Andre Deutsch, 1981, p. 16.

2. Ibn Hisham, quoted in Philip K. Hitti, *History of the Arabs*, 9th ed., New York: St Martin's, 1966, p. 120.

3. John Howard Yoder, *When War is Unjust*, Minneapolis: Augsburg, 1984, p. 26.

4. John L. Esposito, *Islam: The Straight Path*, Oxford: Oxford University Press, 1988, p. 17.

5. S. H. Amin, *The Legal System of Iraq*, Glasgow: Royston Publishers, 1989.

6. Charles Tripp, "The Abuses That Led To War," *Times Literary Supplement*, January 25, 1991, p. 11.

7. Bernard Lewis, ed., *Islam: From the Prophet Muhammad to the Capture of Constantinople*, vol. 1: *Politics and War*, Oxford: Oxford University Press, 1987.

8. "Jihad," in Thomas Patrick Hughes, *A Dictionary of Islam* , Clifton, N.J.: Reference Book Publishers, 1965, p. 243-248.

9. Ibid., p. 244.

10. Francis E. Peters, "The Early Muslim Empires: Umayyads, Abbasids, Fatimids," in *Islam: The Religions and Political Life of a World Community*, ed. Marjorie Kelly, New York: Praeger, 1984, p. 79.

11. See Fazlur Rahman, *Islam*, New York: Holt, Rinehart and Winston, 1966.

12. Fazlur Rahman, *Health and Medicine in the Islamic Tradition*, New York: Crossroad, 1987 (Series Editors: M. Marty, K. Vaux).

13. Quoted in W. Montgomery Watt, *Classic Fundamentalism and Modernity*, London: Routledge, 1988, p. 99-100.

14. Ayatollah Khomeini, *Light of the Path*, quoted in Watt, *Classic Fundamentalism*, p. 102.

15. Ibid., p. 135.

16. Mary Hegland, in *Religion and Politics in Iran*, ed. Nikki Keddie, New Haven: Yale University Press, 1983, p. 226.

17. W. Khalidi, "Iraq vs. Kuwait: Claims and Counterclaims," in Sifry and Cerf, *op. cit.*, p. 60.

18. Falih 'Abd al-Jabbar, "Sword of Islam," *Guardian*, February 11, 1991, p. 21.

19. Robert Fisk, "War Aims," *London Review of Books*, February 21, 1991, pp. 5-6.

20. Ibid., p. 5.

21. Rudolph Peters, "Jihad," in *The Encyclopedia of Religion*, ed. Mircea Eliade, New York: Macmillan, 1989, p. 87-91.

22. "The most extensive and reliable survey of the classical doctrine of *jihad* is Majid Khadduri's *War and Peace in the Law of Islam* (Baltimore, 1955). The same author has translated the oldest legal handbook on *jihad*, written by Muhammad al-Shaybani (749-805) and published under the title *The Islamic Law of Nations: Shaybani's Siyar* (Baltimore, 1966). Muhammad Hamidullah's *Muslim Conduct of State*, 6th rev. ed. (Lahore, 1973), is based on an extensive reading of the classical sources but is somewhat marred by the author's apologetic approach. In my *jihad in Mediaeval and Modern Islam* (Leiden, 1977), I have translated and annotated a classical legal text and a modernist text on *jihad*; also included is a comprehensive bibliography of translations into Western languages of primary sources on *jihad*. Albrecht Noth's *Heiliger Krieg und heiliger Kampf in Islam und Christentum* (Bonn, 1966) and Emmanuel Sivan's *L'Islam et la Croisade: Idéologie et propagande dans les réactions musulmanes aux Croisades* (Paris, 1968) both deal with the *jihad* doctrine in the historical setting of the Crusades. In addition, Noth compares *jihad* with similar notions in Christianity. Hilmar Krüger's study *Fetwa und Siyar: Zur international rechtlichen Gutachtenpraxis der osmanischen Seyh ül-Islam vom 17. bis 19. Jahrhundert unter besonderer Berücksichtigung des "Behcet ül-Fetâvâ* (Wiesbaden; 1978) examines the role of the *jihad* doctrine in Ottoman international relations from the seventeenth to the nineteenth century. Mohammad Talaat Al Ghunaimi's *The Muslim Conception of International Law and the Western Approach* (The Hague, 1968) attempts to apply the notions of modern international relations. The political role and the interpretation of the *jihad* doctrine in the nineteenth and twentieth centuries are the main themes of my *Islam and Colonialism: The Doctrine of jihad in Modern History* (The Hague, 1979). On the Egyptian *jihad* organization see Johannes J. G. Jansen's *The Neglected Duty* (New York, 1986)."
Ibid., p. 9.

5

Christian Traditions of Pacifism and Just War

While U.S. President George Bush was adopting the demeanor of Lawrence Olivier's Henry V at Agincourt and touting the war over Kuwait as just and right, the soldiers on the ground, always suspicious of politicians' rhetoric, found more solid comfort in a popular song based on Psalm 91:

> *Under his wings you will find refuge*
> *His faithfulness is a shield and buckler.*

Life at the front is a song of dark fears, deep pride, lost mail, long waits and improvisation. The white heat of the summer is hard to remember now, when it becomes cold enough at night to leave ice rattling inside canteens . . .

> *You will not fear the terror of the night,*
> *Nor the arrow that flies by day,*
> *Nor the pestilence that stalks in darkness,*
> *Nor the destruction that wastes at noonday.*

The closer to the front, the more raw the nerves. The 'T' rations are hot and a lot better than M.R.E.'s (Meals Ready to Eat) . . . Everyone hates them. Egyptian soldiers refused them. Only ravenous Iraqi prisoners of war wolf them down. . . . Nights are so quiet that a cough can

be heard from 400 yards and the land is so
barren that a single twisted piece of brush
becomes a landmark . . .

*Because he cleaves to me in love, I will deliver him. I
will protect him, because he knows my name.*

The men seem to take the women's presence in
stride. "Once you work with them enough, they
realize that you're a soldier like they are . . . ."

*A thousand may fall at your side,
Ten thousand at your right hand;
But it will not come near you.*

With each passing day, the hasties (fox-holes)
are dug further down, so that by now they are
are armpit deep and flanked by sand bags. This
is low-tech war of the most vital kind.[1]

Sustained by lofty precepts or down to earth guts and courage, all
sought for some reason to be there. In the State of the Union address the
president addressed the nation:

Each of us will measure, within ourselves, the
value of this great struggle. Any cost in lives is
beyond our power to measure. But the cost of
closing our eyes to aggression is beyond
mankind's power to imagine.
This we do know: Our cause is just. Our cause
is moral. Our cause is right.
Let future generations understand the burden
and the blessings of freedom. Let them say, we
stood where duty required us to stand.
Let them know that together, we affirmed
America, and the world, as a community of
conscience.
The winds of change are with us now. The
forces of freedom are united. We move toward
the next century, more confident than ever, that
we have the will at home and abroad, to do
what must be done–the hard work of freedom.
May God bless the United States of America.[2]

In the minds of the Allied forces--U.S., British, and French--the president's rhetoric of war ethics must have rung oddly while they fought alongside Egyptian troops on the sands of the Islamic lands of Saudi Arabia and Kuwait. The song based on Psalm 91 expressed convictions that sustained them day and night on that seemingly endless expanse of sand. There was the nomadic Hebrew poem of Yahweh as the desert companion in struggle against the enemy. Unable to celebrate Christmas, something of the austere Islamic jihad, its passion for liberation of the oppressed, extirpation of unbelief, and strife for peace may have cut across army lines. The Jewish and Islamic notion of the warrior as a purified cultic savior might also have been felt. But in the end it was that mingled patriotism, devotion to the folks back home, and sacred duty to God and humanity in the face of injustice that brought and kept them there. This time there was no equivocation. They were completely free from the doubt and desertion that plagued the U.S. incursion into Vietnam. If this was not holy war, it was just war for sure.

Bush is a graduate of Yale University. We might expect him to live the intellectually and morally reflective life which the university tradition entails. He was a World War II pilot, shot down in the Pacific, and is a practicing Christian of the Episcopalian tradition. Though he was rushed along by events and cautioned by Prime Minister Thatcher's mischievous words, "This is no time to be wobbly, George," he nevertheless gave great thought to the justice and rightness of this war. We are told that he was guided by the following code for conflict:

Principles for Launching War

Just cause. A war can be started only for just reasons. They may include: Vindication of justice, restoring a just international order, protecting innocent life and restoration of human rights.
Competent authority. War can be started only by those with responsibility for public order and legitimate authority for engaging the nation in war.
Comparative justice. The central question should be: Is the justice of our cause greater than theirs?
Right intention. A just war is only a means to gain peace and reconciliation--not humiliation and punishment.

Last resort. All nonviolent alternatives should be exhausted.

Probability of success. If a successful end is futile, war should not be started.

Proportionality of projected results. The good expected from war must be greater than all the foreseen costs.

Right spirit. War must be engaged with an attitude of regret.

Principles for Conducting War:

Proportionality in the use of force. No action should be taken that creates more harm than good. Deadly force should be used only in the proportion needed to achieve a just objective.

Discrimination. There must be no intention to harm innocent civilians.

Avoidance of evil means. No cause justifies evil means, such as executing prisoners, taking hostages, pillaging and desecrating holy places.

Good faith. Enemies should be treated with dignity–as much as possible, in ways that keep open the possibility of eventual reconciliation.[3]

The background of Bush's preparation of this formulary provides an interesting entrée into a consideration of the Christian just war tradition and its relevance to the war over Kuwait. In December 1990, as the president prepared to send hundreds of thousands of Americans to the Gulf, a decision that would make war inevitable, he consulted with six close friends about the morality of his war. He was challenged to this reflection by the presiding bishop of his own denomination, Edmond Browning, who argued that the sanctions, which had been in force about ten weeks at that point, should be given a longer time to work. Struggling already, it would seem, with the last resort theme of just war, a constraint so foreign to the U.S. spirit of "get it over with fast," Bush told Bishop Browning that the Iraqi atrocities in Kuwait brought new urgency to a crisis that normally could have waited for slow diplomacy. Recalling Edmund Burke's oft quoted point that the only thing necessary for the triumph of evil is for good men to do nothing, Bush challenged the bishop with the question, "Where were the churches when Hitler overran Poland?"

Bush overlooked two important considerations: First, though there was terrible silence, even complicity, it was the church, not the politicians, who were the only front of resistance to the Nazis. Many pastors and priests were executed along with the Jews. On this point of argument with Bishop Browning, Bush also failed to register the crucial just war principle that reprisals are illegitimate.[4] Granted, the Iraqi atrocities in Kuwait were horrendous, as sordid as the U.S. atrocities in My Lai and elsewhere in Vietnam, or the Iraqi gassing of the Kurds in July 1988 when Bush was vice president and soon to be elected president.

Bush then took comfort in a letter from Pope John Paul II in which the pontiff said that he "hoped for peace but if hostilities broke out, he hoped that the United States would win quickly and with minimal casualties." This affirmation of "get it over quickly" impatience seems out of keeping with the pope's broader brief on the Gulf crisis, which decried the abrupt nature of the confrontation and the too-easy resort to war. Bush then consulted the "prophets of the civil religion," Robert Schuler and Jerry Falwell, along with the more reflective, though conservative, Billy Graham and Bishop Bernard Law of Boston. One might have thought that on such an important matter he would have consulted other religious leaders as well, such as the teaching ethicists of the church and synagogue or the presidents of the theological seminaries, but he did submit this grave matter to prayer and ethical reflection. Having lived through great crises like World War II, the death of his daughter Robin to leukemia in 1953, the Korean and Vietnam wars, and the U.S. Civil Rights movement, he had learned to lean on his childhood faith and his mother's ethical instruction.

In 1988 Bush had declared that he had been "born again" and had accepted Christ as his personal savior. This shift of faith from one of a formal and nominal kind to one more living and personal intensified the seriousness of his spiritual and ethical quest. This would have been all the more difficult in the United States (or Iraq for that matter) when the semblance of going through the religious motions and emotions was politically so important. As I sit now in the pub where C. S. Lewis talked through his ideas with George MacDonald and J. R. R. Tolkien, I appreciate the words of Lewis that Bush shared with a friend about ostentatious and zealous religious expression: "The greatest sin is pride and all other sins really come from pride."[5]

In a speech to religious broadcasters during the crucial days of the conflict, Bush quoted Augustine and the Christian just war tradition.

> Abroad, as in America, our task is to serve and seek (God) wisely through the policies we pursue.

Nowhere is this more true than in the Persian
Gulf where, despite protestations of Saddam
Hussein, it is not Iraq against the United States,
it's the regime of Saddam Hussein against the
rest of the world. Saddam tried to cast this
conflict as a religious war. But it has nothing to
do with religion per se. It has, on the other
hand, everything to do with what religion
embodies–good versus evil, right versus wrong,
human dignity and freedom versus tyranny and
oppression.

The war in the Gulf is not a Christian war, a
Jewish war, or a Moslem war–it is a just war.
And it is a war with which good will prevail.
(Applause.) We're told that the principles of a
just war originated with classical Greek and
Roman philosophers like Plato and Cicero. And
later they were expounded by such Christian
theologians as Ambrose, Augustine, Thomas
Aquinas.

We seek nothing for ourselves. As I have said,
U.S. forces will leave as soon as their mission is
over, as soon as they are no longer needed or
desired. And let me add, we do not seek the
destruction of Iraq. We have respect for the
people of Iraq, for the importance of Iraq in the
region.   We do not want a country so
destabilized that Iraq itself could be a target for
aggression.[6]

   Reserving comment on Bush's interpretation of Christian just war, let
me review the ethical heritage he mentions and the evaluation it brings
to the war over Kuwait. The compilation of principles said to have
instructed the president comes partially from the Christian tradition and
partially from the secular just war tradition. Were his orders and the
execution of the war consonant with his stated beliefs and values?

Pacifism and Just War

The Christian tradition has generated three approaches to war ethics. The holy war ethic, although on occasion invoked by the extremely zealous, enjoyed widespread legitimacy only in one brief period of Western history, that of the Crusades. The pacifist and just war doctrines have dominated Christian intellectual and ethical history, with the teaching of Jesus and the Apostles, the pastoral instruction of the early church, and the great consolidation of Christian thought by Augustine for the most part elevating to a supernatural plane the warfare of good versus evil, giving a nonviolent and pacifist tone to our temporal life. Yet, as Yoder rightly pointed up, in political conflict throughout Christian history, both the pacifist option rooted in piety, and just war conviction rooted in moral reflection have quickly yielded to holy war rhetoric. "The just war position is not the one taken practically by most Christians since Constantine. . . . In most wars baptised people forsook pacifism (and the just war theory of intellectual and spiritual elites) and have died and killed by thought patterns which derive from the crusade or the national-interest pattern."[7] Pacifism is the pristine conviction of Christian conscience. The Gospel allows the devout soul to hear only this music. But it is purely eschatological. It is primal in that it stands before any corruption or compromise with worldly concern. It is ultimal in that it stands in the transcendent, beyond all earthly affairs. The eschatological lies behind and beyond the veil of all temporal reality.

In preparing this volume I've sought the opinion of several friends who are newly Christian, converts from other cultures, one for example, a traditional Korean. I've also asked persons who have undergone evangelical "born again" experiences such as that acknowledged by Bush in 1988 what they thought of the war over Kuwait and just war theory. "No war can be just," was their uniform and automatic response. The thought of sanctifying war was repulsive to them. Dirty business? Necessary? Perhaps--but it had nothing to do with God, Christ or my-soul-now-committed-to-Him. Just war theory and even pacifist theory in part must be seen as intellectual exercises distanced from Christian experience, reflecting accommodation of faith to the ways of the world.

The primitive Christian community formed in the hub cities of the Roman empire, one of the most powerful yet pacific regimes the world has ever seen. Uprisings and rebellions were quickly quelled in any part of the empire. Christianity was born in the Roman province of Judea in the tumultuous last years of Jewish militant resistance. Pacifism was not only in the best survival interest of the fledgling community, it grew out of their faith in the risen Lord. Exilic and messianic Judaism also offered a way of nonbelligerence and peace as the saving purpose of God with

His people and through them with the whole earth. Thus Matthew
(12:18-21) construed the meaning of messianic announcement in Isaiah
(42:1-4):

> Behold, my servant whom I have chosen,
>   my beloved with whom my soul is well
>   pleased.
> I will put my Spirit upon him,
>   and he shall proclaim justice to the Gentiles.
> He will not wrangle or cry aloud,
>   nor will any one hear his voice in the streets;
> he will not break a bruised reed,
>   or quench a smouldering wick,
> til he brings justice to victory;
>   and in his name will the Gentiles hope.

The word *peacemaker* in the Sermon on the Mount not only equates
the person who brings peaceful salvation to the world through his
witness with Yahweh himself (Isaiah 45:7), but also with Alexander the
Great and Julius Caesar, who were both described as peacemakers and
sons of God. This Gospel about Jesus as the just and righteous king
deliberately says that Christian vocation embodies eternal and earthly
peace:

> You have heard that it was said, "An eye for an
> eye and a tooth for a tooth". But I say to you, [1.]
> *Do not resist one who is evil.* But if any one strikes
> you on the right cheek, turn to him the other
> also; and if any one would sue you and take
> your coat, let him have your cloak as well; and
> if any one forces you to go one mile, go with him
> two miles. Give to him who begs from you, and
> do not refuse him who would borrow from you.
> You have heard that it was said, "You shall love
> your neighbor and hate your enemy." But I say
> to you, [2.] *Love your enemies* and pray for those
> who persecute you, so that you may be sons
> [children] of your father who is in heaven
> (Matthew 5:38 ff).[8]

The evangelists' memories of what Jesus said were focused in their
memory of who he had been, what he had done, and who he continued
to be as their risen companion. Confounding all expectations of one who

would execute political justice or join combative action as might be expected of the Jewish Messiah, he forgave his enemies and silently submitted to their violence, offering only the resistance of forgiveness. Paul the Apostle intuited clearly what Jesus brought to the world as he entered that world in the lives of those who would hear and live the Gospel: Warfare is incumbent on those who join cause and the sword must be lifted against evil. This is a new kind of transcendent warfare against principalities and powers (Ephesians 6:12). When war and peace are thus rendered apocalyptic, as in Wisdom, or eschatologic, as in Paul, readiness, even yearning, for earthly crisis is stimulated, as is radical pacifism.

Pacifism in the Early Church

The earliest Christians objected in conscience to warfare and declined to participate for several reasons: Killing human beings, even in self-defense, was discountenanced because only God could take life. If one's life was taken, as in martyrdom, it was taken by God. As Christ's return was thought to be imminent, there was no call to defend or conquer any earthly state. Military service constituted a false oath and idolatry.

> But now the question is whether a believer can become a soldier and whether a soldier can be admitted into the faith, even if he is a member only of the rank and file who are not required to take part in sacrifices or capital punishments. There can be no compatibility between the divine and the human sacrament (=military oath), the standard of Christ and the standard of the devil, the camp of light and the camp of darkness. One soul cannot serve two masters-- God and Caesar. Moses, to be sure, carried a rod; Aaron wore a military belt, and John (the Baptist) is girt with leather (i.e., like a soldier); and, if you really want to play around with the subject, Joshua the son of Nun led an army and the people waged war. But how will a Christian man go to war? Indeed how will he serve even in peacetime without a sword which the Lord has taken away? For even if soldiers came to John and received advice on how to act, and

even if a centurion became a believer, the Lord,
in subsequently disarming Peter, disarmed
every soldier. No uniform is lawful among us if
it is designated for an unlawful action (*Treatise
on Idolatry* 19; ANF 3:73).[9]

In the year A.D. 211 Tertullian reflected on what had come to be a behavioral canon in the early church. Lingering elements of Jewish cultic and kosher law, as in the case of David, excluded him from temple privilege because his hands were blood-stained from his having been a soldier. There is the rejection of oaths, incantations, or any kind of formulae or confessions that would constitute idolatry or blasphemy. The text reminds us of the fact that Israeli youth today in orthodox theological study come into the army but continue their rabbinical work and are excused from some forms of service.

Like Tertullian, Hippolytus held an apocalyptic and "rigorist" view of the Roman state. Attracted by sectarian community such as he found among the Essenes, he withdrew from the Roman church because even as early as the second century it had become worldly. The document *Apostolic Tradition*, often attributed to him, although surrounded by controversy as to date and author, reflects the war ethics of a growing Christian community whose moral life was instructed by the teaching and ruling office of the church.

Servants of the Pagan State

–A Soldier who is in authority must be told not
to execute men; if he should be ordered to do it,
he shall not do it. He must be told not to take
the military oath. If he will not agree, let him be
rejected.
– A military governor or a magistrate of a city
who wears the purple, either let him desist or let
him be rejected.
–If a catechumen or a baptised Christian wishes
to become a soldier [i.e., a volunteer], let him be
cast out. For he has despised God.[10]

The issue here seems to be idolatry, heretical oath, and misplaced loyalty. The Roman state was well experienced in persecuting synagogues, house churches, and cells from Rome to the far reaches of its authority. Some years later, in the early years of the third century, Origen, the greatest of the church fathers before Anselm and Augustine, rehearsed the tested beliefs and orthopraxy that had become established in the church:

> The assertion that 'certain Jews at the time of Christ revolted against the Jewish community and followed Jesus' is not less false than the claim 'that the Jews had their origin in a revolt of certain Egyptians'. Celsus and those who agree with him will not be able to cite a single act of rebellion on the part of the Christians. If a revolt had indeed given rise to the Christian community, if Christians took their origins from the Jews, who were allowed to take up arms in defense of their possessions and to kill their enemies, the Christian Law-giver would not have made homicide absolutely forbidden. He would not have taught that his disciples were never justified in taking such action against a man even if he were the greatest wrongdoer. [Jesus] considered it contrary to his divinely inspired legislation to approve any kind of homicide whatsoever. If Christians had started with a revolt, they would never have submitted to the kind of peaceful laws which permitted them to be slaughtered 'like sheep' (Psalm 44:11) and which made them always incapable of taking vengeance on their persecutors because they followed the law of gentleness and love (*Against Celsus* 3.8).
>
> To those who ask about our origin and our founder we reply that we have come in response to Jesus' commands to beat into plowshares the rational swords of conflict and arrogance and to change into pruning hooks those spears that we used to fight with. For we no longer take up the sword against any nation, nor do we learn the art of war any more. Instead of following the traditions that made us 'strangers to the covenants' (Eph. 2:12), we have become sons of peace through Jesus our founder (*Against Celsus* 5.33).[11]

By the time of Origen, we can be certain that Christians were in the army. Like slaves who converted during their indenture, these soldiers remained in service. In a gesture that gathers all of this early Christian history into one symbol, Martin of Tours converted while in the service, but stayed in his normal noncombatant post until battle was joined in A.D. 358, when he divided his military garment with two beggars and volunteered to go to the front armed only with a cross. Obviously, he was summarily discharged. He later became a bishop of the church.

According to the Roman-Christian historian Eusebius, a significant turning point in Christian war ethics, indeed in Western history, occurred in A.D. 312 when Constantine finished off the last of a long line of pagan caesars by his cunning at the battle of the Milvian Bridge. Changing his military formation into a Christian symbol (XP) and interpreting a sunspot to be a superimposed cross, Constantine transformed the battlefield into a sanctuary and ultimately the church into a political entity. Cicero's *Res Publica* had now become *Res Publica Christiana.* Following edicts of toleration, then endorsement, the Roman state became the champion of the church.

In an argument refuted by Origen, Celsus pleaded that if all Roman citizens did the same as the Christians, there would be nobody left to defend the empire against barbarian assault (*Contra Celsus* 8:68-69). Both Origen and Tertullian, despite their objections to the pretenses of the pagan state and their commitments to purity of allegiance among the baptized, argued along the same lines as Paul's letter to the Romans that the church was loyal and not seditious to the state. After Constantine it became the task of first Ambrose, then Augustine, to defend the loyalty and new-found partnership, as well as the purity of the church and the worldly mission the state might advance for it. At the same time, urgency to defend the empire mounted as barbarian hordes rushed down from the north and west.

By the late fourth century Christianity was no longer merely tolerated. Rather, the church was adopted as the new cult of the state, displacing the old Roman cults. Emperors now looked to the church to authorize and bless its existence and activity; Ambrose, bishop of Milan, sanctified the Roman emperors with scriptural images of the Israelite kings and identified the invading Goths as the archetype of evil Gog. It remained for Ambrose's student Augustine, weaving a complete philosophical system of thought about the state, divine and human judgment, and politics and warfare as expressions of that judgment, to lay the foundations for just war theory for subsequent history. When Bush alluded to Augustine in his speech to religious broadcasters, he was referring to this turning point in moral history.

Augustine

Following Ambrose, Augustine transformed Cicero's doctrine of the state's assertive power and prerogative into a pattern of judgment and a structure of justice expressive of the righteous benediction (pacification) and punishment of God mediated on earth by church and state. It is within the context of the doctrines of judgment and grace and the virtues of love and justice in *The City of God* that Augustine fashioned his sketch of just war theory. U.S. leaders blame the peace movement and obtrusive media for the U.S. defeat in the Vietnam War and determined that no contrary word would be heard in the Gulf War. Augustine faced a similar charge that the western Roman empire collapsed before the invading barbarian hordes because of Christian pacifism and otherworldliness. This charge became the occasion for the first thorough Christian treatise on social ethics as well as the particular issue of the morality of war and peace. Augustine fathomed the depths and heights of human evil and aspiration. He elucidated the tragic reaches of human pride and fall, both individual and collective. He witnessed the glories of human potential and political association. In Peter Bathory's words, Augustine's project was not an "escape from the world, but a start at living more freely in it."[12] He thus established the spiritual and moral necessity of politics for Christian conscience, a conscience that might prefer to refuse responsibility in favor of the inner life and the world beyond.

Augustine's political theology is enduringly valid. We do not live in, or for, some idyllic or utopian paradise, nor is our own world a despicable, fallen, or illusory veil of tears. The world is good and opportune. Though we incline toward harm and exploitation, the hard work of justice and love redeem life and allow the world to gloriously reflect the creator's will in peace, reconciliation, and mutual service. If war is necessary, it is to restrain violence and restore peace; no other ambition is morally worthy.

Despite his powerful doctrine of citizenship, Augustine lingered in the pristine conviction of the fresh reality of Christ's redemption and the significance of that experience for our life in the world. At the heart of his nonretaliatory ethic, Augustine stood with the primitive Christian community. In this purview war was a tragic necessity; his discussion of the issues of war and peace unfold in what Roland Bainton calls a "mournful mood."[13] The war over Kuwait exhibited the supreme irony of victimless air strikes down the stacks of chimneys, of armaments facilities juxtaposed with piles of massacred and charred bodies of Iraqi soldiers on the Basra road. Like Wilfred Owen and other modern war poets, Augustine was aware that all human suffering and each death bears down on human consciences and grieves the loving heart of God. For Augustine, the state and its juridical and political arms were necessitated by the innate violence of humans and the reign of evil in the world. Only the virtues of justice and love could transform the persistent violence of this world into a semblance of the promised kingdom of order and peace. In the poignant cry of the Credo: *"Crucifixus sub Pontio Pilato."*

Men, as they showed in the crucifixion of Christ, are bent on pride, hatred, injury, violence, warfare, and death. But rather than opting out in apocalyptic rage or pietistic withdrawal, Augustine invited "the members of the Heavenly City to perfect the State, healing its wounded nature and restoring the free character of its rule."[14] Augustine saw the state as a defense against the evil of the world. *Tranquillitas Ordinis* (the peaceful order) is what the state, guided by the church, should provide the world. This peace could only be the fragile and transient "peace of Babylon," but even that penultimate good could enable life and work to go on in the world. It was this political realism that became the basis of Augustine's just war reflections.

Augustine was first and foremost a Christian, loyal to *Civitas dei*. He did not glorify patriotism, secular power, or warfare, earthly loyalties inappropriate as objects of ultimate devotion. But he moved beyond the pacifism and antimilitarism of Tertullian, Origen, and the primitive church in holding that war should not be categorically rejected or condoned. Discernment must be brought to bear to determine when a particular war is just and conscionable. When that decision has been made, conscience must guide its implementation in just conduct.

For Augustine, only three causes justify war: defense against aggression, seeking just reparations for previous wrong, and recovering stolen property. In addition to one or more of these precipitating causes, a rightful and duly constituted authority must declare the war. In the war over Kuwait, President Bush, Prime Minister Major, President Mitterrand--all ministers of state in the Christian tradition--concluded that aggression against Kuwait had occurred. Adding to this composite authority was that of the exiled government of Kuwait, and of the governments of Saudi Arabia, Egypt, and a majority of the United Nations (albeit under some duress), rightful authority was felt to be in place.

In addition to these criteria of just cause, Augustine wrote, the war must be waged with "right intention." Motives of revenge, anger, national power, or acquisition of resources must not prevail. Here obviously the case for the United States making war against Iraq weakens considerably. As to conduct of the war once undertaken, Augustine's rules derive from Greek and Roman just war theory: Faith must be kept with the enemy and there can be no wanton violence, desecration of religious sites, looting, massacre, or conflagration. Hebraic holocaust and its Islamic counterpart, total obliteration of a society and its infrastructure, napalming, scorched-earth tactics, and any effort to exterminate a people from the earth are strictly forbidden. Only history will tell whether the war over Kuwait fell within these bounds of propriety.

The classical theory from which Augustine borrowed was based on the moral experience of both the Greek and Roman empires, that battles could be won and wars lost if the victor was disgraced in the eyes of the world through unworthy intentions or conduct. Augustine's conditions are rigorous, based on his personal conviction that war, indeed all retaliation, is always wrong, even in self-defense: Peacekeeping is the Christian mandate except in a very narrow range of circumstances when war becomes tragically necessary. It remained for Thomas Aquinas and the philosopher theologians of the sixteenth and seventeenth centuries to formulate a more militant and modern platform.

The application and relevance of Augustinian concepts to the geopolitical realities of our day has been questioned by many. The realities of total war, high technology with muted interpersonal engagement and effect, weapons of enormous destructiveness even when nuclear, chemical, and biological capacity is restrained, as well as vast cultural disparities confound application of Augustine's concepts. The danger of Augustine's approach is his distancing of the realm of piety and virtue from the realm of *realpolitik*. The monumental contribution of his thought is that ethics remain grounded in the reality of God and what He is doing in the world as theologians Paul Lehmann and Reinhold Niebuhr would hold. No thinker before or since has seen so clearly what is in the heart of man. Just war theory before or after was never able to deal as well with that most fundamental ethical reality.

Augustine and Boniface

The genius of Augustine's theological and political construal comes into moving personal focus in his correspondence and conversations with Boniface. Boniface was a commander in the Roman army defending the southern border of Numidia, Augustine's own province, who fell into deep grief when his wife died while he was away at battle. A devout Christian, he contemplated abandoning his military career and taking up the monastic life. Augustine, the pastor-bishop extraordinaire, began a remarkable correspondence, and in the year 421 at sixty-seven years of age journeyed 400 miles to visit Boniface at the front. The conversation and counsel which ensued established for Christendom a new normative position of citizenship and military commitment. In a broader sense it conveys a sensibility about Christian existence in the fallen world that yet remains home and God's good creation. In reminiscence of Israel's holy war, Augustine reminded Boniface that military and monastic vocation both fight against enemies; both involve austerity, chastity, and temperance (a lesson studied again by U.S. troops in Saudi Arabia, until the "joy ships" arrived for R and R in the Mediterranean). Both vocations involve a kind of withdrawal from worldly affairs. Bodily strength and a strategic mind find godly service on either battlefront. In Augustine's words:

> This is what I can say in a short space: "Love the Lord your God in all your heart, all your soul, and all your power; love your neighbor as yourself" [Mt. 22:37, 39]. This is the summary which the Lord gave when he spoke on earth in the Gospel: "The whole Law and Prophets depend on these two commands" [Mt. 22:40]. Grow in this love every day by prayer and good works. The Lord both commanded and gave this love to you; by his help may it be nourished and increased in you, so that by reaching its own fullness it may perfect you as well. This, indeed, is the charity which "is poured forth in our hearts through the Holy Spirit who is given to us."

> Do not suppose that a person who serves in the army cannot be pleasing to God. The holy David, a soldier, was given high praise by our Lord. Many of the just men of his time were also soldiers. Another soldier, the centurion, said to the Lord, "I am not worthy to have you enter under my roof but only speak a word and my servant will be healed. I, indeed, am a man subject to authority and have soldiers under me. I say to one, 'Go' and he goes; to another, 'Come' and he comes; to my servant 'Do this' and he does it." The Lord said to him "Amen, I say to you, I have not found such faith in Israel" [Mt. 8:8-10].

When you are arming yourself for battle, therefore, let this thought be foremost in your mind: even your bodily strength is God's gift. Think about God's gift in this way and do not use it against God. Once you have given your word, you must keep it to the opponent against whom you wage war and all the more to your friend for whom you fight. You must always have peace as your objective and regard war as forced upon you, so that God may free you from this necessity and preserve you in peace. You must, therefore, be a peacemaker even in waging war so that by your conquest you may lead those you subdue to the enjoyment of peace. 'Blessed are the peacemakers,' says the Lord, 'for they shall be called children of God' [Mt. 5:9].

What, indeed is wrong with war? That people die who will eventually die anyway so that those who survive may be subdued in peace? A coward complains of this but it does not bother religious people. No, the true evils in warfare are the desire to inflict damage, the cruelty of revenge, disquiet and implacability of spirit, the savagery of rebellion, the lust for domination, and other such things. Indeed, often enough good men are commanded by God or a lawful ruler to wage war precisely in order to punish these things in the face of violent resistance.

When humans undertake war, the person responsible and the reasons for acting are quite important. The natural order which is directed to peace among mortals requires that the ruler take counsel and initiate war; once war has been commanded, the soldiers should serve in it to promote the general peace and safety. No one must ever question the rightness of a war which is waged on God's command, since not even that which is undertaken from human greed can cause any real harm either to the incorruptible God or to any of his holy ones. God commands war to drive out, to crush or to subjugate the

> pride of mortals. Suffering war exercises the
> patience of his saints, humbles them and helps
> them to accept his fatherly correction. No one
> has any power over them unless it is given from
> above. All power comes from God's command
> or permission.[15]

In June 430, while Boniface remained in command of his distant troops, the Vandals fell upon the fortified town of Hippo, for a siege that was to last fourteen months. In the heat and deprivation of that summer siege, the great bishop died. Boniface was killed in battle in Italy a few years later.

The legacy of Augustine is profound. Even today any academic treatise or course on political theory, theology, or war ethics must consider his thoughts. That politicians and military leaders from many of the Allied nations in the Gulf War were drawn to his reflections attests his lasting influence. The responsibility of individuals and nations--theistically or humanistically conceived--finds compelling formulation in his thought.

Two themes stand out in *The City of God* and the correspondence with Boniface: peace and providence. These themes have profound impact on any war ethic that seeks to be true to the Augustinian spirit. The peace of God is the natural order and aim of all secular society. The soldier and politician, like the priest and homemaker, is a peacemaker. This is the central purpose of human learning, work, conviviality. Wars can be justified as acts of making justice, love, and peace. But peace sometimes means taking up the sword. It is to be done only with great reticence and prayer and the knowledge that those who "take the sword will perish by the sword" (Matthew 26:52). Peace is not the absence of strife but the presence of justice and love. When public or ecclesiastic leaders call upon the people on patriotic occasions to peace without a call to the rough sacrifices and disciplines that freedom from aggression and compassion with those who suffer entail, they merely banter that peace that is no peace (Jeremiah 6:14).

Providence is a more confounding belief. Probably no idea is more deeply felt in time of war. Augustine's comfort that we are all going to die anyway may have worked in the fifth century. It comes harder in the twentieth. Soldiers and loved ones at home, victors, vanquished, and victims all reach for comfort and the assurance that even in the spray of shrapnel no harm can come to God's holy ones. In persecution, fire, and sword--nothing can separate us from the love of God (Romans 8:35).

The notion of providence affirms the nearly incredible, uncanny, and persistent faith that nothing in the creation--even a lonely death in a sandy bunker under a dark foreign sky--nothing can sever a person from God's love and His life. Providence in its radical form declares that all eventuality, even all war, is embraced, even willed by God. Just as no sparrow falls outside this omniscience and omnipotence, no Scud missile or M-119 Howitzer shell falls beyond the reach of this judgment and grace. The doctrine of providence is dangerous. It can lead to fatalistic resignation or, worse, the abdication of accountability. But sensitively and rightly conceived, omniscient and omnipresent destinarianism prompts high responsibility and human care. In war ethics, the doctrine of providence harks back to Augustine's moral system and, indeed, the biblical way of life on which he based his system. We are to act as if everything depended on us, because we know that in the end nothing does. God is a man of war because we are people of war. All shall one day be people of peace because He is the prince of peace.

Medieval Just War Teaching

Augustine's central tenet that war and peace are God's dispensation and history's events pattern the inscrutable purposes of His will dominated Western thought for centuries, reaching new heights in the synthesis of Christ and culture exposited by Thomas Aquinas:

> Thomas Aquinas . . . like Plato and Aristotle before him . . . came at the end of the social development whose inner rationale he set forth . . . . In his system of thought he combined without confusing philosophy and theology, state and church, civic and Christian virtues, natural and divine laws, Christ and culture. Out of these various elements he built a great structure of theoretical and practical wisdom, which like a cathedral was solidly planted among the streets and marketplaces, the houses, palaces, and universities that represent human culture, but which, when one had passed through its doors, presented a strange new world of quiet spaciousness, of sounds and colors, actions and figures, symbolic of a life beyond all secular concerns.[16]

Though a monk living the ascetic life of mortification, Aquinas was not nearly as disenchanted with this failing world as his father-in-faith,

Augustine. Aquinas believed that broad principles of human reason could find concord with revelation in the working out of philosophical and political systems. Embracing Aristotle in ways unavailable to Augustine and only made possible by the Islamic renaissance in early medieval Europe, Aquinas spoke of natural rights and gifts and the pursuit of appropriate human ends and fulfillments in the civil community: Civil law was the instrument through which human freedom would be perfected. Aquinas's rehearsal of Augustine's just war theory must be seen in this light.

In the *Caritas* section of the *Summa Theologica*, Aquinas began by pondering the Gospel imperatives of nonretaliation and peace. He then presented the opposing case, that war is not always sinful, but because it does incline toward sin and evil, war to be waged must be just.

> Three things are required for war to be just. The first is the authority of the sovereign on whose command war is waged. . . . Secondly, a just cause is required, namely that those who are attacked are attacked because they deserve it on account of some wrong they have done. So Augustine wrote, "We usually describe a just war as one that avenges wrongs, that is, when a nation or state has to be punished either for refusing to make amends for outrages done by its subjects, or to restore what has been seized injuriously. . . ." Thirdly, the right intention of those waging war is required, that is, they must intend to promote the good and to avoid evil. . . . Now it can happen that even given a legitimate authority and a just cause for declaring war, it may yet be wrong because of a perverse intention. So again Augustine says, "The craving to hurt people, the cruel thirst for revenge, the unappeased and unrelenting spirit, the savageness of fighting on, the lust to dominate, and such like--all these are rightly condemned in wars."[17]

Returning to Gospel peace in his afterthought, Aquinas reminded us that the purpose of war is to establish peace. These words may ring hollow in a century blighted by nearly unbroken war, but his stern reminder is vital to any martial policy that seeks to ground itself on ethical principles.

The Revival of Holy War in the Crusades

From the time of the Crusades to the late twentieth century, the great majority of wars in the world have been waged by Christians against other Christians. In contrast with Islamic and Judaic ethics (although it became a theme in sixteenth- and seventeenth-century just war theory), the Christian just war tradition was strangely silent about killing one's own siblings-in-faith. It must be admitted that the bloody history of the West evidences that Augustine and Aquinas did their job well in justifying war. The Christian Crusades of the eleventh to the fourteenth century are perhaps the epitome of the abdication of the Christ spirit of love for one's enemies, "turn the other cheek" ethics, and refraining from returning evil for evil. When the Crusaders massacred the Jews in German cities or the Muslims in Palestine, they were carrying out the dictates of *Realpolitik* but violating the deepest law and spirit of Christian ethics. The Crusades show the patent moral absurdity of the "Onward Christian Soldier" ethic.

From 1095, when Pope Urban II proclaimed the first crusade at Clermont to the pathetic Children's Crusade (1212), the portentous fifth crusade against Saladin, and the misadventures of the excommunicated Frederick II and sainted Louis IX in the sixth and seventh crusades, we see the Western Christian empire imbued with a thoroughly comingled Christian pacifism and barbarian militance. Through it all is the search for the social and political meaning of Christian faith. When pilgrimage routes to the Holy Land were interrupted by the Muslim conquests, holy war zeal fired up as it had when the Philistines intruded against the Israeli landtaking promised in the Covenant, or when pagan Arabic Meccans threatened nascent Islam.

"God wills it!" shouted the congregation at Clermont after Pope Urban's sermon in 1095. Soon 5,000 fighting men were on the move toward Constantinople in Christian just war, in which Yoder finds five distinctive elements:

- Its cause has transcendent validation.
- This transcendent quality is known by revelation.
- The adversary has no rights.
- The criterion of last resort does not apply.
- It need not be winnable.[18]

Initially the Crusades exhibited this distinctly religious and revelatory flavor. Bernard of Clairvaux organized the second crusade in 1147, which ended in defeat at Damascus. Francis of Assisi accompanied the fifth crusade into Egypt in 1219. It must be remembered that these

movements of European peoples into Asia Minor, Arabia, and Palestine
were like the Hebrew tribal migrations to Egypt and back to Palestine.
They could be seen as a restoration of safe pilgrimage access such as Iran
now seeks in its renewed diplomatic relations with Saudi Arabia. There
was no question of the fighter-bombers Israeli defense officials say can
fly in twelve minutes from Baghdad to Jerusalem. By the time of the
third crusade, called the Crusade of Kings, secular leaders Frederick I,
Philip II, and Richard I (the Lionheart) were at the forefront; interests of
territory, influence, and dominion began to supersede spiritual causes.

Already in the eleventh century, tension was being felt between
secular and sacred authority. The peace of God and truce of God were
understandings built on the just war idea of sanctuary and the keeping of
certain places and persons pure and undefiled by war. From the eighth
to the thirteenth century, the Clunine and Cistercian orders alone
claimed the adherence of 100,000 monks throughout Europe. As late as
the fourteenth century, it was estimated that 25 percent of the population
of Spain was in Holy Orders. Bainton makes vivid the accompanying
pacifist backdrop of just war militancy:

> The first half of the eleventh century was
> marked by a great campaign--mainly in France,
> but also in Germany--to promote the Peace of
> God and the Truce of God. The first category
> limited those involved in war by increasing
> enormously the category of the exempt. The
> Council of Narbonne in 1054, for example,
> decreed that there should be no attack on clerics
> [a medieval canonical category considerably
> broader than our contemporary notion of
> 'clergy' as sacramentally ordained deacons,
> priests, and bishops], monks, nuns, women,
> pilgrims, merchants, peasants, visitors to
> councils, churches and their surrounding
> grounds to thirty feet (provided that they did
> not house arms), cemeteries and cloisters to sixty
> feet, the lands of the clergy, shepherds and their
> flocks, agricultural animals, wagons in the fields,
> and olive trees.
>
> The Truce of God limited the times for military
> operations. There should be no fighting from
> Advent through Epiphany, nor from
> Septuagesima until the eighth day after

> Pentecost, nor on Sundays, Fridays, and every
> one of the holy days throughout the year.[19]

The church also sought to implement its peacemaking vocation by serving as mediator and arbitrator in disputes. Just as the Church of England sent emissary Terry Waite to Lebanon in the 1980s, church leaders, in the name of the peace of God, often assumed roles of admonition, reconciliation, and arbitration. In radical circles of Franciscans, Waldensians, and Hussites, pure pacifism was maintained as it is today in movements such as those of the Quakers and Mennonites. But holy war zeal persisted throughout the Middle Ages, surfacing again in the religious wars of the Reformation and Counter-Reformation. Holy war resolve again combined with an acquisitive spirit in the sixteenth and seventeenth centuries when commerce called Western entrepreneurs to the far reaches of the globe, a legacy we will review in the next chapter on the secular tradition of just war. The Middle Ages came to a close with Christian faith yielding to an empire building ethic as even the holy orders became militant with the Templars, Hospitalers, Knights of St. John, and other such societies.

An underlying impulse to pacify the world built on the Augustinian and Thomistic idea that the purpose of war was to bring peace. The forceful Augustinian doctrine of pacification, formulated as barbarians closed in from all sides, would in subsequent centuries be spoken of as colonization, civilization, conversion, education, and numerous other euphemisms about bringing order out of chaos and civility out of barbarity. Crusaders of any age fail to realize that the methods they use to evangelize and bring faith to unbelievers betray the very message they seek to convey. To quote from Pope Urban's sermon at Clermont in 1095:

> Oh race of the Franks, we learn that in some of
> your provinces no one can venture on the road
> by day or by night without injury or attack by
> highwaymen, and no one is secure even at
> home. Let us then re-enact the law of our
> ancestors known as the Truce of God. And now
> that you have promised to maintain the peace
> among yourselves you are obligated to succor
> your brethren in the East, menaced by an
> accursed race, utterly alienated from God. The
> Holy Sepulchre of our Lord is polluted by the
> filthiness of an unclean nation. Recall the
> greatness of Charlemagne. O most valiant
> soldiers, descendants of invincible ancestors, be

> not degenerate. Let all hatred depart from you,
> all quarrels end, all wars cease. Start upon the
> road to the Holy Sepulchre to wrest that land
> from the wicked race and subject it to
> yourselves.[20]

An unholy mixture of worthy imperatives of defending and propagating the faith and unworthy impulses of aggressing and destroying people with differing beliefs and values is found in this early modern revisitation of holy war ethics. As the modern age dawned, the mixture grew still more complex. In Paul Johnson's summary: "The idea that Europe was a Christian entity, which had acquired certain inherent rights over the rest of the world by virtue of its faith, and its duty to spread it, married perfectly with the need to find some outlet both for its addiction to violence and its surplus population."[21] An age of universal history was about to dawn.

Neoscholastic Just War Ethics

The Greek *oikumene* and the Roman empire were vast consolidations of peoples conjoined by a semblance of peace (*Pax Romana* in the latter case) and by some measure of linguistic and cultural cohesion. But the explorers from Spain and England, France and Holland, Italy and Germany circumnavigated the globe, opening trade routes to the Orient, colonizing the New World, and finally engaging not only Islamic regions but the Hindu and Buddhist realms along with vast enclaves of aboriginal and non-Abrahamic peoples. Concepts of just war evolved first from the faith contexts of the restless, inquisitive, and acquisitive European peoples.

The first modern just war theorists were Jesuits in Spain who articulated the dual ambition of missionizing and commercializing the New World. Francisco de Vitoria (1492-1546) and Francisco Suarez (1548-1617) took the position of Christian realism found in Augustine and Aquinas as the basis for a complex theory of the rights of nation-states to extend their interests to other peoples, especially those where governmental, legal, and ecclesiastic systems had yet to develop, at least in a form Europeans were willing to acknowledge. People have rights not only to defend their possessions and interests but to extend their needs to other realms. Cultivating what was virgin land, educating people who were preliterate, evangelizing where superstition and nature worship prevailed were now seen as divine responsibilities under the rubric of stewardship. Suarez articulated a just war doctrine that had not been a central theme since Cicero: "If the end is permissible, the necessary means to that end are also permissible."[22]

The doctrines of these Spanish Jesuits retained the gentle spirit of Aquinas and Augustine on just war, holding that conflict should be prevented if at all possible, that innocents should not be harmed, that peace and accommodation should be the ultimate purpose of any incursion into another land, and that respect for the divine soul of persons who were "given over to" one's authority should be maintained. The harsher doctrines of enslavement, commercial exploitation, even the baptizing/head-bashing (cf. Psalm 137) of children to assure them instant salvation and freedom from temptation intruded from the alien spirit of expediency. As we shall see in the development of the secular just war doctrine of these emerging and competitive nation-states in the thought of writers like Hobbes and Locke, ambitions were to arise that were inimical to the spirit of religious ethics. But first I will touch on the ethics of war and peace in the Reformers, the modern Protestant and Catholic traditions of just war, and finally a sample of very recent Christian ethics concerning the unfolding crisis in the Middle East.

Luther on War

Theological ethics today are those which have been refined by the protestant and catholic reformations. Martin Luther's salient work bridged the late medieval and the early modern worlds. The scholastic synthesis was yielding to the critical intellectual inquiry and theological and political protest that accompanied the rise of powerful ethnic-linguistic states in Europe. Machiavelli's prince was instructed in Ciceronian power politics, but cautioned to bow to religious interests and to feign rituals if necessary to further secular purposes. Throughout Europe voices were beginning to be raised against crown and church. John Wycliffe and the Lollardist movement in England, Peter Waldo and the Waldensians in southern Europe, Jan Hus in Bohemia, and a large community of clerics and scholars across Europe questioned the authority of the state, its relationship to the church, and its right to wage war.

For Luther the consideration of legitimate war returned to the Augustinian belief in "two kingdoms," which in turn rested on the Pauline tension between the "two loves": the love of God and love of the world, a basic spiritual/material dichotomy that animated the human soul and framed the drama of human history. Speaking of the "irrational susceptibility to war," Antoine de Saint-Exupéry showed that bloodlust, greed, and stubbornness as well as justice, love, and sacrificial service come into play in human warfare.[23] (The emotive and spiritual impulses to war and peace will be addressed in the final chapter.) Continuing the realist heritage, which sees human pride and violence (love of death) always intertwined with justice, love, and peace (love of life), Luther argued that as in education love is joined to discipline and punishment, in war and politics love must be joined to force. If the world is unjust and if some persons or groups want to hurt, rob, and destroy others, then our love for our neighbors requires that we protect and defend them. As Paul Ramsey often quipped, "We can't turn our neighbor's cheek." In the world we protect each other with police, courts, and armies. The church, though, lives by another law. In *Table Talk* Luther was asked whether he would strike back if he was attacked by robbers:

> Yes—of course. I should then act the prince and wield the sword, since there would be no one else around who could protect me; I should strike out for all I was worth, and then go to Communion feeling I had done a good work. But if I were attacked as a preacher and on account of the Gospel, with folded hands I should say: "Well my Lord Christ, here I am; it is you I have preached; if it is now time, I commit myself into thy hands and then I would die."[24]

Luther here goes beyond Augustine's doctrine of self-defense (where violence against one's own person is not to be revenged), and speaks a more modern notion of rights against harm to one's person or property. In his doctrine of the state, Luther goes beyond this teaching about checking and countering aggression to suggest that in a fallen world, one full of fulminant violence, only the threat of violence maintains order and peace. This radical doctrine of two warring and antithetical kingdoms (*Zweireiche Lehre*) has led to the accusation that Luther was the precipitating cause of the rise of Adolf Hitler. If aggression is constantly required to check the propensity of us all to aggress on others, we are in a vicious circle. What modern Lutherans have learned following the Nazi period is that human compulsions about order and controlling disorder, and manias about nipping rebellion in the bud may indeed be the major cause of war on God's earth. Perhaps the Christian doctrine of the right to check aggression has itself become the major stimulus to aggression. As Americans learned in Vietnam, the German people after World War II and its holocaust learned to use great care in taking up the sword to prevent being taken by the sword. It may be better to be red than dead, and "My country right or wrong" is blasphemous. More introspective doctrines of justice and peace are called for.

Calvin

The gentle political experiment under John Calvin provides us a more self-critical doctrine of war ethics. In *The Institutes of the Christian Religion* , Calvin positioned the rights and restraints about war making in the realm of the law and the hands of the lawful magistrates. Power, he wrote, has been vested in "rightful authority" to maintain the "tranquility of their subjects," and to bring about "the repression of seditious movements" and "the assistance of those violently oppressed." "Natural equity and duty demand that princes be armed not only to repress private crimes by judicial inflictions, but to defend the subjects committed to their guardianship whenever they are hostilely assailed."[25]

Calvin followed Augustine's pacifist line in warning magistrates against pretensions of power, lashing out in anger, and "burning with implacable severity." The Calvinist warrior, unlike the Lutheran, is, in the spirit of Seneca, the peaceful yet stern guardian of the weak and vulnerable. In Calvin we find an ascetic civil servant who quietly defends the lives of his or her people without the bombastic lashing out that seems so often to lead to war. Recently in a small town in England, a civil servant who guarded a public building was accosted and killed. The story came out that this was not the first but the last of a long series of assaults. He had been attacked a dozen times before and had been hospitalized on several occasions, but he bore no malice, and went back to his post, calmly claiming that was his duty. This is the spirit of defense and of war making in Calvin's ethos.

Modern Christian Ethics of War

With the exception of a small contingent of pure pacifists[26] and a dissenting tradition of Christian realists,[27] the dominant traditions of Christian ethics in our time have inclined against war making. The new conditions of warfare, especially nuclear weaponry, the recovery of New Testament ethics, and the pragmatic realization that throughout history we have too readily claimed our prideful ambitions as just war have converged to create this new ethos.

The Roman Catholic tradition, in a remarkable intellectual reversal of the just war heritage derived from Augustine, Aquinas, and the early Jesuits' war ethics, has moved in our time to a more pacifist position.

From the American Revolution through the Vietnam War, U.S. bishops were unswervingly loyal to the nation in its war making. I recently asked a colleague who holds the prowar position to go through the list of the dozen or so U.S. wars and tell me how each was justified in Christian ethics. While he could present compelling arguments for World Wars I and II and the Korean War, with some less convincing points about the revolution against Great Britain, for the rest he had difficulty. The wars against the Native Americans (chronicled at last in a film that some native communities have endorsed, *Dances with Wolves*), the Civil War, the wars against Mexico, Vietnam, Panama, and Grenada were more questionable both in cause and conduct. But Catholic war ethics through the Vietnam War (that South Vietnam was a Catholic society has bearing) were for the most part unequivocally bellicist. What happened?

In 1962 Pope John XXIII convened the Second Vatican Council. Putting the church firmly on the side of a new order of peace and hope, the deliberations of the council issued in the monumental encyclical of 1963, *Pacem in terris*, embarked on several themes that diverge from traditional just war theory. The council recognized a new era of history in which common men and women throughout the world were forming a new human community, an interdependence that necessitated a new vision of reciprocity and common good to bind all the earth's peoples into one family. The nineteenth-century assumption of competitive nation-states was yielding to a new concept of "the inhabited earth" on which peace must be established on an international scale. The implementation of basic human rights required structures of international authority to maintain peace. In this encyclical published just before his death, Pope John went on to chide the world for constructing myths about "evil empires" and calling to engage and dismantle other nations. Even communism and fascism may be more the demonizing projections of European and U.S. power urges than real threats to world order and peace. Finally, the pope questioned the current ethics of war, the latest mutation of secular just war theory, which held, somewhat in the radical spirit of Luther's reign of terror against latent chaos, that deterrence would check violence and keep peace. The pope questioned the cold war stockpiling of weapons not only as a threat to global peace but as an unjust siphoning off of resources needed for human liberation.

The culmination of the council's work was its 1965 promulgation, Pastoral Constitution on the Church in the Modern World (*Gaudium et spes*). This document reinstated Gospel values above political expediency as the centerpiece of ethical reflection. "What does the Gospel require?" was the central question, assuming human history in the world, it stated, was the formation of a global family, a new humanity that would be the alpha and omega, the initiating and consummating purpose of God's intrusion into the life of the world in Christ. After a review of the modern state of war technology, the council called for "an entirely new attitude" in the realm of war and peace, arguing that we are now facing "the supreme hour of crisis" in the progress of the global human family toward maturity. Affirming the classic just war stipulates of reason and restraint, the coucil went on to decry the arms race and the mounting commitment around the world to prohibitive terror. The only preventative to war in our time was the establishment of justice, the council claimed. Only when the lesser part of the world that controls so great a proportion of world resources comes to the aid of that greater part subsisting in poverty would the conditions that make for war cease and peace become possible. We must hope that Bishop Law forcefully communicated his church's official teaching to President Bush.

As we reflect religiously on 1990 and 1991, one reality is painfully clear. Though just war and even holy war rhetoric abounded, the hard commitments to do justice, love mercy, and make peace were too easily set aside in favor of national interest and military expediency. In the war over Kuwait, the Jewish ethic was eerily silent. Though Christians sought to speak out in their national and international assemblies and associations, their voices were hollow in the worn out rhetoric of liberal and liberationist nostalgia and were ignored. Even though we shouted amen to their salubrious words at the myriad parades, the caricature of religious ethics espoused by the civil religionists nauseated the thoughtful, and in Kierkegaard's memorable words reduced the God of Abraham, Isaac, and Jacob again to. . . "ludicrous twaddle." Like Santayana, we were mainly bemused by the pseudo-religious rhetoric, but we did ask the right question when we raised the issue of just or holy war. That question may yet save us.

Case Study: Modern Christian Ethics
and the War in the Gulf

The case of the war in the Gulf provides a concrete measure of contemporary Christian ethics. Debate in the Church of England parallels that in the United States. In a joint meeting with the prime minister on the eve of the air war over Iraq, the archbishop of Canterbury and the Roman Catholic Cardinal Hume agreed that all attempts to find a "diplomatic resolution to the crisis" should be sought and that military means to oust Saddam Hussein from Kuwait would be tragic and likely a "human, environmental and political disaster."[28] Acknowledging that resort to war was sometimes necessary, they counseled that "minimal force" be used and that "indiscriminate damage" not be inflicted on Iraq and its citizens.

Looking back on the campaign, we note that Prime Minister Major, President Bush, and especially generals Colin Powell and Norman Schwarzkopf failed to heed this cautionary admonition. With their construal of the earliest opportunity as a last resort, deliberate exaggerations of Iraqi strength, and interpretion of just war constraint and proportionate damage as "get it over as fast as possible," unimaginable destruction of the social infrastructure and the fabric of life of Iraq was wrought by the air assault. On Thursday, March 21, 1991, the United Nations Commission, led by Under Secretary-General Martti Ahtisaari, assessing the damage in Iraq, reported:

> With the Iraqi summer temperatures of 50°C only weeks away, there is very little time left to avert a major human tragedy in Iraq. It is unmistakable that the Iraqi people may soon face a further imminent catastrophe which could include epidemic and famine, if massive life-supporting needs are not rapidly met the recent conflict has wrought near-apocalyptic results upon the economic infrastructure.[29]

Most political commentators see the pronouncements and admonitions of the churches as largely ceremonial, unprophetic, and generally ineffective. When it comes to a choice between pleasing the people (who in this war were 80-90 percent committed to swift and decisive warfare) and standing up for prophetic, gospel, or even traditional just war values, gratification of the populace generally wins out.

After the outbreak of the war, a courageous statement was issued by church leaders, theologians, academics, and twelve bishops, which expressed a more critical, if still ambiguous view: "We accept that Iraq must fully abide by all the UN resolutions and withdraw from Kuwait. But although war in the Gulf has now begun, we remain firm in the belief that, because of the scale and horror of destruction which will be caused, recourse to war remains totally unacceptable." The report went on to admonish both sides not to use nuclear or chemical weapons, to avoid civilian and carpet bombing, and not to target oil wells. In a short statement that, as later events would show, deserved elaboration, the report claimed, "Demanding unconditional surrender instead of negotiating a peace can lead to unnecessary loss of lives and must be rejected."[30] The report then called for an end to the media censorship that had become oppressive both in Great Britain and the United States. It called for a conference after the war to end the grievances and policies that had made war necessary, such as supplying Western arms to the region. Reflecting the warning in the pope's Christmas message *Urbi et orbi*, theologians such as Oxford Regius Professor Rowan Williams argued that the conflict was one of disproportionate power against weakness, "a one-way adventure" in the pope's words, and that this imbalance of power made even more urgent the imposition of just war and pacifist restraints.

Other Oxford theologians, including the bishop of the Anglican church and the Regius Professor of Morals, Canon Oliver O'Donovan, supported the war. The church in general remained staunchly bellicist as it had in the United States. Britain's responsibility in creating the perpetual injustice of an Iraqi state with no access to the sea may also have fueled a self-justifying posture; yet once a country's sons and daughters are in the military theater it is hard to voice dissent or objection. As I write in late 1991, it remains for the returning soldiers to tell their story, for the casualties to be tallied up, for the bitter residue of war to fade away, for the rumors of war to be sifted out until we see what really happened in those one hundred hours, forty days, and eight months. This much is clear: Christian war ethics were out on the table again in ways that made everyone in the West take a new look at them, and perhaps even come to terms with them.

Notes

1. Nancy Gibbs, "Life on the Line," *Time*, February 25, 1991, p. 36-37.

2. George Bush, "State of the Union," January 29, 1991, in *Vital Speeches of the Day, 57*, no. 9 (February 15, 1991), p. 261.

3. "Bush's 'Just War' Doctrine," *US News and World Report*, February 4, 1991, p. 52-53.

4. On this point see Michael Walzer, *Just and Unjust Wars*, New York: Basic , 1977, p. 207 ff.

5. Ibid., *US News and World Report*, p. 53.

6. George Bush, "Remarks by the President in Address to the National Religious Broadcasters Convention," The Sheraton Washington Hotel, Washington, D.C., January 28, 1991. (Document supplied by the White House Office of the Press Secretary.)

7. John Howard Yoder, *When War Is Unjust*, Minneapolis: Augsburg, 1984, p. 71.

8. William Klassen, *Love of Enemies: the Way to Peace*, Philadelphia: Fortress, 1984, p. 126-127.

9. Quoted in John Helgeland, Robert J. Daly, and J. Patour Burns, *Christians and the Military: The Early Experience*, London: SCM, 1985, p. 22-23.

10. From Hippolytus, *The Apostolic Tradition*, in *Christians and the Military*, ed. Helgeland, Daly, and Burns, p. 37.

11. Ibid., p. 39.

12. Peter Dennis Bathory, *Political Theory as Public Confession: the Social and Political Thought of St. Augustine of Hippo*, New Brunswick, N.J.: Transaction, 1981, p. 20.

13. Roland H. Bainton, *Christian Attitudes Toward War and Peace: A Historical Survey and Critical Re-evaluation*, Nashville: Abingdon, 1960, p. 98.

14. Augustine, *The City of God*, trans. M. Dods, New York: Random House, 150, xix, 13.

15. Augustine's letters to Boniface, quoted in *Christians and the Military*, ed. Helgeland, Daly, and Burns, p. 76-82.

16. H. Richard Niebuhr, *Christ and Culture*, New York: Harper and Row, 1951, p. 130.

17. Thomas Aquinas, *Summa Theologica*, London: Blackfriars, 1972, II,II Q 40 Art. 1, p. 80-85.

18. Yoder, *When War Is Unjust*, p. 26-27.

19. Bainton, *Christian Attitudes*, p. 110.

20. George Weigel, *Tranquillitas Ordinis*, Oxford: Oxford University Press, 1987, p. 89.

21. Paul Johnson, *A History of Christianity*, Harmondsworth, U.K.: Penguin, 1978, p. 244.

22. "Selections from Three Works of Francisco Suarez" (see especially disputation 13: On war, sec. 7, p. 840) in *The Classics of International Law*, ed. James Brown Scott, Oxford: Clarendon, 1944, p. 840.

23. Antoine de Saint-Exupéry, *A Sense of Life*, New York: Funk and Wagnalls, 1965, p. 134.

24. Martin Luther, *Werke* (Kritische Gesamtausgabe Weimar, 1883), TR. 2 No. 1815, TR. 1 No. 1023, TR. 2 No. 2666 (*Tischrede*).

25. John Calvin, *The Institutes of the Christian Religion*, London: James Clarke, 1957, Vol. 2, Chapter 20, p. 661ff.

26. John Howard Yoder and his fellow Mennonite ethicists have presented the most compelling case for religious pacifism in our time. See, for example, Yoder's *The Politics of Jesus*, Grand Rapids: Eerdmans,

1972; *Nevertheless,* Scottdale: Herald, 1972; and *When War is Unjust,* Minneapolis, Minn.: Augsburg, 1984.

27. The three leading studies of martial realism (though certainly not bellicist positions) are Paul Ramsey, *The Just War: Force and Political Responsibility,* New York: Scribner's, 1968; Oliver O'Donovan, *Peace and Certainty,* Oxford: Oxford University Press, 1989; and George Weigel, *Tranquillitas Ordinas,* Oxford: Oxford University Press, 1987.

28. "The Terrible Choice: Joint Statement of the Archbishop of Canterbury and Cardinal Hume," *The Tablet,* January 19, 1991, p. 85.

29. "U.N. Report Describes Catastrophe in Iraq," *Independent,* March 22, 1991, p. 13.

30. "The Just Conduct of the Gulf War: A Christian Statement," *The Tablet,* January 26, 1991, p. 116.

6

Secular Just War Theory

Wars are often fought over religion–to defend or spread the faith. The voice of God is often heard to say, "Move into this land or against this people." That same voice has also been heard to say, "Be still and refrain from violence." Divine holiness has given impetus to eradicate nonbelievers, to cleanse warriors for cultic purity, to isolate those tainted by blood guilt in war, or to prohibit killing as blasphemy. This variety of interpretations has led some observers to dismiss the theological dimension as irrelevant to any meaningful formulation of ethics. Religious ethics, it is sometimes urged, are parochial and mystical, sectarian, and subjective, incompetent to guide public decisions in secular or pluralistic communities. On good evidence, those morally concerned have often seen religions as epicenters of strife and war throughout history. It could also be said that secular authority is established when feuding religious bodies agree that a neutral means of restraint is required: Secular rule arises in the vacuum left by the loss of belief in divine right.

Holy war and just war theories capture some moral truths. Public war ethics also take many wrong notions and seek to make them right. The undergirding leitmotif in my ethical scheme confirms the good of any value if it accords with redemptive purpose as love, suffering, and death yield renewal. I have reviewed the substance of this normative ethic for war and peace, through a chronicle of the war itself. After a review of the secular heritage of just war ethics, we will join our composite review of the ethical heritage to our analysis of the war itself and project the kind of moral future which that ancient tradition and recent trauma provide.

Background to the Secular Tradition

Until the sixteenth and seventeenth centuries, most societies on earth lived with what might be called "ontocratic" patterns of political belief. God's will and immutable natural law constituted the state, gave it its raison d'être, and justified its actions. The body politic was a being in which all cohered under the leadership of a ruler, and all were guided by a divine pattern of action. Right inhered in this corporate being and its action. By the sixteenth century in Europe, when Francisco Suarez, Francisco Vitoria, and Giagiovanni Gentili were articulating a new political theory, rights had begun to be identified with territories. With Hobbes and Locke in the seventeenth century, this right also focused in individuals. By the seventeenth century throughout Europe political and theological theory were in tension. On the one hand, state prerogative was extrapolated from individual natural right and affirmed by thinkers like Grotius, Hobbes, and Locke. On the other hand, conscientious objection to the state's power was found in the Protestant monarchomachi and tyrannicidal thinkers like Calvin, Buchanan, Poynet, and Knox.

Sovereignty had by now become a very complex doctrine. It both undergirded the independence and assertiveness of states and checked that same right and power on grounds that the state, too, was subject to a higher sovereignty. If *majestas* belonged to the people, there could be no ruler. If *majestas* belonged to the ruler, the people had only to obey. If *majestas* belonged to God, both people and state were subject. How these fundamental beliefs worked out in concrete political order from the sixteenth to the twentieth century determined the ethics of war, revolution, and rebellion. To deal with this tension various schemes of division and dispersal of power have been proposed over the last three centuries. Leagues of nations, alliances, concordats, and a body of international law have emerged to guide modern states in the use of power and restrain its abuse.

In secular theory, the theology of warfare became a philosophy of warfare. Divine commands to go to war or not to kill turned toward the rights of aggressive interests, of offended parties, and of those under attack. Some bridging thinkers like Grotius, in *De Jure Belli ac Pacis* (1625), sought to reconcile divine right/natural law ethics with the new sense of the sovereignty, power, and expedient interest of states. Grotius attempted to remain faithful to Suarez and Aquinas, Augustine and the Gospels, but also support the Dutch mercantilists seeking to open markets in the East Indies. Grotius projected the natural right of individuals to defend themselves and secure what was necessary for their well-being (life, liberty, and property) into the collectivity of the state and ruler. If the state had to expand its interests to new lands and new markets, and if naval and military power was necessary to secure those incursions, these actions were legitimate. The words of Cicero were revived: The liberty and opportunity of the individual was the supreme value. Now the autonomous or sovereign being was Plato's individual writ large–the state. The sovereign right of individuals to maintain themselves against an aggressive world became in Hobbes's *Leviathan* the prerogative of the state. Anticipating Darwin by 200 years, Hobbes affirmed that nature was a condition of warfare of all against all and only those states that could protect and assert their will would prevail.

Renaissance Beginnings of Just War Theory

Hence, therefore, every leader to his charge;
For on their answer will be set on them,
And God befriend us as our cause is just!
Shakespeare, *King Henry IV, Part 1,*
Act 5, Scene 1

By 1597, when Shakespeare wrote *King Henry IV, Part 1*, much thought, sacred and secular, had been given to the glorious and gruesome necessity of war. As Prince Hal, Sir John Falstaff, and other warriors more or less impressive set forth to confront Hotspur, the Scottish Earl of Douglas, and their rebellious company in the north, King Henry took the words for his commission from sources that stretched from Israeli holy war, Cicero, and Augustine to the Crusades and Richard the Lionheart, Thomas Aquinas, and perhaps even Francisco de Vitoria: "God befriend us as our cause is just!" By the dawn of the seventeenth century, a complex notion of righteousness, the state, and warmaking had emerged. King Henry and even Prince Hal, the future Henry V, would no longer see Constantine's cross shimmering in the sunlight. War justification became a matter of harsh necessity and civil remedy, not divine or natural law. Citing Cicero in *De Inventione*, Hobbes wrote of men who once "roamed the field like animals" now gathered into domestic and civil systems, ordering their lives by reason and law. Principal among the functions of this completely human construction of culture were the restraint of violence, defense against enemies, and the securing of well-being for the people.

Ius gentium and *ius civile* now gained importance over the medieval *ius divina* and *ius naturale*. *Dominium*, that life-giving and life-taking claim made on all under one's authority, was no longer a divine dispensation but a rightful possession based on natural reason. Settled law, covenant, and contract between people and the sovereign justified the state in all its endeavors. As we have already seen, religious theory retained currency in this otherwise humanist period. It was conscience in Luther, divine command in Calvin, and revised natural law in Vitoria and Suarez that justified statesmanship and militancy in states shaped by those faiths. But even with this religious ground, political ambitions of princes, civil needs of magistrates, and expansionary economics of new and powerful mercantile interests aligned with government took precedence. Freedom, not determinism or subservience, was now posited as the primary moral quality of persons and states. Liberty was seen as the primary qualification of responsibility of individuals and nations. This liberal spirit animated Lutheran and Calvinist, Dominican and humanist alike. The seminal exponent of modern secular political and war theory was a man whose roots were in the Calvinist and Thomist world view, but whose thought pressed out toward a universalist and humanist perspective. Hugo Grotius, a brilliant student of Calvinist Aristotelianism at Leiden, took the classical theme of liberty from Greece and Rome and wove it into the Renaissance/Reformation commitments of the Netherlands to form a doctrine of safeguarding and adventurous liberty. His *Mare Liberum* (1609) proclaimed a law for the seas that would eventually ground what is called international law in the twentieth century. In *De Jure Belli ac Pacis* (1625), Grotius reflected on colonial expansion and conflicts and rules to govern such enterprises. His political ethic transformed Aristotelian natural law and Calvinist divine command and will into a modern exposition of law and policy.

Grotius felt that God's will for humankind was surely a sociality that maximized distributive and commutative justice in Aristotle's sense. The world offered expanse and provision for the sustenance of human freedom (αυτε ζουσιον, "self governing"). The acquisition of material things by persons and nations fulfilled this rightful desire. Open space or opportunity of any sort was an invitation for a person or a people to extend themselves into that realm and lay claim to it. In a famous illustration, Grotius spoke of theatre seats that, if left unoccupied, could be claimed by someone else. If the purchasers of the seats arrived late, they could not claim them from the squatters. As we shall see in the specific events leading up to the war over Kuwait, the question of occupancy and occupation became crucial. What was the status of the disputed islands and the land overlying the Rumaila oilfield? Did the United States assure Iraq that it would not interfere in a border dispute? In case of hostilities over borders between Iraq and Kuwait, what were the rights or duties of remote states to protect and intervene? Grotius began to lay out a doctrine of proper ownership and expropriation of land and resources that would justify and rationalize four centuries of world history as the West made war, redrew maps, and divided and renamed the remote parts of the world that it visited and occupied.

Not only do peoples have the natural and imputed right of dominium--occupation and ownership through striving and work--they have the right to punish, Grotius argued. Not only could states punish, but individuals or corporations could exact retribution or inflict punishment for wrongdoing. The right to chastise resided in individuals before it was appointed to the state: "The state inflicts punishment for wrongs against itself, not only upon its own subjects, but also upon foreigners."[1] When John Locke wrote his second treatise, this "very strange doctrine" of Grotius played a prominent part particularly in the justification of English colonial discipline, even war, in colonies like South Carolina where Locke happened to be a stockholder. This doctrine of chastisement, especially against aborigines, aliens, or those who had become alienated, eventually turned into the Dutch doctrine of *Stadholdership*, which was used to imprison the Arminians and other suspect persons and eventually Grotius himself. The romantic escape of the tiny man bearing the great name, borne in a clothesbasket from the castle of Lowenstein where he had been imprisoned for two years, symbolizes the reverse side of the dangerous equation he set forth of liberty to claim and chastise. Ironically, Grotius and Descartes, seen by many as the two founders of the Enlightenment, both forged their insights in small cells, Descartes in his winter quarters with the French army and Grotius at Lowenstein.

Grotius's law of war was grounded in the respect for rights that is necessary for people to live in a community. Participation in a society of individuals or a society of nations implies a fundamental principle of acknowledgment of mutual rights.

> This sociability or this case of maintaining Society in a manner comfortable to the light of human understanding, is the fountain of right, properly so called, to which belongs the abstaining from that which is another's and the restitution of what we have of another's, or of the profit we have made by it, the obligation of fulfilling promises, the reparation of a damage done through our own default, and the merit of punishment among men.[2]

Justice enforcement and exertion of the will of a state is imposed on citizens by virtue of the bonds they have assumed as citizens. Persons must take up arms in defense of the state in the same way that they uphold domestic laws. The power of the sovereign may break down, even an absolutist like Grotius has to admit, when the law of love interposes itself over statute: "To impose on all citizens the hard necessity of dying" or actions that might involve "the destruction of many innocents" cannot be made law. "For what charity recommends in such a case to be done, may, I doubt not, be prescribed by a human law."[3]

The theologian in Grotius often came to the forefront in his thought, leading the reader to wonder whether his concern was to justify or condemn European exploits in the New World. The goal of any warfare is always the achievement of peace. The relative justice of a cause increases the legitimacy of warmaking. Preemptive or anticipatory intervention is only licit in the face of "immediate and imminent" threat. Defensive war, in other words, is the only ground for violence. Anticipating our present world of manifold independent yet interdependent states which constantly need to learn to live in reciprocal provision and respect, Grotius helped us see the moral contours of an emerging world order. In full sympathy with the conviction of his critical follower Immanuel Kant, Grotius set forth a political philosophy in keeping with the best traditions of his northern European lowlands home, where peace was to be preserved unless severe injustice and harm was visited on one's own or another nation. By the time Grotius wrote *De Jure Belli ac Pacis* in 1625, he had come to affirm the validity of divine and natural law even in the face of positive and civil law. In *De Jure*, the primary discernment of rightness or justice in a cause was, of course, according to Luther's and Calvin's doctrines of conscience. *Iustitia interna* was the discerning conscience, which must weigh, in case of war, the injustice inflicted and the remedy (war) being proposed (III c.25). But courage may tell us to go on when conscience tells us to stop. A tension between just war and pacifism thus arises.

Throughout the month of April (1991) the newspapers spoke of a controversy between the Allied field commander in Iraq, General Schwarzkopf, and the political leaders in the United States, President Bush, Secretary of Defense Cheney, and Secretary of State Baker. Schwarzkopf, concerned with the turmoil developing in Iraq, with Kurdish rebellion in the north and Shiah uprising in Basra and the south, and conscious of how history would deal with the war, is said to have wanted to march (à la General MacArthur) all the way to Baghdad. Here, one surmises, the Allied forces were to depose Saddam Hussein and supervise the establishment of a new government. Courage, as a military virtue, animates people to risk their lives to defend or prosecute their cause. In courage, we seek to act swiftly, decisively and completely so that we can "get the thing over with." Common sense, a more reflective and less bellicose virtue, may also convince us that the just thing to do is to "finish the job well." Conscience, however, raises other questions: What is right, just, fair, and kind. It raises the question of compassion, uncomely to those who gaze intently "into the eyes of the cannon" (Shakespeare, *As You Like It* II,I,143ff). Conscience also asks: "What will be the feedback?" "How will this action reverberate and create unforeseen and regrettable consequences?"

Grotius was a moralist about war who insisted that we examine this full range of reflection. If war is to be conducted with credibility and respect in a world where, because of the media, everyone is watching, it must be initially justified and continually transacted within a moral framework. War that is misconceived and misconducted will rebound as shame on its perpetrator. Grotius's just war theory lays the necessary groundwork for moral discourse and for resolution of conflict. Perhaps more than ever before, given UN deliberations and authorization of the Gulf conflict in both General Assembly actions and Security Council resolutions, a "community of moral perception"[4] is audience to all modern warmaking. In continuity with the prophets of Israel, modern secular just war theory seeks to define the parameters of righteousness in national and international action.

The genius of Grotius is in his secularization of the moral virtues of remembrance and hope. In his use of historical examples he achieves for the first time a feat unreproduced until Michael Walzer's *Just and Unjust Wars*. Moral remembrance, what the Greeks called *anamnesis*, is the quality of recounting events so that their lessons are appropriated into the present. George Santayana's concept of normative history--Those who ignore history are doomed to repeat it--helps us refine a sense of what is appropriate in warfare. The proportionate use of force would be an example. Like Walzer, Grotius used frequent examples from the Roman and Greek wars and from medieval campaigns to illustrate his doctrines of justice, charity, and proportionality.

When the judges appointed by the the victorious Allies convened the Nuremberg trials in 1946 and 1947, they were called on to assess morally the culpability of Nazi officers and physicians. In the spirit of Grotius, they invoked "principles of Humanity" (Grotius: Charity) to evaluate what the soldiers and doctors had done. Charity is the proleptic actualization of hope. Do unto others as you would have others do unto you. The idea of anticipated reciprocity functions ethically via feedback expectation, exactly as memory functions from past action. James Johnson summarizes Grotius's contribution:

By setting forth a historically and rationally
grounded secular foundation for restraint in war
he made it possible for international law on war
to develop as it did, receiving steadily greater
elaboration in succeeding centuries right up to
and including the humanitarian law of armed
conflict of our time. Perhaps we in the West
have lost, as a culture, the sense of charity that
calls us to think well of an enemy (still possible
for Grotius); yet we remain bound by limits
based in consideration of fairness and
proportion, just insofar as we are human.[5]

Thomas Hobbes took political theory one more step in the direction
of secular war ethics. In his landmark books *De Cive* and *Leviathan*,
Hobbes argued that human beings by nature are ruthless and
exploitative and therefore have joined in social compact. By contract,
they renounced personal aggression and retaliation for wrong done and
committed that role to the state. Justice as a domestic sword, and war
and international policy as an interstate sword displaced personal self-
defense and aggression. Security and peace were only possible with
such an external threat:

Forasmuch as they who are amongst themselves
in security, by the means of this sword of justice
that keeps them all in awe, are nevertheless in
danger of enemies from without; if there be not
some means found, to unite their strengths and
natural forces in the resistance of such enemies,
their peace amongst themselves is but in vain.
And therefore it is to be understood as a
covenant of every member to contribute their
several forces for the defence of the whole.[6]

The law and ethics of war were clear for Hobbes. Security requires
constant vigilance against the aggressive desires of all competitive
nations. People cannot be trusted at their word, and when it comes to
the affairs of state what one calls cruelty is for another justice. Anarchy
is the natural state of humans, which is and must be supervised by "the
natural kingdom of God" and the articulated law of the sovereign. If
lawlessness erupts through any of these membranes, punishment ensues.
In *Leviathan*, Hobbes articulated this chain of consequences:

Having thus briefly spoken of the natural
kingdom of God, and his natural laws, I will add
only to this chapter a short declaration of his
natural punishments. There is no action of man
in this life, that is not the beginning of so long a
chain of consequences, as no human providence
is high enough, to give a man a prospect to the
end. And in this chain, there are linked together
both pleasing and unpleasing events; in such
manner, as he that will do any thing for his
pleasure, must engage himself to suffer all the
pains annexed to it, and these pains, are the
natural punishments of those actions, which are
the beginning of more harm than good. And
hereby it comes to pass, that intemperance is
naturally punished with diseases, . . . negligent
government of princes, with rebellion; and
rebellion with slaughter. For seeing
punishments are consequent to the breach of
laws; natural punishments must be naturally
consequent to the breach of the laws of nature;
and therefore follow them as their natural, not
arbitrary effects.[7]

Hobbes was the consummate realist. His political theory marked the
beginning of a new era in the ethics of politics and war. His monumental
Leviathan is an argument fashioned on Thucydides' *History of the
Peloponnesian War*, which he had translated. When the tiny island-state
of Melos, a Spartan colony, was attacked by the Athenians, the
inhabitants refused to submit. Both sides used arguments that Hobbes
would later employ as "the necessity of nature." The island people said
that if they submitted to the mighty Athenians the humiliation itself
would destroy their independence and foment constant unrest.
Weakness necessitates response, it was argued. In words like those
Saddam Hussein used in the war over Kuwait, "at least if we lose (as we
certainly will of necessity) we will not lose face and will have some
semblance of victory in having stood up to a mighty power" (BBC). The
powerful victor also acts under necessity. Essentially this side argues
that if another party is weak and can be overwhelmed, it must be
overwhelmed. In Walzer's words:

If they do not conquer when they can,
they only reveal weakness and invite attack;

and so, "by a necessity of nature", they
conquer when they can.[8]

Leaping across the Christian ages of just war theory, including
Aquinas and Augustine, Hobbes appealed to a secular heritage that
considered war as its own justification. Although Hobbes concluded
Leviathan with a discussion of the Christian state and even mentioned the
eternal kingdom of Christian faith, he fundamentally argued that
warfare and conquest are, at the end of the day, not matters of ethics,
philosophy, or theology, but of political necessity.

Hobbes extended this ethic to the question of uninhabited or
sparsely inhabited areas. Two necessities come into play, according to
Hobbes: The "not sufficiently inhabited land" (*terra nullius*) invites
habitation, and a people searching for a habitat follow a natural necessity
to make it their home. Land is not the Lord's received in gratitude or
taken at divine command in holy war. Land is a realm for human
occupation and exploitation; it is there for the appropriation and
fulfillment of human prospects. Hobbes's doctrine of the sovereign and
the rights of a resident populace becomes a point of war ethics
disallowing aggression and protecting the peace, although in lands not
fully filled up with human habitation and culture (cultivation) the
sparsely dispersed out inhabitants might be ordered to group themselves
closer together and allow others to move into the vacated land. Even
today in international law occupation remains one of the measures of
establishing sovereignty along with annexation, accretion, cession,
prescription, and acquisition.[9] Assuming the worst instincts and
intentions in people, Hobbes would have the sovereign or the contractual
state (1) in a constant state of readiness to defend its properties, (2)
always ready to exploit *Lebensraum* that comes available, not only
adjacent, but distant; and (3) always vigilant to "keep the peace" by
stilling aggressive urges wherever they arise.

Hobbes was writing in one of the most turbulent eras of British and
European history. The English Civil War would prove but the first in a
long chain of popular rebellions seeking to establish democracies, or at
least governments responsive to the will and sovereignty of the people.
John Locke became the architect of this modern notion of democratic
sovereignty. Wars of revolution, wars for freedom against tyranny, and
wars to establish representative government were to mark the period
extending from the late sixteenth to early twentieth century. Indeed, all
of the world's wars from the English and American revolutions through
the French and Russian revolutions down to the two world wars in
Europe and the more recent struggles in Korea and Vietnam consisted

for the most part of popular or peasant rebellions against oppressive internal or externally manipulated regimes.

War in the modern era became a mean and dirty business. The ancient Chinese invention of gunpowder paved the way for rifles, bullets, and cannon. Hand-to-hand combat as the final consummation of bow-and-arrow conflict between representative or even mercenary groups gave way to what would be called "total warfare," involving entire nations, conscripted armies, and civilian populations. In the early nineteenth century, the first fully modern philosopher of war, the Prussian General Karl Maria von Clausewitz, reflected on what warfare had become in Napoleonic France. In his massive and monumental work *Vom Kriege* (On War)--a writing still studied in military academies and therefore familiar to Gulf War commanders like Norman Schwarzkopf, Colin Powell, Peter de la Billière, Michel Henri Roquejeoffre, and Sultan Hasheem Ahmad--Clausewitz blended a philosophical notion of "absolute (ideal) war" and the sordid and imperfect reality of war. When we "pass from abstractions to reality," Clausewitz held, "we find that war is an act of violence pursued to its utmost bounds. To introduce into the philosophy of war a principle of moderation would be an absurdity."[10]

It is secular, Clausewitzian war ethics that are taught today in the military academies, officer training schools, and boot camps. This view of swift, unprincipled war, where expedience is the preeminent value, was exemplified along with its tension with humanistic and religious values in a press interview with General Schwarzkopf at the height of the war. "What do you think about the thousands of Iraqi boys who are being killed?" he was asked by a reporter. With a tear in his eye, the West Point graduate responded, "I can't allow myself to think about that" (BBC, March, 1991).

War, in its modern secular sense, has become a clear and admitted "act of violence to compel our opponent to fulfil our will," although, in practical terms, war always ends in some kind of compromise far short of total victory. Clausewitz looked with derision on the generals ("Brahmins") of the eighteenth century who sought just and fair wars between their picturesque small dynasties and "looked upon war as an evil." These idealists he saw caught up in a "morbid paroxysm" in which a "spirit of benevolence"[11] was allowed to interfere with the brutal yet noble necessity of war making. War must be conceived and conducted justly if only for reasons of expediency, yet war is not the venting of vengeance and hatred. It is a rational, political act in which the objective is to disarm and remove the destructive power of an enemy. The spirit of Grotius and Montesquieu thus endured into the modern age in that "the law of nations is naturally founded on this principle, that different nations ought in time of peace to do one another all the good they can, and in time of war as little injury as possible without prejudicing their real interests."12

The Modern Legacy of War Ethics

For the reasons discussed in the last section, the modern experience of war has become one of profound ambivalence. Beginning in the nineteenth century civilized society began to construct conventions about the causality and conduct of war. It is as if the potential for brutality increases concomitantly with the uncertainty of rightness of cause which is, in turn, reflected in the rhetoric of convention. Even with the great wars of the twentieth century, if one pauses to think of the absurdity of a country lad from Saint Omez, France, being killed by the son of a merchant in Heidelberg or the history graduate from Freiburg dying in the trenches of Verdun at the hands of a promising classics graduate of Cambridge, the pain is unbearable.

While the war over Kuwait and its terrible aftermath in ecological and human catastrophe runs its course, a striking film called *Dances with Wolves* has captivated the hearts of millions in the West. The film reflects on one of the tragic chapters of U.S. war history as the Civil War came to an end and the U.S. military turned its attention to the western frontier and a "liberation" of a vast *terra nullius* from Native Americans. A soldier who received a leg wound in battle against the Confederates avoids the dreaded amputation of his leg to dance back and forth in front of the enemy lines in a death frenzy on his horse. Miraculously he eludes the rain of bullets and survives. He is honored and chooses as reward to go to a far outpost on the western frontier. Here he finds soul affinity with nature--the great land, Chico, his wise steed, Two-Socks, the wild wolf, and the Sioux tribe. He finds love with a white woman who has been raised by the tribe after hiding as a girl from the massacre of her family. The film ends with the brutal and inevitable destruction of the tribe's sacred lands first by the marauding soldiers and then by the settlers who follow in their wake. War against any fellow humans, be they Sioux, Vietnamese (cf. the film *Good Morning Vietnam*), or Iraqi is fought today with gnawing doubt and equivocation.

With the passing of the age of chivalry and the emergence of modern technological anonymity in combat, certain rules have been codified to minimize the misguided inception and vicious execution of war. From the time of the American Civil War and the Crimean War in Europe, conventions were articulated to safeguard the threads of humanity embodied by persons like the soldier-hero in *Dances with Wolves* and

Florence Nightingale even in the midst of the cruel inevitability of war. Beginning with the Declaration of Paris (1856), Lieber's Code in the American Civil War (1863), the Geneva Convention for the Amelioration of Wounded Armies in the Field (1864), the Declaration of St. Petersburg (1868), and ending with the Geneva protocols of 1974-1977, a long sequence of secular war ethics has been expressed. These beliefs and the general ethical principles derived from their implementation shape recent moral conviction about war.

Reporting on the conferences of 1898 and 1907 in The Hague (which he observed with meticulous detail), Joseph Conrad called the proceedings "a solemnly official recognition of the Earth as a House of Strife."[13] With the American Civil War and the Franco-Prussian War in Europe, the world came to realize its apparently irresistible propensity toward violence, its irrevocable entrapment in what theology calls the fall, and its inability, in Paul the Apostle's language, to do the good clearly known and avoid doing the evil likewise self-evident (Romans 7). Conventions now became house rules for the wounded *oikumene*.

War history since the mid-nineteenth century confirms Paul Johnson's depiction of our times as an epoch of megaviolence. In 1859 France defeated Austria and liberated Italy. In 1864 Prussia and Austria defeated Denmark and liberated Schleswig-Holstein. In 1861 Karl Marx cautioned Abraham Lincoln against pursuing war against the Confederacy, arguing that the abolitionist intelligentsia had yet to emerge. In 1866 Prussia defeated Austria and in 1870-1871 the new north German confederation defeated France and established the Second German Reich.

In 1863 the divided states of America and the U.S. Army (Union) issued General Order No. 100, which summarized civilized wartime behavior in early modern European history under the authorship of the German-born writer Lieber. In 1864 the first Geneva Convention drafted rules protecting the sick and wounded, and four years later the St. Petersburg Convention prohibited the use of certain missiles. The contemporary custom of engaging in combat with weapons less fierce than those at one's disposal anticipates the tradition of *jus contra bellum* starting to emerge--by the time of the Nuremberg and Helsinki conventions at the close of World War II, the rules almost seemed to outlaw war. In 1898 and 1907 the Hague conventions were formulated against the background of the Boxer Rebellion in China, the Japan-Russia war, and the colonial wars of Britain against the Boers, Somalia, and Nigeria, and France against Chad. The Hague Convention IV on The Laws and Customs of War on Land defined the status of civilians and belligerents: Soldiers must be under legitimate command, wear visible uniforms and insignia, carry their arms openly, and conduct all operations in accord with the historic body of war ethics.

In early 1914, General Hugh L. Scott, commander of the U.S. troops on the Mexican border, sent a copy of the pamphlet containing "The Hague Rules" (1907) across the border to Pancho Villa, general of the Mexican insurgents. After contemplating the document for many hours, Villa sent word in Clausewitz's spirit, "What is this Hague Conference? Was there a representative of Mexico there? It seems to me a funny thing to make rules about war. It is not a game. What is the difference between civilized war and any other kind of war?"[14] Despite the quasi absurdity, if not oxymoronic character of "civilized war," the Lieber and Hague conventions have endured as appropriate rules for armed conflict among nations.

But the will to preserve peace and restrain war was countered by another cache of beliefs and values. As Clausewitz wrote, war is a matter of morale and strategy. Philosophical, theological, and ethical thought converged with an increasingly sophisticated military technique. In Prussia Hegel taught that the process of history, including wars, was the working out of a divine plan. In France the biblical scholar Ernest Renan thought that war was one of the conditions of refinement and advancement of human progress. In Britain the social Darwinists saw conflict and war as a survival and strengthening process in which the weak yielded to the mighty. This moral thought grounded the ideology of Otto von Bismarck, Louis Napoléon, and Benjamin Disraeli as each in turn sought to establish the ascendency and supremacy of their nations. Kaiser Wilhelm II wrote in 1912 of "the struggle for existence which the German people in Europe will eventually have to fight against the Slavs, supported by the Latins."[15] President Theodore Roosevelt felt that destiny and future influence required that the United States assume a "greater part in the world" and "perform those deeds of blood and valor which above everything else bring national renown" for "by war alone can we acquire the virile qualities necessary to win in the stern strife of national life."[16] The sense of necessity, even desirability of war in Europe and the United States as the nineteenth turned into the twentieth century combined with a sensibility that war must be justified in inception and execution. In 1859, Louis Napoléon claimed that he must have a *causus belli* to justify war nationally and in the eyes of the world. Bismarck that same year said that war should come only if "all other means had been exhausted."

Probably the most important convention regarding *causus belli* was not to start a conflict as aggressor. When there existed a lust for conflict as we have noted in the nineteenth century, this cynically meant that states had to make sure that the other side started it. Hitler's henchmen burned the Reichstag and blamed it on the socialists. Ultimata, especially unconditional ultimata, were favored devices to precipitate a war, making it look like the party that could not accept an ultimatum was really at fault. Russia thus threatened Turkey in 1853. Austria announced that no negotiations were possible in 1859. France would not take no for an answer in 1870. As we will see when we rehearse the features of *ius ad bellum*, the just war requires genuine violation, not just perceived and feigned threat. Certainly there is no place in just war tradition for the contrived initiation of conflict for some imaginary pretense of power. As the diplomatic transactions in the war over Kuwait show, in retrospect, certain ambiguities were purposely left hanging, and ultimata, calculated to make response impossible, offered.

The Hague conventions of 1907 marked the first significant initiative in the twentieth century to define in a secular way and backed with legal and political force, restraints on the war temperament rapidly growing in Europe. Rules were formulated regarding the initiation of war: A declaration of war had to be made that articulated the grounds for war or, even better, an ultimatum stating the conditions which, if not met, would result in war. Neutral states were to be notified and assurance given that their rights to noninterference would be honored. This stipulate was centrally involved in the war over Kuwait, especially with regard to the nations of Iran and Israel. The convention outlawed poisoned weapons and projectiles that could cause unnecessary suffering, and it outlawed bombing of civilian sites.

In 1928 the General Treaty for the Renunciation of War sought to codify the moral lessons learned in World War I, attempting to ameliorate both the tragedy of that war and the new violence and depredation following the Versailles settlements of 1919-1920. Affirming the beginning doctrines of the League of Nations and the Pact of Paris, the Briand-Kellogg Pact disallowed any treaty or agreement among nations to conspire against any other nation(s): The nonrecognition of aggression and occupation, even pursuant to an extant treaty, was an enormous leap in ethics.

The treaties, conventions, and even structures (League of Nations, World Court) of the twentieth century were seminal and formative for the emerging world order, but their practical efficacy proved to be shortlived. In 1931 Japan invaded Manchuria and the world failed to respond. Less than a decade later the world was again engulfed in total war. The Geneva Convention of 1864, the Hague conventions of 1898 and 1907, the 1925 Geneva protocol on gas warfare (following the poison gas attacks at Estaires in 1918), the Red Cross practices and regulations were all in force at the dawn of World War II in Europe and Asia. In the churches and political circles in Europe and the United States, strong voices of pacifism, noninterventionism, war realism, and strident holy war passion were heard. The grimy horrors of trench warfare at Verdun now yielded to high-tech fire power in tank battles in the Bulge and North Africa, fighter bombing over France, Germany, and England; bitter inch-by-inch ground combat in the jungles of the Japanese-occupied islands; and finally the carpet bombing of Hamburg, Dresden, and Cologne. The fire-filled winds of Dresden and Tokyo mortally anticipated the scorching atomic fires over Hiroshima and Nagasaki that forever changed the face of war ethics.

In 1945 the UN Charter with its myriad declarations on human rights was adopted. The International Court at The Hague was given renewed power to hear and resolve conflicts between nations. The Nuremberg trials gave concrete secular meaning to the "laws of humanity." Starting in 1945 with the UN Charter there has entered into world political consciousness an antipathy to border changes, occupations, or violations of territorial integrity. Obviously this value has been violated time and again in the subsequent forty-five years. The lingering shame of the invasions of Tibet, Cyprus, Palestine, and countless other similar violations of that value attest not to its irrelevance but to its growing importance. One hope the world might draw from the resolute and swift ejection of Iraq from Kuwait is that territorial aggression will not again go unchallenged. We probably cannot undo the seizure of Tibet or the West Bank, but any future aggression or occupation will be hard pressed for justification. Indeed, the years since World War II have seen the change of warfare in the world from boundary redrawing and occupation to internal uprising within nations and more subtle forms of economic and political pressure and capitulation. When the European Community affirmed the 1991 British proposal to cordon off a safe haven zone in northern Iraq where the bewildered and persecuted Kurds might find refuge, and when Allied and UN peacekeeping forces implemented it, this ethic was realized. This initiative is fully in keeping with the war ethics derived from World War II, with various international bodies encouraged to assume mediating and reconciling roles in the resolution of conflict.

Other procedures to preserve the peace, reduce the inhumanity of war, and restore peace were also formulated in the years immediately following World War II. The Nuremberg trials of 1945-1948 added several important values to the international canon:

- Crimes of aggression or treaty violation are condemned.
- Crimes against humanity, e.g., genocide of racial or religious groups are condemned.

- Individuals (political or military) are responsible for their actions and not immune by virtue of office or "obeying orders."
- Conspirators (industrialists, financiers, etc.) can be found guilty of war crimes.
- Persons or nations can be guilty of crimes against the peace and security of mankind.

The 1946 and 1949 Geneva Red Cross conventions elaborated requirements for the care of sick and wounded combatants, and the care and safe return of prisoners. These "laws of humanity" were refined and intensified in the Korean armistice agreement of July 1953.

The 1960s saw nuclear test ban treaties and rules regarding nuclear weapons. By now it had become clear that all humanity, discrimination, and ethics are abandoned if any nation ever reverts to the use of nuclear devices. Civilians cannot be protected, innocents cannot be spared, and unpredictable consequences cannot be avoided. War ethics began to focus on the absolute discountenance of nuclear engagement, and even militant and realist proponents of war as a national right became nuclear pacifists. The Helsinki declarations adopted by the UN in 1975 completed the human rights work of the postwar period by affirming the right of self-determination of peoples and their territorial integrity and national sovereignty.

Of the large list of international laws about conflict and war that have particular bearing on the war over Kuwait, we need mention the rules from The Hague through the 1980s that define the duties of nations in hostilities or occupation: They are to maintain order, administer the resources of the region to serve both civilians and occupying forces, and not harm or exploit the inhabitants of occupied land. Here the radical and ideal nature of recent conventions comes into focus. From time immemorial, forces overrunning territory necessarily create disorder, inevitably take resources–food, water, animals, vehicles, whatever–for their own purposes, and usually mistreat, even harm, the inhabitants. Pillage, rape, and exploitation are assumed to be the privilege of conquest. We might recall at this point the holy war stipulate of *herem* or holocaust, calling for destruction of everything in sight in tribute to the divine conquest, rather than making off with the booty.

The Vietnam Experience and the Morality of War

The agony for humane conscience in the Vietnam War derived from just war ethics in both conception and execution, and the inability to honor those ethics in situations like the U.S. invasion of Vietnam. The "rules of engagement" in Vietnam illustrated this moral impossibility: In that jungle guerrilla war a typical engagement would be for a U.S. commander to call down artillery and air strikes on a peasant village from which his forces had received small arms-fire. In honor of the long history of war ethics we have received here, civilians might be warned by loudspeaker or air-dropped pamphlets--which they probably could not understand--announcing something to the effect: "The U.S. Marines will not hesitate to destroy immediately any village or hamlet harboring the Viet Cong . . . The choice is yours. If you refuse to let the Viet Cong use your village and hamlets as their battlefield, your homes and your lives will be saved."[17]

The desire to protect civilians is noble, but now impossible. How could peasants resist armed Viet Cong forcing their way into a village? The villagers were scared to death, huddled in the scant shelter of their modest homes. The enemy hiding in entrenchments, chicken coops, and cellars, were indistinguishable to Americans from villagers. The Hague conventions about uniforms and open carrying of weapons may pertain; it may not. Finally in exasperation and desperation, the Americans strafe-bombed or burned out the villages, finding perhaps a few Viet Cong among the bodies of old men, women, and children.

What that war did to the conscience of the world, and the American people in particular, is inestimable. I remember serving as a young pastor in a conservative rural area and noting how often otherwise patriotic farm families worried about the rightness of the war. Sons or friends were sent to Vietnam and loyalty and love followed them. Yet the justifying cause and conduct were never fully known and were not morally convincing. In part because the justification was abstract: to "defend freedom." The reluctance was often unworthy: "Why should we care about yellow people on the other side of the world?" The ethics of isolationism and noninvolvement in problems elsewhere in the world prevailed for a quarter-century, until in August 1990 President Bush asked the American people, "If we don't come to the aid of Kuwait and stop aggression–who will?" Even that obvious appeal met with significant resistance in the U.S. Congress and was only made palatable with the assurance "This will not be another Vietnam."

During and after the Vietnam conflict, war ethics from theistic and humanistic perspectives moved decisively toward pacifism. The killing of people, destruction of their culture, and devastation of the natural world make war unconscionable for most who reflect on the issues, although political, legal, and economic evaluations of the necessity or value of war take their own course regardless of these reflections. The countless books and pronouncements by theologians, philosophers, and religious bodies are generally dismissed as naive and uninformed. The one exception to this cultural schizophrenia on war ethics is the small circle of thinkers who provided justification for "deterrence" theory during the cold war of the 1970s and 1980s. Chief among these are prominent British conservative ethicist Oliver O'Donovan and Paul Ramsey in the United States.[18] The position of these thinkers is that deterrence and the arms buildups which allow deterrence is justified because the fear of total nuclear war is the only force that will prevent it. The argument, in my view, is misguided, as it divorces intent from action in conflict with most of the ethical heritage. Toward the end of his life, Ramsey abandoned this "cold-warrior ethic," and reaffirmed classical just war theory.

The final word on just war ethics pertaining to the war over Kuwait can be found in the sequence of UN resolutions which defined the nature of the wrong committed by Iraq and projected the judgment that that wrong would incur. But before reviewing the key elements of those resolutions, I must acknowledge, as Clausewitz did almost two centuries ago, that war is principally a political action. The law of courts, even international courts, and the policy of deliberative bodies, even the UN, are inevitably political. To the victors go the spoils, and to the mighty often go the very definitions of justice. The Nuremberg tribunals defined justice from the perspective of Anglo-U.S. and French values. The UN expresses the will of those select nations who are members of the Security Council and, given their veto powers, often of a single member of the Security Council. At its very best the council can only reflect the unanimous convictions of the five permanent members of the council. The early UN Security Council resolutions on the war over Kuwait were impressive for their unanimity. Even Cuba and Yemen joined in Resolution 660 condemning Iraq's incursion into Kuwait. Subsequent resolutions were more ambiguous.

Just War Ethics as Reflected in the UN Resolutions

Beginning with the Iraqi invasion in August 1990 and continuing into early summer 1991, the UN was the focal point of ethical, legal, and political assessment of the situation in Kuwait. That this fledgling and often-derided institution became the epicenter of dialogue and maneuvering among the nations of the world is certainly a cause for hope. That it was amenable to manipulation by the United States and the great powers and that in the end it was unable to assert its founding and guiding values in negotiation, reconciliation, and peace is a cause for concern. The residue of just war ethics as reflected in international law and policy about aggression, territorial rights, and humanitarian principles was the milieu within which the war issues were defined and discussed. The relevance of this tradition to the war itself will be the subject of our concluding chapters. The moral heritage embraced by holy war and just war traditions affected decisions through informal discussions in the halls, formal envoys, negotiations such as those undertaken by Pérez de Cuéllar and Terry Waite, and formal declarations of UN bodies. The sequence of twelve resolutions offered by the Security Council during the nine months from August 1990 through April 1991 offer a window to view the present moral force of just war views on the crisis before us.

Resolution 660 condemned the annexation of Kuwait by Iraq in the first days of August 1990. Affirming the principles discussed earlier of national sovereignty and territorial integrity, the resolution, along with subsequent clarifications, required that Iraq withdraw unconditionally from Kuwait and that the rightful government of the al-Sabah family be restored. This resolution rightly defended the inherent right of nonviolence of states and their right to appropriate defense and punishment for aggression. Regrettably, because the resolution was formulated under the influence of U.S. Secretary of State Baker and U.S. and British diplomacy, it did not direct Iraq to take its grievances against Kuwait to the World Court or give any assurance of UN support for that course.

Resolutions 661 to 669 initiated land, sea, and air embargoes and boycotts of all goods to or from Iraq except medicines. From the start, these resolutions were equivocal. Were foodstuffs and other humanitarian supplies included? Apparently and regrettably the Western powers made several contradictory judgments at this point: The sanctions were to be severe, including foods. Trucks carrying food into Iraq were bombed, and as with decisions to bomb the Iraqi civilian infrastructure, the desire was to place severe hardship not only on the military but on the Iraqi people. The combination of severe sanctions plus the unwillingness to give them time to work clearly violated just war standards. In holy war ethics in the Jewish tradition, as interpreted by Maimonides, siege must be limited to three sides, enabling combatants to escape and vital supplies to be delivered. The ethics of siege, blockade, and embargo are obviously complex. Modern states and armies tend to abuse this principle of civilian rights. Just as scavengers among the dead on a battlefield exploit conventions and wear red crosses, soldiers will disguise themselves as civilians and exploit the open door. In the same cynical way a communications and command center will be placed under the cross or crescent of hospitals.

On December 7, 1990, a crucial Security Council resolution was passed authorizing the use of force and setting an ultimatum for Iraqi withdrawal from Kuwait by January 15, 1991. With this action a furious yet creative process of negotiation began. Again, the resolution contained no provision for a dignified and orderly withdrawal, although it was clear by this time that Saddam Hussein wanted only a face-saving way out. He released all international hostages and responded positively to initiatives from France, the Soviet Union, and Egypt to begin a process of negotiation and disengagement. Ironically, these initiatives to comply with the UN were accompanied by a massive U.S. troop buildup in the region, with personnel doubled to more than 400,000. Was the purpose the initially articulated goal of removing Iraq from Kuwait, or had a decision already been made in the White House and 10 Downing Street to incapacitate Iraq's military, severely damage the nation's infrastructure, and depose Saddam Hussein, if possible?

The political character of the UN resolutions was made clear when they were punctuated on October 20 by another expressing alarm at the violence perpetrated by all sides in the Temple Mount killings in Jerusalem. It was clear that the vast majority of the world's nations wished for a clear and forceful condemnation of Israel for the unconscionable atrocities, but the United States and Great Britain threatened a veto, making only a watered-down statement possible. The resolutions about Kuwait at times embodied the just war and humanitarian ethics proper to the UN, but at other times expressed more the utilitarian expediency of the Western powers.

As the war came to an end, UN resolutions were negotiated to provide terms of a cease-fire. The main points were the return of all Allied prisoners of war and abducted Kuwaitis; cessation of hostile or provocative actions; rescinding the annexation of Kuwait; accepting liability under international law for war damage in Kuwait and elsewhere; the return of all seized Kuwaiti property; help in the rebuilding of Kuwait; and disclosure of the location of mine fields and booby traps. The final resolutions also reaffirmed all twelve previous council resolutions.

In late 1991, the UN was facing the problem of Kurds fleeing northern Iraq over the mountains into Turkey and Iran. Discussion is under way about establishing a safe haven for Kurds within the borders of Iraq, an enclave that would be protected by Allied or UN forces. Some voices go so far as to argue that existing international law respecting the territorial integrity and sovereignty of Iraq should be set aside and a new independent republic of Kurdistan be created. These developments point to the inherent ethical tension in the principles of freedom and benevolence/justice. In the case of the ongoing suffering of the Kurds, do humanitarian principles override the rights of a sovereign state to quell internal resistance and disturbance, even with gross brutality? Just war, as it has been formulated in international law, has focused more on order than on social justice. One of the areas of just war ethos that will need amplification in the aftermath of the war over Kuwait will be the right and obligation of nations to intervene in a state's internal affairs when people's rights are being violated.

Two new crises have surfaced in postwar Iraq. The United States and its allies have committed themselves to the territorial integrity of Iraq, fearing the political consequences of dismembering Iraq into Kurdish and Shiah states. At the same time, the Allies have encouraged opponents of Saddam Hussein to resist and attempt to overthrow the president, albeit warning them not to expect Western aid in their rebellion. The ambiguity of policy is painfully evident in this nation where the state seems to despise its own people. The moral resolution of this ambiguity can only come through clarification and amplification of humanitarian principles such as protection, justice, and consideration of needs even to the extent of limiting other values like state prerogative and civil order.

Will the war end as it began, denying human responsibility and projecting blame and responsibility on the deity? Abbas Amanat, a historian at Yale University, fears this very evasion as the agony of what some call the Kurdish genocide unfolds before the eyes of the world on these summer days of 1991. The ambiguity of the U.S. message: "Topple Saddam, but don't look to us for help" is now, in Amanat's words, the fulfillment of Iraq's Ba'athist regime's long-held ambition to "clear Iraqi Kurdistan of its inhabitants":

> Mr. Bush and his chief ally, Prime Minister John Major of Britain seem to have converted to a politics of divine intervention. They appear to be waiting for the hour when the heavens are torn asunder and the sinner of Baghdad is miraculously removed from power. The saviors in this scenario are the Iraqi officers–who right now are busy massacring Kurds and Shi'ites by the thousands.[19]

Human ethics, especially political ethics, are always a curious blend of active control and responsibility and accession to inevitable force, fate, or providence. Dietrich Bonhoeffer, the German theologian who lost his life because of his complicity in one of the most difficult of questions of war ethics, "Shall we assassinate Hitler?" (a question we shall return to in our analysis of war's morality), warned against returning to God what should remain our own responsibility. This we must avoid as assiduously as we avoid claiming divine prerogatives in Promethean or Adamic fashion: We are to take the responsibility that is rightly ours, but leave those matters that are beyond our control to divine mystery and will. Critical discernment is required to know the difference. Americans, say Europeans, are "decadent puritans," combining ducking responsibility with telling everyone else what to do.[20] This flaw in the national character must be overcome.

Summary: An Ethical Tableau of Just War Values

The task remains to sum up the composite religious and secular heritage of war ethics. Have the values accrued in the tradition proved adequate to preserve justice, fairness, and humanity in this crisis? Do the particular details of this conflict--technology, human suffering, proportionality--show us the need for new conventions? The following typology of war ethics according to sacred and secular sources provide a moral matrix for our evaluation of the war over Kuwait:

Just Cause   (*Jus ad bellum*)

- The righteousness and judgment of God as ultimate cause (holy war)
- Purpose of war to gain peace (Augustine)
- Love of neighbor overriding aim (Augustine)
- Absence of ulterior motives, such as acquisition of goods, e.g., oil
- Desire for peace and reconciliation (Christian pacifism)
- Hatred, prejudice, or punishment must not be purpose (Christian pacifism)
- Right spirit of humility, hesitancy, regret, accession to higher purpose (holy war)
- Defensive purpose, countering aggression (Augustine after Greeks, Romans)
- No threat of aggression or preemptive strike (just war)
- Protecting innocent life
- Restoring human rights
- To gain just reparations for previous wrongs (Augustine)
- Properly constituted authority declaring and directing war (Aquinas)
- Last resort–all peaceful means have failed
- Probable success
- Proportionality: the good to be achieved outweighs human cost (just war, utility theory)

Just Conduct (*Jus in bello*)

- Leave vengeance and war to God; instead love neighbor and enemy (holy war, pacifism)
- Wage war only to attain peace (Aquinas)
- Keep faith with enemy; retain dignity of enemy (Christian just war)
- Avoid wanton violence
- Do not fight with great disparity of power (pacifism)
- Do not profane or destroy religious sites
- Avoid looting, massacre, executing prisoners, conflagration, destruction of ecology, taking hostages, vengeance, atrocities, reprisals
- Do not shoot a wounded enemy or those surrendering or in retreat
- Avoid harm to noncombatants
- In siege do not block food, water, or medicines
- End war as swiftly as possible
- Warn civilians when indiscriminate harm is necessary
- Maintain magnanimity in victory (holy war)
- Avoid humiliating defeated people
- Seek just and lasting settlement and restoration of peace

The war over Kuwait has reinforced the ethical importance of most of these values, pointing up the difficulty or obsolescence of some of the old values as well as a need to articulate some new ones. In the final chapter, I will offer an ethical critique and commentary toward these ends. I have used the war over Kuwait as an occasion to reexamine the relevance of just war ethics for wartime decisions in the contemporary world. Like our world leaders, we have called on that honorable tradition to evaluate what happened during the course of that conflict. Has the exercise been worthwhile? Some argue that we are moving from the more ethically sensitive 1960s and 1970s into a morally apathetic if not amoral 1980s and 1990s. One hears many voices, even of respectable and concerned persons, say that even though we know what is right and wrong in fundamental areas such as economic justice, racial discrimination, and war and peace, we are not able to do right. Reality in the form of scarce resources, limited opportunities, and national interests, forces us, it is argued, to act in submoral ways. This cynical view is unacceptable for two reasons, one pragmatic, one principle. Practically speaking, an age of global awareness requires that we act justly, or our injustice will backfire and take its toll, if only in diminished trust and credibility. Right now the war is a *cause celèbre* in the United States, England, France, Israel, and the anti-Iraq alliance in the Middle East. In the rest of western Europe, especially Germany, Switzerland, and Scandinavia, in eastern Europe and the former Soviet Union, in Asia, Africa, and Latin America, a deep consciousness of the war's impropriety and an increased mistrust of U.S. foreign policy has grown. Enlightened self interest alone should prompt us in the future to gauge our adventures more carefully, especially in the Middle East. At the same time, we must be true to our principles. If our rhetoric invokes just war theory founded on Judeo-Christian values, we must study these same beliefs and try to live them out more carefully.

Most experts on the Gulf region feel that the United States has now established itself as the dominant power, and that it will now have to provide sound leadership in the decisions and policies that must evolve in the region in areas such as security, arms control, and social justice vis-à-vis the distribution of oil revenues. The opportunity in this war to lay hold of a vital ethical heritage and square that with practical demands of national interest may serve the United States well as it now assume our broadened responsibilities.

Notes

1. Hugo Grotius, *De Jure Praedae* , ed. H. G. Hanaker, The Hague, 1868, p. 91.

2. Hugo Grotius, *The Rights of War and Peace*, ed. J. Bar Beyrac, London, 1738, p. xvii-xviii.

3. Ibid., p. 105.

4. James Turner Johnson, "Grotius' Use of History and Charity in the Modern Transformations of the Just War Idea," *Grotiana*, Vol. 4, 1983, p. 26.

5. Johnson, Ibid., p. 33.

6. Thomas Hobbes, *Elements of Law*, quoted in Richard Tuck, *Natural Rights Theories*, Cambridge: Cambridge University Press, 1979, p. 121.

7. Hobbes, *Leviathan, quoted* in Tuck, Ibid., p. 126.

8. Walzer, *op. cit.*, p. 5.

9. J. G. Starke, *Introduction to International Law*, London: Butterworths, 1989.

10. *Clausewitz on War*, ed. Roger Ashley Leonard, London: Weidenfeld and Nicholson, 1967, p. 7.

11. Ibid., p. 11-12.

12. Montesquieu, *The Spirit of the Laws*, New York: Harper, 1940, p. 5.

13. Joseph Conrad, "Aristocracy and War," in *Notes on Life and Letters*, London: Littleworth, 1921, p. 143.

14. Pancho Villa, quoted in *Restraints on War*, ed. Michael Howard, Oxford: Oxford University Press, 1979, p. 17.

15. Kaiser Wilhelm II, quoted in Evan Luard, *War in International Society*, London: L.B. Tauris Ltd., 1986, p. 357.

16. Theodore Roosevelt, quoted in Evan Luard, *War in International Society*, London: L.B. Tauris Ltd., 1986, p. 356.

17. Walzer, *op. cit.*, p. 190.

18. Oliver O'Donovan, *Peace and Certainty*, Oxford: Oxford University Press, 1989; Paul Ramsey, *The Just War*, New York: Scribners, 1968.

19. Abbas Amanat, "A Dangerous Mess is Left for the Almighty to Fix," *International Herald Tribune*, April 11, 1991, p. 4.

20. "America's Decadent Puritans," *The Economist*, July 28, 1990, p. 11.

7

Justice, Peace, and the Future of War

In this final chapter, I will sum up the moral views I have put forward throughout this book, and set before the reader not only an account of the composite wisdom of holy war, just war, and pacifism for evaluating this war but also a vision of the future toward which this assessment could lead. I believe just war ethics in the last years of this millennium will not only synthesize past teachings from holy war, just war, and pacifist ethics but also incorporate some new ingredients. Ethics is a matter of seeking the coincidence of a range of parameters. I will begin by weighing biological, technological, psychological, political, and spiritual concerns of war ethics that this particular war presented. I will offer a vision of a new world order in which peace and justice can make war obsolete--an eschatology that I hope will inspire a creative ethic.

Biology/Ecology

The war over Kuwait could be seen as an effort to evade interhuman responsibility by driving the violence downward into the natural world and upward into technology. As I write in the days following the ceasefire with UN Resolution 688 cautioning the Iraqi government to refrain from harming Kurdish and Shi'ah dissidents or interrupting the humanitarian safe haven enforced by residual Allied and UN forces, it is becoming clear that one lasting stigma of the war will be an ecological and biological crisis.

What will be the toll of the air and water pollution of the Gulf War? Unprecedented violence against the biosphere was inflicted by Saddam Hussein in his unholy fury and the sin that blinded him to his own fault as well as the justifiable rage he bore because of the deaf ears the world turned to his rightful cause. The double jeopardy of a contaminated sea and a blotting out of the sun by smoking oil-well fires will despoil the intricate web of life in the Persian Gulf for decades to come. This double-edged ecocatastrophe, combined with the demolition of the life-sustenance infrastructure, is also creating an immediate health crisis. Unless safety zones are extended south of the thirty-sixth parallel and throughout the entire country as the UN proposed, so that clean water, adequate food, medicines, sanitation systems, and other hygienic measures are made available to all people, an ecological crisis will ravage Iraq in the near future. This health disaster will result from Western sanctions, Allied bombing of Iraq's infrastructure, and Saddam Hussein's continuing oppression and neglect of the Iraqi people.

Already in the mountain camps, people, especially the very young and old, are dying from exposure, hypothermia, starvation, dehydration, weakness and exhaustion, pneumonia, cholera and other waterborne and airborne infections. As drinking water and sewage intermingle, these contaminations and epidemics will spread throughout the country, the inevitable result of high-tech, indiscriminate warfare against a people who even in the best of times lived an impoverished and fragile existence. High-tech, smart-weapons warfare against a developing nation lacking a sophisticated public health infrastructure of necessity pushes morbidity and mortality down into the realm of the natural environment and the biological substance. How ironic that the war that began with the threat of Saddam Hussein using mustard and other poison gases as well as anthrax and other biological warfare should end with a biological threat posed by the Allied assault, the Allies having adamantly cautioned against that very vector of harm!

Biological warfare and the biological side effects of conventional warfare have long been a part of war. The ancient Romans contaminated the water wells of their enemies with the carcasses of animals. In 1347 during the counter-Crusade, the Tartars captured Caffa by catapulting corpses of soldiers who had died of bubonic plague over the city walls. European-Americans distributed blankets contaminated with infectious material to Native Americans. When the Japanese invaded China during World War II, they used a range of biological agents, killing thousands of people.

This history prompted the United Nations to renew the 1925 Geneva protocol on chemical and biological weapons in the 1972 convention on biological and toxic weapons. This was the first time in history that an entire class of weapons was outlawed. But if we set aside the question of anthrax or other biological weapons which mercifully were not employed in the Gulf conflict, if we bracket for the moment the range of DNA-modified organisms that could eventually be employed in warfare, surely new and more stringent conventions will be required to regulate those possibilities. And what of the biological trauma that was unleashed in the war over Kuwait? Do belligerents have responsibilities in the name of just war to see that disease is not stimulated by their wastage of the natural environment and damage to the hygienic infrastructure? Starting with World Wars I and II, the victors in war assumed an obligation to restore health and well-being to the vanquished when the war was over. The rapid and awesome recovery of Germany and Japan after World War II give new meaning to those nineteenth-century ideas that war can dramatically renew and invigorate a people. Marxist ideas that capitalist nations require perennial war to stimulate economic vitality also finds substantiation here. The Gulf War, unlike World War II, in which nearly 10 percent of the population of the European continent was killed, largely spared civilians, but devastated both the natural and civilized fabrics of life sustenance and maintenance. In the war over Kuwait it is very likely that as many persons will die from the results of war as from the war itself. If this is the case we will need to write into the canons of just war what might be called cybernetic conventions. At the very least we will need to postulate feedback cycles to calculate the total costs and damages for assessing both proportionality and whether the good to be achieved justifies the evil necessary to achieve it.

Recollection of the ecosanctity of holy war found in Deuteronomy (the tree of the field is man's life [20:19]), Maimonides' explication of that theology of nature in the Talmud, Franciscan nature holiness, and Islamic reverence for the world will be necessary in an age where high-tech warfare can penetrate so destructively into the very heart of mother earth. The secular versions of just war theory from Descartes onward will not help much because of the mind-matter dichotomy that fosters a materialistic-mechanistic mania and overrides all nature mysticism. We need a renewed sacramental ethic of nature. If we are bound to a secular war ethics heritage, our best hope would be a more refined utilitarian war ethic that could accurately read consequences and thereby correct initial actions.

War in the ancient and medieval world was one of three scourges, disease and famine being the others. The sad tragedy of war and its uniqueness among the trilogy was that war was not natural. Without human vengeance and violence, war would not exist. Though starvation and disease could be prevented in part by human action, their occurrence could not in most cases be attributed to human malevolence; and of the three, war was the first that humans came to believe they could see through and vanquish. Holy war, pacifism, and just war were attempts to quell the insatiable human appetite for violence and mitigate its rancor once loosed.

One of the strong international fellowships today opposing nuclear proliferation and the resort to war is the International Physicians for Social Responsibility Organization (IPSRO). For this fellowship, war is the epidemic of our time, the primary disease that we must seek to prevent. War destroys life, cultivation and culture, growth and development. It is the antithesis of *zoes* and *bios*, the flourishing of life. With Aquinas and Augustine and against Aristotle and Cicero, we can now say that war is unnatural, a violation of natural law. Far from being either holy or just, the action of the Iraqi government in inciting this war, of the Allies in exacerbating it, and of both parties in despoiling the creation must be seen as a violation of natural and human order.

Technology

In modern warfare life and the tree that supports life can be "cut down" from within or without. Bacteriological agents and recombinant organisms make it possible to assault and destroy life at the molecular level. The U.S. atomic bombings of Nagasaki and Hiroshima proved to be genetic assaults in that they caused not only genetic breakage and delayed diseases like cancer, but they also adversely affected germinal substance and offspring. Because this threat has since been vigorously, and so far successfully, banned in war conventions, since war in the 1990s relies on external destruction from increasingly more sophisticated technology. The war over Kuwait was inspired by a certain tantalus factor, with the Western Allies seeking to try out, under real war conditions, the weaponry fashioned in the cybernated computer age that began around 1970. Deriving from cold war competition with the Soviet Union, an enormous buildup and upgrading of military capacity took place under the conservative governments of the West during the 1980s (e.g., Reagan and Thatcher). In the war over Kuwait it was finally given a chance to "show its stuff."

The exquisite communications technology available in 1990 changed the face of war, shifting the intelligence balance to the side that had access to satellite and aircraft monitoring. It was now possible to build a comprehensive geography of buildings; factories; roads; bridges; electrical, water, and sewage systems; communications systems; military installations; and troop emplacements with dynamic programs that could incorporate any shifts or movements. Gridding all of these stationary items on coordinates allowed precise guidance of weapons to targets. Although the continually mobile Saddam Hussein frustrated former President Nixon's suggestion that a "contract" be put out on him by the CIA, every other strategic possibility was mapped and made vulnerable.

It could be argued that the war over Kuwait was won not only by supreme power but by superior intelligence, surveillance, and communication. It may have been the first war in history in which information, guidance, and feedback processes were the real victors. Indeed, this war may portend future conflicts in which DNA sensors or radio-sensitive tags such as paroled prisoners have been fitted with in some places are used to trace the movement of individuals. When this sphere of cybernetic technology is combined with the capacity to disarm the enemy's counter efforts, the war will be won. For just war morality, we might ask if the ancient Greek convention of the sacrosanctness of the messenger that prevailed through the ages might need reemphasis. Breaking down the enemy's communication and simultaneously demanding instant response to ultimata is unfair. Such tactics also raise the larger and very ambiguous question of whether it is morally licit to disable or handicap an enemy before war begins. This notion, which was unconscionable in the age of chivalry, might also conflict with the Hague convention of respect for and nonengagement with the wounded.

It was computerized cartography that made it possible for smart weapons systems like the F-117 Stealth fighter-bombers to fulfill their missions. With infrared nighttime instrumentation, "smart" bombs could be dropped into a basket in which they were guided on a laser string into a specific chimney or other target. The romantic days of British biplanes chasing the whirling, diving Red Baron over German skies are gone forever. Now there is no adversary on the ground or in the air, and good aim and luck no longer matter.

The Star Wars fantasy of bullets hitting bullets was presaged by a remarkable weapon that saved countless lives and prevented the potential monumental disaster of Israel entering the war. Called the Robocop hero of the war, Patriot missiles intercepted dozens of Scud missiles heading for Israel and Saudi Arabia; only one Scud--tragedy enough--got through to the Dharan barracks. With a Patriot's sights cybernetically leveled by radar on an incoming Scud, at just the right moment the twenty-foot-long rocket launched, then within seconds accelerated to 3,000 miles per hour as it was guided to its intercepting rendezvous by its own radar antenna. The M-I-AI tank, with its unprecedented technology of "reactive armor" repelling incoming explosives, also first saw action in the Gulf War. This tank, which travels at forty miles per hour and carries a crew of four to operate the 120-mm guns, was the main U.S. ground weapon employed, with 1,400 in the theater.

How does this new technology change war? Weapons like those described here not only remove an opponent from contact at a human level, but change the humanity of the users. The man who pulled the lever on the U.S. bomber *Enola Gay* over Hiroshima scarcely could have felt the moral impact that King Henry V did wielding a heavy sword in hand-to-hand combat at Agincourt. Those who watched this electronic wizardry on television tended to interpret the conflict as a vast video game, so removed was the actuality of those who suffered and died. Rudolf Otto coined a phrase for the perception of the holy--"*tremendum et fascinans.*" This awestruck fascination vested in technology must be examined if we are to understand what surgical and technological warfare does to those who use it. Against international law, both Iraq and Israel seem to have surreptitiously developed advanced nuclear plans. Does techno-bloodshed[1] have the same opprobrium? Is it the same abomination as other modes of bloodshed, or do its perpetrators keep their hands clean?

Psychology

Robert Lifton, a psychiatrist who has studied the Nazi holocaust and the Hiroshima bombing, claims that what happens to people in wartime is a kind of dissociation, a psychic splitting and numbing. The U.S. pilot who ponders for a moment over the circumstance that the Iraqi plane he just blew up carried a pilot "who had a family like I do" must return, like a surgeon, to a disinterested apathy, or he will cease to be able to function. This psychic repression is why General Schwarzkopf, in his inimitable way, refused to talk about enemy casualties and why Prime Minister Thatcher was offended when the Falklands memorial service acknowledged the grief of Argentinian families. Lifton reports that Vietnam War veterans he interviewed spoke of "learning to feel again" and "becoming human again."[2] Sparing the victor from the trauma of self-dehumanization that follows from dehumanizing another person is part of the psychology of the restraints of war in holy and just war ethics.

W.P. Paterson wrote in his excellent essay on that subject in *The Hastings Encyclopaedia of Religion and Ethics*, "even a just war sets the heart of a nation aflame with hatred, malice and revenge. War makes its influence felt later on in a certain hardening of a people's hearts, and a perversion of their moral sentiments."[3] The best evidence of this phenomenon in the aftermath of the Gulf War is the waning of commitment to Oxfam, Save the Children, and other Western agencies concerned with relieving the famine in Africa. Not only have governments curtailed their support, but individual philanthropy has fallen off since the war over Kuwait began. Augustine knew in the fourth century that war had its origins in the worst of passions: "*Noscendi cupiditas, uiciscendi crudelitas, impacatus atque implacabilis animus, territas rebellandi, libido dominandi, et si qua similia.*"[4]

Of the British theologians who have addressed the ethics of the war over Kuwait, Rowan Williams of Oxford has best highlighted the issue of what the war did to the victors. Westerners allowed their sensibilities to be dulled, he claimed, by the video-game aspects of the war. Watching people being killed at long distance inured viewers to mortal cries near at hand. The Western public came to tolerate lies, admitting the ubiquity of disinformation, exaggeration, and censorship, and lost the sense of connection between acts and consequences. People told themselves that the attacks were precision efforts and no great numbers of people suffered or died. People claimed that the Western addiction to oil--and the lifestyle it is expected to support--was good and necessary. But what happens to an individual or a people who learns to live with lies? War conventions in the format of holy war and just war theory attempt to diminish the brutality inflicted on one's own people as well as an enemy. In the epilogue to his monumental study on the psychology of war, psychiatrist Jerome Frank concluded, "Survival today depends on reducing, controlling, channelling and redirecting the drive for power and the impulse to violence and fostering the countervailing drives toward fellowship and community."[5]

Politics

Prosecuting a war against another nation is the international equivalent of prosecuting murder domestically. All political judgment is the expression of the justice and mercy of a given jurisdiction. Holy war, just war, and pacifist guides are meant to contour and constrain justice so that it is fitting. They are also meant to enhance mercy. An initial political implication of just war, then, is that only a crime as grievous as murder justifies going to war, which is the equivalent of imposing the death penalty many times over. This warning against prosecuting a war for trivial or ulterior reasons is one of the major themes of just cause ethics. Militating against this is the old maxim of statecraft that "a foreign war is the best recipe for domestic dissensions." Francis Bacon argued that just as exercise is necessary for a beautiful body, so "no Body can be healthful without exercise, neither natural body or politique."[6]

The propensity of nations in economic or political trouble to wage war in order to distract the citizenry is a strong reason for the ethic of only declaring war in concert with a family of nations such as the United Nations. If avoidance of domestic crisis is the precipitating cause, international bodies should be able to expose that fallacy. But the increasing economic interdependence of nations increases the persuasive and coercive power that one nation has over others. In the war over Kuwait it is clear that both Iraq and the United States were experiencing severe economic and other domestic crises. Iraq had the rebellious Kurds in the north and a Shi'ah stronghold in the south to deal with. The economic crisis precipitated by some members of the international oil cartel with over-quota production and lower prices also endangered the Iraqi government. In the United States the domestic crises of poverty, racism, and inadequate education cut into the administration's popularity—until the war came along.

The political consciousness within a state can make war abhorrent and unacceptable. In the case of the Gulf War, the participation of Germany and Japan was legally and popularly proscribed, although both powers were "invited" to put up part of the cost. Many nations view the death penalty as unethical, and it is difficult to justify war within this ethos. The conscience of a people can shift slowly or suddenly from endorsement and enthusiasm to profound disagreement and dissent. The Vietnam War was transformed in this way in the psyche of the U.S. people. This took on considerable political import when civil rights leaders like Martin Luther King began to condemn the war. Black and Hispanic communities supported the war over Kuwait in part because military service is a strong source of dignified employment for the poor and in part because of the conservatism of these ethnic communities. Baptists love their country, but the balance could have changed suddenly if, the thought arose that dark-skinned people were fighting other dark-skinned people to protect white people's oil. War remains a consensual and political act.

Another political dimension of the war over Kuwait is the global political order that it affirmed. Regardless of the pressure brought to bear on member nations, the fact that the United Nations is now recognized as the only legitimate vehicle to authorize war is an enormous accomplishment for the community of nations. The fact that representatives of all of the nations of the world debated and voted on the legitimacy of the war, the imposition of sanctions, and on the myriad resolutions and conclusions of the war meant that all were accepting the notion of a higher law of world order in their own affairs also. That the Iraqi ambassadors to the UN remained involved throughout the crisis is a tribute to that beleaguered country and an encouragement for the future efficacy of the UN. Of course, the process failed at critical junctures. The Allies moved ahead on their own, for example, when the French, British, and U.S. forces set up safety zones for the Kurds even as the Iraqi government was negotiating with the United Nations for the same humanitarian aid throughout the country. Yet despite these qualifications, the world body took significant strides toward becoming the focal point of global order and peacekeeping that has always been its mission.

Theology

The prospect of a lasting moral order emerging from the war over Kuwait depends on how the nations of the world intertwine the political and spiritual experiences and expressions of their cultures. Has ethnic and theophanic holy war yielded to national-interest war and then to internationally sanctioned war? Although vestiges of war as crusade and holy campaign could be seen in Iraq and the United States, most Islamic nations involved in the conflict refused to label it jihad and most Western nations desisted from seeing it as a Christian crusade. In Oliver O'Donovan's words, the theophany assumption of holy war, the expectation of God appearing as advocate and warrior of a particular cause, has been transmuted into belief in the death and resurrection of Christ, a cosmic event.[7] Now a rationalized universal context is sought for war and peace.

The theology of war in the Western Christian world, shaped by the firm resolve to avert a third world war and a recurrence of the destruction of Hiroshima, was formulated by the Presbyterian layman, John Foster Dulles. Called "deterrence," the theory was based on the assumption, "The heart of the problem is how to deter attack. This, we believe, requires that a potential aggressor be left in no doubt that he would be certain to suffer damage outweighing any possible gains from aggression."[8] God is no longer the active warrior, the executioner of justice. He is now the god of power and security. If might makes right in Thrasmachian and Machiavellian ethics, now right makes righteous. Godly defense for Israel today is not the shield of Yahweh but a sure nuclear shield against Arab retaliative resentment and *Intifada*. Godly defense for the West is not Paul's shield of faith, but the defensive nuclear shield of missiles arched toward Moscow or the heavenly panoply of Star Wars. Bush, Major, and Mitterrand possessed this shield yet chose to use the conventional chariots with wings and wheels in the Gulf War, although their rhetoric was that of deterrence. Saddam Hussein was sternly warned, the catastrophic demolition was outlined in gory detail before hostilities began, and yet he was not deterred. Hussein knew that deterrence is based on the internal contradiction of possessing massive strength and disavowing its use. He seemed not only to doubt that the Allies would use their overwhelming destructive and decisive power, he also assumed that threat and inaction were inseparable elements in the logic of deterrence.

The eschatology of the Swiss Reformed pastor-theologian Karl Barth was misconstrued by latter-day Calvinists to provide a basis for deterrence theory. War was unthinkable; therefore it had to be made impossible. It is categorically disproportionate, therefore unjust and impossible by virtue of internal logic. Much is already gained with the admission that, whatever may be the purpose or possible justice of a war, it now means that not only individuals or even armies, but whole nations as such are out to destroy one another by every possible means. It only needed the atomic and hydrogen bombs to complete the self-disclosure of war in this regard.[9]

Human sin is ineradicable. Human destructive intent is unavoidable. Maximal articulation of power is inescapable. Therefore the only hope for peace is to suspend the world at the brink of (only) threatened annihilation. The theology of deterrence comes unraveled over Kuwait. Its eschatology of end time and doomsday is presumptuous and blasphemous.

Another Vision of Peace

The world of nuclear weapons stockpiling, the arms race, and belligerent diplomacy is not the peaceable kingdom envisioned by Isaiah in his prophecies or Henri Rousseau in his painting, a world in which swords (or rifle butts) are beaten into plowshares and "they will study and learn war no more" (Isaiah 2:4).

The news on BBC carried a fascinating picture. A U.S. soldier, assisted by several Kurds, was pushing around large stones with his rifle butt and together they formed them into a large circle near Zakho. They were outlining areas for toilets and cooking, tents and recreation areas for the protective encampments being set up by the Allies which they hoped would lure the fleeing and dying Kurds down from the mountains of the Turkish border. The Allied action made Iraqi officials furious and the prospect of violence such as pot shots at Allied soldiers or Kurdish rebels killing Iraqi soldiers remains high. But the image of a rifle butt being beaten into a plowshare was moving. One was led to wonder why we do not employ all of the armies of the world in such peace-building and peace-keeping missions. With the money and person-power of the U.S. military, think what could be done in westside Chicago or the lower Bronx, to say nothing of the Third World.

Peace is not the mere absence of war and certainly not the defensive huddling under the nuclear shield. It is the presence of justice. Justice is the lifting of subjugation, the empowerment of the poor, the liberation of the oppressed. Human acts of healing the sick, giving sight to the blind, helping the poor, and insuring human rights to all are the precursors of peace. The kingdom of God or messianic age will come about as "They beat their swords into plowshares, and their spears into pruning hooks; nation shall not lift up sword against nation, neither shall they learn war any more" (Isaiah 2:4).

This eschatological hope has been given historical form in the modern world through agencies like Oxfam, Save the Children, Amnesty International, and Famine Relief. It is embodied in a secular form in the moral philosophy of the modern age expressed by Immanuel Kant: "The greatest problem set to the human race is the formation of a political organisation under which justice will be dispensed to all, and a branch of this is the subordination to law of the external relations of the particular states."[10]

The idea of a league of nations as the structure of world order and peace can be traced at least to Henri IV of France and the Abbé of St. Pierre who proposed the *Projet de la paix universelle*, in which the governments of the world would all contribute resources to the maintenance of a grand alliance that would negotiate treaties, reconcile differences, prosecute judgment, and take offensive arms against any nation that broke the pledge to govern affairs and affiliations peacefully. Amazingly, in that age of dawning European nationalism, the league and project were to insist on prior renunciation of arms, even disarmament. The present-day United Nations, highly active during the war over Kuwait, has inherited this worldly version of a heavenly peaceable kingdom. Its precursor, the League of Nations, condemned the actions against Manchuria (1931), Ethiopia (1936), and Finland (1939) by Japan, Italy, and Soviet Union, but had little power to counter the aggressions or aid the victims. In the cases of invasions of Hungary (1956) and Afghanistan (1979), the UN condemned aggression but took no effective action. Over incursions into Guatemala (1954), Cuba (1961), and Goa (1961), it turned a blind eye. Only in Korea (1950-1953) and Egypt (1956) did the organization contribute effectively to ending conflict and restoring peace.[11] The action of the UN in the war over Kuwait awaits the analysis of historians. In my preliminary view the peacemaking and peacekeeping accomplishments were impressive, but the capacity to reconcile differences and address underlying problems of injustice proved sadly deficient.

The most serious impediment to an effective United Nations in the arena of war and peace is the ambivalence and equivocation of the United States and the Soviet Union. From 1980 to the war over Kuwait, most UN resolutions seeking to censure aggression and secure peace were vetoed by one of these powers. In 1979 the Security Council resolution deploring Soviet intervention in Afghanistan and calling for withdrawal was vetoed by the Soviets. In 1982 the Security Council resolution calling for Israeli withdrawal from Lebanon was vetoed by the United States. In 1982 the Security Council resolution condemning the U.S. mining of Nicaraguan ports and the use of Honduras as a base of insurgency was vetoed by the United States. In 1983 the Security Council tried to condemn the U.S. attack on Grenada and call for the withdrawal of foreign troops; the United States vetoed the resolution. This pattern continued up to the eve of the war over Kuwait. Perhaps the people of the world have never been quite sure what kind of world order we seek through this body. Do we seek relief from oppression and the institution of human rights? In South Africa we long supported white rule; now we impose sanctions and demand an end to apartheid. In the case of Israel we supported occupation of Palestinian lands, then we reversed our position. As a nation, the United States seems uncertain whether it seeks freedom, equity, justice, human rights, and liberation for the poor and oppressed, and especially torn when our national economic and security interests seem threatened by the advocacy of such values. Now that United States is the single dominant world power, with the diffusion of power in the former Soviet Union and its international brotherhood of communist states in Eastern Europe and elsewhere, we will need to declare which values we will stand for, defend, and promulgate throughout the world.

The closest agenda to the noble kingdom of justice and peace envisioned in the Bible, the Quran, and more recent documents on the "rights of man" would be the pronouncements of the churches, especially the Roman Catholic bishops, on economics, war and peace, poverty, and other social issues, or the agenda proposed by the Russian scientist-prophet Andrei Sakharov. Sakharov argued that the human rights agenda of the French Revolution and the modern democratic nation-states, combined with the moral substance of Judaism and Christianity and the ethical legacy of Marxist and secular humanism, is the best hope for peace in our world. The world is challenged by forces of disunity and destruction, including the threat of nuclear war, instability in East Asia and the Middle East, tensions in the international economy, hunger, overpopulation, racism, pollution of the environment, police dictatorships, and threats to intellectual and scientific freedom. Our best hope to counter these threats is a strong United Nations grounded on a substantive ethical agenda and armed with the means to defend and enforce these values.

The ethical values embodied in the UN Universal Declaration of Human Rights (1948) were explicated in two covenants, the International

Covenant on Civil and Political Rights and the International Covenant on Economic, Social and Cultural Rights, adopted by the United Nations General Assembly in 1966. These rights synthesize three sources of value: the substantive ethical righteousness of Abrahamic religion (freedom, social justice, care for the poor); the rights of autonomy and liberty derived from the Western liberal revolutions (freedom, speech, press, worship); and the recast Hebraic economic values of Marxism-Leninism (equity, opportunity, abolition of class oppression and exploitation). In Sakharov's view (shared by many powerful statist thinkers, especially in the USSR and Germany), the UN should have power to move in and enforce civil liberties in Romania, South Africa, Kurdistan, Uzbekistan, New York City, or Mississippi.[12] Against these views coming from such a courageous man who, with Aleksandr Solzhenitsyn and Anatoli Sharansky, showed the world the meaning of intellectual freedom and moral integrity, one is hesitant to level the charge of utopianism. Yet Sakharov would probably admit the charge. Hope for a newer and better world may be idealistic, fantastic, an impossible to realize. Yet the attempt is required, and he would warn us as we despair of his solution that the alternative is perpetual strife and eventual global destruction.

The war over Kuwait has been another chapter in humankind's halting struggle to find international justice and world peace. The wastage of this latest war surely shows us again the silence and wrath of the world's creator that we continue to despoil His handiwork and especially His people: Iraqi, Kurdish, Shi'ah, white, black, brown, men, women, children, grandparents, orphans, so many lying in the hastily dug trenches throughout Iraq, forgotten to men and women but not to God.

Two texts from morning matins at Christ Church will serve well to bring this chapter to a close. The boys' choir sang the psalm from the Old English Gradual:

> The seas are His for He made them
> With His hands he fashioned the Dry Land.

And the lesson from the Acts of the Apostles:

> God that made the world and all things therein
> hath made of one blood all nations of men for to
> dwell on all the face of the earth and hath
> determined the times before appointed and the
> bounds of their habitation (17:24, 26).

Closing Reflection

The war over Kuwait, rightly warns former U.S. National Security Adviser Zbigniew Brzezinski, threatens to end in "geopolitical disaster and moral disgrace." Although invoking the righteousness of moral cause and just war, by the intensity of the air assault, the demolition of the life-support environment and the callous massacre of retreating troops the United States displayed the "view that Arab lives are worthless." With the conclusion of the mission a "catastrophe of epidemics and undernourishment," the only way that the West could truly salvage a "moral enterprise" would be to provide "massive scale relief," "not only for the Kurds but for the Shi'ites and other Iraqis as well" and then to energetically pursue several goals: "a regional security arrangement; a process for redistribution of regional wealth and for enhanced economic cooperation among all the region's states (including Israel); and a serious movement towards Arab-Israeli peace."[13]

The wrongs of the war over Kuwait cannot be undone. Judgment has been stirred up in the world and the divine wrath has been let loose on the world. The war has seen a crisis in the biblical sense of that word, a rupture into our presence of profound meaning. Now we have within our power the pursuit of justice and peace as the war's reconciling purpose. A new dawn of ecological, humanistic, political, and religious sensitivity can emerge from this dark day.

Notes

1. Robert J. Lifton, "Techno-Bloodshed," *Guardian*, February 14, 1991, p. 21.

2. Lifton, Ibid., p. 21.

3. W. P. Paterson, "War," *Hastings Encyclopaedia of Religion and Ethics*, 1922, New York: Charles Scribners' Sons, p. 685.

4. Augustine, *Contra Faustum*, xxii, viii, 405a.

5. Jerome D. Frank, *Sanity and Survival: Psychological Aspects of War and Peace*, New York: Vintage, 1967, p. 289.

6. Francis Bacon, "Of the True Greatness of Kingdomes and Estates," *Essays*, ed. W. A. Wright, London: Knox Press, 1865, p. 127.

7. Oliver O'Donovan, *Peace and Certainty*, Grand Rapids: Eerdmans Press, 1989, p. 47.

8. Quoted in O'Donovan, Ibid., p. 55.

9. Karl Barth, *Church Dogmatics*, III 4, M.G.W. Bromily, Edinburgh: T & T Clark, 1961, p. 149.

10. Immanuel Kant, "Idee zu Einer Allgemeinen Geschichte in Weltbürgerlicher Absicht," *Gesammelte Schriften*, Berlin: Gurch Verlag, 1902, viii, 24.

11. Evan Luard, *Conflict and Peace in the Modern International System*, New York: Macmillan Press, 1988, p. 59.

12. Andrei D. Sakharov, *Progress, Coexistence and Intellectual Freedom*, New York: New York Times Book, W.W. Norton, 1968, p. 102.

13. Zbigniew Brzezinski, "The U.S. Victor has an Obligation to the Middle East," *International Herald Tribune*, April 22, 1991, p. 6.

Afterword

As spring rushes to its heights in America and Western Europe and yellow daffodils and jonquils shimmer their graceful glory against the yellow-ribbons tied on trees, Van Gogh's "Potato Eaters" is stolen from the museum in Amsterdam and sobbing mothers lay their dead babies outside a makeshift mosque on a frigid mountainside on the Turkish border. In the end war reaps its apocalyptic harvest on the poor and wretched of the earth. Dying seeds give rise to new spring growth on earth. The Al-Sabah family have returned with their stock-market computer screens to Kuwait City. Uncontrolled oil-well blazes still blanket the sky with that eerie spectre. Red Adair and his Texas team of "blowout" cappers now vie with British, Canadian and even Chinese contractors for the lucrative opportunity to undo that ravage. Meanwhile, American and British contractors scramble for the contracts to rebuild Kuwait and ultimately Iraq. Many who sent us to war now eye their stock portfolios, making sure they get a piece of the action. The European Community meeting in Strasbourg hears a motion from German foreign minister Genscher that Saddam Hussein be tried for war crimes and genocide under the 1948 Nuremberg Convention. Time to get the monkey off your shoulder onto the new Hitler.

But it is the 17-year-old construction worker whose charred body lies in a hastily hollowed grave in the desert who bears the war's final toll. It is the lonely, young wife whose new husband never returns to the bed-chamber, the child who must now grow up without a father to roll with on the floor -- these are the war's final casualties. After the welcome home rock-concerts and cathedral services we will in the end have only the voices of the war-poets and lamentation:

On the dark night before the dawn of St. Crispen's day Shakespeare portrayed King Henry V stealing quietly among the campfires of his men, cloaked in disguise, testing incognito the source of their hope, the fibre of their will. At dawn in the shadow of Agincourt Castle, despite reluctance and fear, they rose to the occasion and seized the day. The King had his doubts and secret turmoil, as did his men, who had little hope of surviving the day against mighty France.

Surely the same anguish and prayer filled the soul of George Bush, Saddam Hussein, John Major, François Mitterrand, Fahd, Shamir, and all other kings on the eve of the Gulf War. Inevitably morning comes and you must put on your boots and move out. To discern the will of God, to extricate it from your own ambition and foolishness, and to act on the best light that you have is, in the end, all that a ruler or a foot-soldier can do.

Any epilogue to the chronicle of war is horror, resignation, and silence. We meditate on those thoughts with the help of three poems of a soldier killed at the Sambre canal in France one week before the Armistice in November 1918: *Dulce et Decorum Est, Asleep,* and *The Unreturning.*

Dulce et Decorum Est

Bent double, like old beggars under sacks,
Knock-kneed, coughing like hags, we cursed
    through sludge,
Till on the haunting flares we turned our backs,
And towards our distant rest began to trudge.
Men marched asleep. Many had lost their boots,
But limped on, blood-shod. All went lame, all
    blind;
Drunk with fatigue; deaf even to the hoots
Of gas-shells dropping softly behind.

Gas! Gas! Quick, boys! - An ecstasy of fumbling,
Fitting the clumsy helmets just in time,
But someone still was yelling out and stumbling
And floundering like a man in fire or lime.
Dim through the misty panes and thick green
    light,
As under a green sea, I saw him drowning.

In all my dreams before my helpless sight
He plunges at me, guttering, choking, drowning.

If in some smothering dreams, you too could
pace
Behind the wagon that we flung him in,
And watch the white eyes writhing in his face,
His hanging face, like a devil's sick of sin;
If you could hear, at every jolt, the blood
Come gargling from the froth-corrupted lungs,
Bitter as the cud

Of vile, incurable sores on innocent tongues, -
My friend, you would not tell with such high zest
To children ardent for some desperate glory,
The old Lie: Dulce et decorum est
Pro patria mori.
(Wilfred Owen)

The memory of schoolchildren in Jerusalem, both Jewish and Palestinian, in the winter of 1991, will be filled with gas-masks. Fumbling to get them on in morning exercise brought dreams of horror that reechoed at night to air raid alerts to incoming Scuds. These masks, like those of Greek tragedy, symbolized our exaggerated fears that were our best response to exaggerated threats. The central meaning of holy war and just war reflection is to mute the propensity to war by amplifying its horror. All war is forbidden in Israel and for Islam—except holy war. Calling an unholy war holy does not make it so. It merely betrays our unbelief. The only war that is licit for modern humanity is just war. Calling a war unjust does not make it so. It merely betrays our poverty of conscience. At war's end the actual horror "plunging at us guttering, choking, drowning" should mingle with the good dreams of our own premonitions of death, fashioning a moral imagination that will study war no more. And when the speeches extol the nobility of peace achieved, order restored, and patriotism exhibited, let us remember silently the old lie: "Dulce et decorum est Pro patria mori."

Asleep

Under his helmet, up against his pack,
After the many days of work and waking,
Sleep took him by the brow and laid him back.
And in the happy no-time of his sleeping,
Death took him by the heart. There was a
    quaking
Of the aborted life within him leaping . . .
Then chest and sleepy arms once more fell slack.
And soon the slow, stray blood came creeping
From the intrusive lead, like ants on track.

Whether his deeper sleep lie shaded by the
    shaking

Of great wings, and the thoughts that hung the
     stars,
High-pillowed on calm pillows of God's making
Above these clouds, these rains, these sleets of
     lead,
And these winds' scimitars;
- Or whether yet his thin and sodden head
Confuses more and more with the low mould,
His hair being one with the grey grass
And finished fields of autumns that are old . . .
Who knows? Who hopes? Who troubles? Let it
     pass!
He sleeps. He sleeps less tremulous, less cold,
Than we who must awake, and waking, say
     Alas!

   The Gulf War was a war where a "Polack" from Chicago, a "bloke"
from Liverpool, and a "Frog" from St. Omer became Lawrence. The fiery
sand and starry, starry nights, the languid Gulf and billowed-smoke
edged clouds recalled for each Lawrence the swift camel-treks across the
Arabian desert or the fateful Sinai wanderings of another people
millennia before. "If I should die before I wake. . . " he prays each night
as he learned on his mother's knee. Will his "deeper sleep lie shaded by
the shaking of great wings . . . high-pillowed on calm pillows of God's
making . . . or will his thin and sodden head confuse more and more
with the low mould"? Who knows? The desert and clouds, the rains and
"sleets of lead" disclose the face of God! There will be foxhole
conversions and foxhole tombs. Resignation is his serenity and our
resolve. "He sleeps less tremulous, less cold, Than we who must awake."

The Unreturning

Suddenly night crushed out the day and hurled
Her remnants over cloud-peaks, thunder-
     walled.
Then fell a stillness such as harks appalled
When far-gone dead return upon the world.

There watched I for the Dead; but no ghost
     woke.
Each one whom Life exiled I named and called.
But they were all too far, or dumbed, or thralled;
And never one fared back to me or spoke.

Then peered the indefinite unshapen dawn
With vacant gloaming, sad as half-lit minds,
The weak-limned hour when sick men's sighs
    are drained.
And while I wondered on their being
    withdrawn,
Gagged by the smothering wing which none
    unbinds,
I dreaded even a heaven with doors so chained.[1]

The Chinese believe that the dead still linger with us. Christians affirm the communion of saints but scarcely believe it. We ought not seek the dead in seance but heed their sacrifice in renewed peacemaking. Let our Remembrance Sunday recite the living names we cherish. That we can't bring back Sam or Sarouk or tiny Fatima, who shuddered to her death on the cold hillside, can fashion in us a resolve to heal the wounds of war, to better know and love all of God's children, and dread a heaven with doors so chained.

Notes

1. *Collected Poems of Wilfred Owen,* ed. Edmund Blunden, London: Chatto and Windus, 1972, p. 46, 66, 69. Reprinted by permission of New Directions Publishing Corp.

References

Ajami, J. 1981. *The Arab Predicament.* Cambridge.

al-Jabbar, F.A. 1991. "Sword of Islam." *The Guardian*, Feb. 11, 1991.

Amanat, A. 1991. "A Dangerous Mess Is Left for the Almighty to Fix," *International Herald Tribune*, April 11, 1991.

American Friends Service Committee. 1967. *In Place of War: An Inquiry into Nonviolent National Defense.* New York: Grossman.

Amin, S.H. 1989. *The Legal System of Iraq.* Glasgow: Royston Publishers.

Aquinas, T. *Summa Theologica.* London: Blackfriars, 1972.

Augustine. *The City of God.* Translated by M. Dods. New York: Random House, 1950.

Aukerman, D. 1981. *Darkening Valley: A Biblical Perspective on Nuclear War.* New York: Seabury.

Bacon, F. 1624. *Touching a War with Spain.* In *Collected Works.* London: Pickering.

Bacon, F. 1865. "Of the True Greatness of Kingdomes and Estates." In *Essays*, W.A. Wright, ed. London: Knox Press.

Bainton, R.H. 1960. *Christian Attitudes Toward War and Peace: A Historical Survey and Critical Re-Evaluation.* New York: Abingdon Press.

Barnet, R.J. 1973. *The Roots of War.* Baltimore: Penguin Books.

Barth, K. 1961. *Church Dogmatics.* Edinburgh: T & T Clark.

Bartor, H. 1984. "The New Messiah." *Ma'ariv*, May 4, 1984.

Bathory, P.D. 1981. *Political Theory as Public Confession: The Social and Political Thought of St. Augustine of Hippo.* New Brunswick: Transaction Books.

Bennett, J.C. 1975. *The Radical Imperative: From Theology to Social Ethics.* Philadelphia: Westminster Press.

Bennett, J.C., ed. 1962. *Nuclear Weapons and the Conflict of Conscience.* New York: Scribner's.

Beres, L.R. 1982. *Apocalypse: Nuclear Catastrophe in World Politics.* Chicago: University of Chicago Press.

Berkhof, H. 1962. *Christ and the Powers.* Scottdale: Herald Press.

Berrigan, D. 1978. *Uncommon Prayer.* New York: Seabury.

Berrigan, P. 1978. *Of Beasts and Other Beastly Images: Essays Under the Bomb.* Portland: Sunburst Press.

Best, G. 1980. *Humanity in Warfare.* New York: Columbia University Press.

Beyer, L. 1991. "Three Ethical Dilemmas." *Time*, February 4, 1991.

Boettner, L. 1940. *The Christian Attitude Toward War*. Grand Rapids: Eerdmans.

Bondurant, J.V. 1958. *Conquest of Violence: The Gandhian Philosophy of Conflict*. Princeton: Princeton University Press.

Borosage, R. 1990. "The Peace Movement: Countering Bush's Gambit in the Gulf." *The Nation*, September 24, 1990.

Brock, P. 1968. *Pacifism in the United States: From the Colonial Era to the First World War*. Princeton: Princeton University Press.

Brodie, B. 1973. *War and Politics*. New York: Macmillan Company.

Bronowski, J. 1968. *The Face of Violence*. New York: The World Publishing Company.

Brown, P. 1969. *Augustine of Hippo*. Berkeley: University of California Press.

Brueggemann, W. 1976. *Living Toward a Vision: Biblical Reflections on Shalom*. Philadelphia: United Church Press.

Brzezinski, Z. 1991. "The U.S. Victor Has an Obligation to the Middle East," *International Herald Tribune*, April 22, 1991.

Brzezinski, Z. 1991. "U.S. Aid Dismissed over Iraq," *International Herald Tribune*, April 11, 1991.

Bush, G. 1991. "Remarks by the President in Address to the National Religious Broadcasters Convention," The Sheraton Washington Hotel, Washington, D.C., January 28, 1991. (Document supplied by the White House Office of the Press Secretary.)

Bush, G. 1991. "State of the Union." In *Vital Speeches of the Day*, vol. LVII, no. 9.

Calder, N. 1982. *Nuclear Nightmares: An Investigation into Possible Wars*. New York: Penguin Books.

Caldicott, H. 1981. *Nuclear Madness: What You Can Do*. London: Bantam Books.

Calvin, J. 1957. *The Institutes of the Christian Religion*. London: James Clarke Ltd.

Cassidy, R.J. 1978. *Jesus, Politics, and Society: A Study of Luke's Gospel*. Maryknoll: Orbis.

Childress, J.F. 1978. "Just War Theories: The Bases, Interrelations, Priorities, and Functions of Their Criteria." *Theological Studies* 39.

Church of England Working Party. 1982. *The Church and the Bomb*. London: Hodder and Stoughton.

Clancy, W., ed. *The Moral Dilemma of Nuclear Weapons*.

Clark, R.E.D. 1976. *Does the Bible Teach Pacifism?* New Malden: Fellowship of Reconciliation.

Clausewitz, Karl von. 1976. *On War*. Princeton: Princeton University Press.

Clouse, R., ed. 1981. *War: Four Christian Views.* Downers Grove: InterVarsity Press.

Cohen, A. and S. Lee, eds. 1986. *Nuclear Weapons and the Future of Humanity: The Fundamental Questions.* Totowa: Rowman & Allanheld.

Conrad, J. 1921. "Aristocracy and War." In *Notes on Life and Letters.* London: Littleworth.

Craigie, P.C. 1978. *The Problem of War in the Old Testament.* Grand Rapids: Eerdmans.

Crossman, R.H., ed. 1983. *The God That Failed.* Chicago: Regnery Gateway.

Cullmann, O. 1963. *The State in the New Testament.* London: SCM Press.

Curry, D.C., ed. 1984. *Evangelicals and the Bishops' Pastoral Letter.* Grand Rapids: Eerdmans.

Drinan, R.F. 1970. *Vietnam and Armageddon: Peace, War, and the Christian Conscience.* New York: Sheed and Ward.

Durnbaugh, D. 1978. *On Earth Peace.* Elgin: Brethren Press.

Ehrlich, P.R., C. Sagan, D. Kennedy, and W.O. Roberts. 1984. *The Cold and the Dark: The World After Nuclear War.* New York: W.W. Norton & Company.

Eller, V. 1980. *War and Peace: From Genesis to Revelation.* Scottdale: Herald Press.

Ellul, J. 1976. *The Ethics of Freedom.* Grand Rapids: Eerdmans.

Ellul, J. 1978. *Violence: Reflections from a Christian Perspective.* Oxford: Mowbray.

Elon, A. 1971. *The Israelis: Founders and Sons.* London: Weidenfeld and Nicholson.

Epstein, J. 1935. *The Catholic Tradition of the Law of Nations.* Washington: Catholic Assn. for International Peace.

Esposito, J.L. 1988. *Islam: The Straight Path.* Oxford: Oxford University Press.

Ferguson, J. 1973. *The Politics of Love: The New Testament and Non-Violent Revolution.* Cambridge: James Clarke and Co.

Ferguson, J. 1977. *War and Peace in the World's Religions.* London: Sheldon Press.

Finn, J. 1965. *Peace, the Churches, and the Bomb.* New York: Council on Religion and International Affairs.

Finn, J., ed. 1968. *A Conflict of Loyalties: The Case for Selective Conscientious Objection.* New York: Pegasus.

Fisk, R. 1991. "War Aims." *London Times Review of Books,* February 21, 1991.

Ford, H.P. and F.Y. Winters, eds. 1977. *Ethics and Nuclear Strategy.* Maryknoll: Orbis.

Frank, J.D. 1967. *Sanity and Survival: Psychological Aspects of War and Peace.* New York: Vintage.

Furnish, V.P. 1972. *The Love Command in the New Testament.* New York: Abingdon.

Gallie, W.B. 1978. *Philosophers of Peace and War: Kant, Clausewitz, Marx, Engels, and Tolstoy.* Cambridge: Cambridge University Press.

Gardiner, R.W. 1974. *The Cool Arm of Destruction: Modern Weapons and Moral Insensitivity.* Philadelphia: Westminster Press.

Gentili, A. 1933. *De Jure Belli: Libri Tres.* In *The Classics of International Law*, J.B. Scott, ed., trans. J.C. Rolfe. Oxford: Clarendon Press.

Gessert, R.A. and J.B. Hehir. 1976. *The New Nuclear Debate.* New York: Council on Religion and International Affairs.

Geyer, A. 1982. *The Idea of Disarmament: Rethinking the Unthinkable.* Elgin: Brethren Press.

Gibbs, N. 1991. "Life on the Line," *Time,* February 25, 1991.

Ginsberg, R., ed. 1969. *The Critique of War: Contemporary Philosophical Explorations.* Chicago: Henry Regnery Company.

Grannis, C., A. Laffin, and E. Schade. 1981. *The Risk of the Cross: Christian Discipleship in the Nuclear Age.* New York: Seabury.

Greet, K. 1982. *The Big Sun.* London: Marshall, Morgan, & Scott.

Gremillion, J., ed. 1976. *The Gospel of Peace and Justice: Catholic Social Teaching Since Pope John.* Maryknoll: Orbis.

Grotius, H. 1925. *The Rights of War and Peace.* Oxford: University Press.

Grotius, H. 1925. *De Jure Belli ac Pacis Libri Tres.* In *The Classics of International Law*, J.B. Scott, ed., trans. F.W. Kelsey, Oxford: Clarendon Press.

Guinan, E. 1973. *Peace and Nonviolence.* New York: Paulist.

Hallie, P. 1979. *Lest Innocent Blood Be Shed: The Story of the Village of Le Chambon and How Goodness Happened There.* London: Michael Joseph.

Hamilton, M.P., ed. 1977. *To Avoid Catastrophe: A Study in Future Nuclear Weapons Policy.* Grand Rapids: Eerdmans.

Harnack, A. 1981. *Militia Christi: The Christian Religion and the Military in the First Three Centuries.* Philadelphia: Fortress Press.

Hehir, J.B. 1978. "The Catholic Church and the Arms Race." *Worldview,* July-August 1978.

Helgeland, J., Robert J. Daly, and J. Patour Burns. 1985. *Christians and the Military: The Early Experience.* London: SCM Press.

Hiro, D. 1989. *Holy Wars: The Rise of Islamic Fundamentalism.* New York: Routledge, Chapman, and Hall.

Hirsch, R.G. 1974. *The Most Precious Gift: Peace in Jewish Tradition.* New York: Hebrew Congregations.

Hitti, P.K. 1966. *History of the Arabs.* New York: St. Martin's Press.

Hobbes, T. *Elements of Law*. Quoted in Richard Tuck, *Natural Rights Theories*. Cambridge: Cambridge University Press, 1979.

Hobbes, T. *Leviathan* . Quoted in Richard Tuck, *Natural Rights Theories*. Cambridge: Cambridge University Press, 1979.

Holmes, A.F., ed. 1975. *War and Christian Ethics*. Grand Rapids: Baker.

Hornus, J. 1980. *It Is Not Lawful for Me to Fight: Early Christian Attitudes Toward War, Violence, and the State*. Translated by A. Kreider and O. Coburn. Scottdale: Herald Press.

Hostetter, P., ed. 1974. *Perfect Love and War: A Dialogue on Christian Holiness and the Issues of War and Peace*. Nappanee: Evangel Press.

Howard, M., ed. 1979. *Restraints on War*. Oxford: Oxford University Press.

Hughes, T.P. 1965. *A Dictionary of Islam*. Clifton: Reference Book Publishers.

Hunter, A.A. 1958. *Christians in the Arena*. Nyack: Fellowship Publications.

Hunter, A.A. 1962. *Courage in Both Hands*. New York: Ballantine.

Johnson, J.T. 1975. *Ideology, Reason, and the Limitation of War: Religious and Secular Concepts, 1200-1740*. Princeton: Princeton University Press.

Johnson, J.T. 1981. *The Just War Tradition and the Restraint of War: A Moral and Historical Inquiry*. Princeton: Princeton University Press.

Johnson, J.T. 1983. "Grotius' Use of History and Charity in the Modern Transformations of the Just War Idea." In *Grotiana*, vol. 4.

Johnson, J.T. 1984. *Can Modern War Be Just?* New Haven: Yale University Press.

Johnson, P. 1978. *A History of Christianity*. Harmondsworth: Penguin Books.

Joseph, P. and S. Rosenblum, eds. 1984. *Search and Sanity*. Boston: South End Press.

Kant, I. 1902. "Idee zu Einer Allgemeinen Geschichte in Weltbürgerlicher Absicht." In *Gesammelte Schriften*. Berlin: Gurch Verlag.

Katz, A.M. 1982. *Life After Nuclear War*. Cambridge: Ballinger.

Keddie, N., ed. 1983. *Religion and Politics in Iran*. New Haven: Yale University Press.

Kennan, G. 1985. "Morality and Foreign Policy." Foreign Affairs 64, no. 3.

Khadduri, M. 1960. *Independent Iraq: A Study in Iraqi Politics from 1932 to 1958*. London: Oxford University Press.

Khadduri, M. 1969. *Republican Iraq: A Study in Iraqi Politics Since the Revolution of 1958*. London: Oxford University Press.

Khadduri, M. 1978. *Socialist Iraq: A Study in Iraqi Politics Since 1968.* Washington: The Middle East Institute.

Kirk, J.A. 1980. *Theology Encounters Revolution.* Leicester: InterVarsity Press.

Klassen, W. 1984. *Love of Enemies: The Way to Peace.* Philadelphia: Fortress Press.

Kownacki, M.L., ed. 1980. *A Race to Nowhere: An Arms Race Primer for Catholics.* Chicago: Pac Christi.

Kraybill, D. 1982. *Facing Nuclear War: A Plea for Christian Witness.* Scottdale: Herald Press.

Lasserre, J. 1962. *War and the Gospel.* Translated by O. Coburn. Scottdale: Herald Press.

Lawler, J.G. 1965. *Nuclear War: The Ethic, Rhetoric, the Reality: A Catholic Assessment.* Westminster: Newman Press.

Lens, S. 1978. *The Day Before Doomsday: An Anatomy of the Nuclear Arms Race.* Boston: Beacon Press.

Lewis, B., ed. 1974. *Islam: From the Prophet Muhammad to the Capture of Constantinople,* vol. I: Politics and War. Oxford: Oxford University Press.

Lider, J. 1977. *On the Nature of War.* Westmead: Saxon House.

Lider, J. 1979. *The Political and Military Laws of War.* Westmead: Saxon House.

Lifton, Robert J. 1991. "Techno-Bloodshed." *The Guardian,* February 14, 1991.

Lind, M.C. 1981. *Yahweh Is a Warrior: The Theology of Warfare in Ancient Israel.* Scottdale: Herald Press.

Long, E.L. 1968. *War and Conscience in America.* Philadelphia: Westminster Press.

Luard, E. 1986. *War in International Society,* London: L.B. Tauris Ltd.

Luard, E. 1988. *Conflict and Peace in the Modern International System.* New York: Macmillan Press.

Luther, M. 1883. *Werke.* Kritische Gesamtausgabe Weimar.

Maalory, A. 1984. *The Crusades Through Arab Eyes.* Schoecken.

Macgregor, G.H.C. 1960. *The New Testament Basis of Pacifism and the Relevance of an Impossible Ideal.* New York: Fellowship Publications.

Mayer, A.J. 1990. *Why Did the Heavens Not Darken? The Final Solution in History.* New York: Pantheon.

McSorley, R. 1979. *New Testament Basis of Peacemaking.* Washington: Centre for Peace Studies, Georgetown University.

Melzer, Y. 1975. *Concepts of Just War.* Leyden: A.W. Sijthoff.

Merton, T. 1968. *Faith and Violence.* Notre Dame: University of Notre Dame Press.

Merton, T., ed. 1962. *Breakthrough to Peace: Twelve Views on the Threat of Thermonuclear Extermination*. New York: New Directions.

Milford, T.R. 1967. *Christian Decision in the Nuclear Age*. Philadelphia: Fortress Press.

Miller, J. and Mylroie, L. 1990. *Saddam Hussein and the Crisis in the Gulf*. New York: Times Books/Random House.

Miller, W.R. 1964. *Nonviolence: A Christian Interpretation*. New York: Association Press.

Montesquieu. 1940. *The Spirit of the Laws*. New York: Harper.

Morris, L. 1976. *The Cross in the New Testament*. Exeter: Paternoster Press.

Mouw, R. 1980. *Called to Holy Worldliness*. Philadelphia: Fortress Press.

Nagle, W. 1960. *Morality and Modern Warfare*. Baltimore: Helicon.

Naipaul, V.S. 1981. *Among the Believers: An Islamic Journey*. London: Andre Deutsch.

Niebuhr, R. 1935. *An Interpretation of Christian Ethics*. New York: Harper.

Niebuhr, R. 1946. *Christianity and Power Politics*. New York: Scribner's.

Niebuhr, R. 1951. *Christ and Culture*. New York: Harper and Row.

O'Brien, W.V. 1967. *Nuclear War, Deterrence, and Morality*. New York: Newman Press.

O'Brien, W.V. 1981. *The Conduct of a Just and Limited War*. New York: Praeger.

O'Brien, W.V. and J. Langan, eds. 1986. *The Nuclear Dilemma and the Just War Tradition*. Lexington: Lexington Books.

O'Donovan, O. 1989. *Peace and Certainty*. Grand Rapids: Eerdmans .

Osterle, W.H. and J. Donaghy, eds. 1980. *Peace Theology and the Arms Race: Readings on Arms and Disarmament*. College Theology Society, 1980.

Owen, W. 1972. *Collected Poems of Wilfred Owen*. ed. Edmund Blunden. London: Chatto and Windus.

Paterson, W.P. 1922. "War." *Hastings Encyclopaedia of Religion and Ethics*. New York: Charles Scribner's Sons.

Peters, F.E. 1984. "The Early Muslim Empires: Umayyads, Abbasids, Fatimids." In *Islam: The Religions and Political Life of a World Community*. Marjorie Kelly, ed. New York: Praeger.

Peters, R. 1989. "Jihad." In *The Encyclopedia of Religion,,* Mircea Eliade, ed. New York: Macmillan Press.

Physicians for Social Responsibility. 1981. *The Final Epidemic: The Medical Consequences of Nuclear Weapons and Nuclear War*. Chicago: Educational Foundation for Nuclear Science.

Piper, J. 1979. *"Love Your Enemies": Jesus' Love Command in the Synoptic Gospels and in the Early Christian Paraenesis.* Cambridge: Cambridge University Press.

Rad, G. von. 1947. *Deuteronomium Studien.* Göttingen: Vandenhoeck.

Rad, G. von. 1951. *Der Heilige Krieg.* Göttingen: Vandenhoeck.

Rahman, F. 1966. *Islam.* New York: Holt, Rinehart and Winston.

Rahman, F. 1987. *Health and Medicine in the Islamic Tradition.* New York: Crossroad Press.

Ramsey, P. 1961. *War and the Christian Conscience: How Shall Modern War Be Conducted Justly?* Durham: Duke University Press.

Ramsey, P. 1968. *The Just War.* New York: Scribner's.

Ramsey, P. 1973. "A Political Ethics Context for Strategic Thinking." In *Strategic Thinking and Its Moral Implication,.* Eds., M. Kaplan. Chicago: University of Chicago Centre for Policy Study.

Ramsey, P. 1983. *The Just War: Force and Political Responsibility.* Lanham: University Press of America.

Rankin, W.W. 1981. *The Nuclear Arms Race: Countdown to Disaster: A Study in Christian Ethics.* Cincinnati: Forward Movement Publishers.

Raven, C.E. 1951. *The Theological Basis of Christian Pacifism.* New York: Fellowship Publications.

Rees, D. 1964. *Korea: The Limited War.* New York: St. Martin's Press.

Rockman, J., ed. 1979. *Peace in Search of Makers: Riverside Church Reverse the Arms Race Convocation.* Valley Forge: Judson Press.

Rogers, P. 1981. *As Lambs to the Slaughter.* London: Arrow.

Rohr, J.A. 1971. *Prophets Without Honor: Public Policy and the Selective Conscientious Objector.* Nashville: Abingdon.

Russett, B.M. 1972. "Short of Nuclear Madness." *Worldview,* April 1972.

Rutenber, C.G. 1950. *The Dagger and the Cross: An Examination of Christian Pacifism.* New York: Fellowship Publications, 1950.

Said, E.W. 1981. *Covering Islam: How the Media and the Experts Determine How We See the Rest of the World.* New York: Pantheon.

Saint-Exupéry, Antoine de. 1965. *A Sense of Life.* New York: Funk and Wagnalls.

Sakharov, A.D. 1968. *Progress, Coexistence and Intellectual Freedom.* New York: W.W. Norton.

Schelling, T.C. 1966. *Arms and Influence.* New Haven: Yale University Press.

Schnell, J. 1982. *The Fate of the Earth.* New York: Knopf.

Schrag, M.H. and J.K. Stoner. *The Ministry of Reconciliation.* Nappanee: Evangel Press.

Scott, J.B., ed. 1944. "Selections from Three Works of Francisco Suarez." In *The Classics of International Law.* Oxford: Clarendon.

Seifert, H. 1965. *Conquest by Suffering.* Philadelphia: Westminster Press.

Shannon, T.A. 1980. *War or Peace? The Search for New Answers.* Maryknoll: Orbis.

Sharp, G. 1970. *Exploring Non-Violent Alternatives.* Boston: Porter Sargent Publishers.

Sharp, G. 1975. *Making the Abolition of War a Realistic Goal.* Boston: Porter Sargent Publishers.

Shelly, M. 1979. *New Call for Peacemakers: A New Call to Peacemaking Study Guide.* Newton: Faith and Life Press.

Sider, R. and R. Taylor. 1982. *Nuclear Holocaust and Christian Hope: A Book for Christian Peacemakers.* Downers Grove: InterVarsity Press.

Starke, J.G. 1989. *Introduction to International Law.* London: Butterworths.

Stein, W., ed. 1961. *Nuclear Weapons and Christian Conscience.* London: Merlin Press.

Stone, R.H. and D. Wilbanks. 1985. *The Peacemaking Struggle: Militarism and Resistance.* New York: University Press of America.

Swartley, W. 1983. *Slavery, Sabbath, War and Women.* Scottdale: Herald Press.

Teichman, J. 1986. *Pacifism and the Just War.* Oxford: Basil Blackwell.

Tripp, C. 1991. "The Abuses That Led to War." *Times Literary Supplement,* January 25, 1991.

Tucker, R.W. 1979. *The Just War: A Study of Contemporary American Doctrine.* London: Greenwood Press.

Wallis, J. 1981. *Call to Conversion.* New York: Harper & Row.

Wallis, J., ed. 1982. *Waging Peace: A Handbook in the Struggle to Abolish Nuclear Weapons.* San Francisco: Harper & Row.

Walters, L.B. 1971. "Five Classic Just War Theories: A Study in the Thought of Aquinas, Vitoria, Suarez, Gentili, and Grotious." Unpublished Ph.D. dissertation, Yale University.

Walzer, M. 1977. *Just and Unjust Wars.* New York: Basic Books.

Wasserstrom, R., ed. 1970. *War and Morality.* Belmont: Wadsworth Publishing Company.

Watt, W.M. 1988. *Classic Fundamentalism and Modernity.* London: Routledge.

Weigel, G. 1987. *Tranquillitas Ordinas.* New York: Oxford University Press.

Weiler, G. 1988. *Jewish Theocracy.* Leiden: E. J. Brill.

Woodward, T. 1991. *The Commanders.* New York: Simon & Schuster.

Woolsey, R.J., ed. 1984. *Nuclear Arms: Ethics, Strategy, Politics.* San Francisco: Institute for Contemporary Studies.

Wright, E.G. 1953. *The Interpreters Bible.* Nashville: Abingdon.

Wright, R. 1985. *Sacred Rage: The Wrath of Militant Islam.* New York: Simon & Schuster.

Yoder, J.H. 1972. *Nevertheless.* Scottdale: Herald Press.

Yoder, J.H. 1972. *The Politics of Jesus.* Grand Rapids: Eerdmans.

Yoder, J.H. 1984. *When War Is Unjust.* Minneapolis: Augsburg.

Yoder, J.H. *The Christian Witnesses to the State.* Newton: Faith and Life Press.

Zahn, G.C. 1963. *An Alternative to War.* New York: Council on Religion and International Affairs.

Zahn, G.C. 1967. *War, Conscience, and Dissent.* New York: Hawthorn Books.

Zimmerli, W. and J. Jeremias. 1957. *The Servant of God.* Naperville: Alec R. Allenson.

About the Book and Author

The war on the ground and in the air over Kuwait and Iraq was not the only Gulf War being fought in early 1990. George Bush and Saddam Hussein were also battling for public opinion and for the perception of legitimacy for their actions. In this effort, both men as well as their spokespersons appealed to the just war theory of their religious traditions.

In this perceptive and wide-ranging book, Kenneth Vaux elucidates the great just war traditions of Judaism, Christianity, and Islam, evaluating the key events of the war in light of the religious rhetoric used by both sides. From the first stirrings of conflict to its uncertain aftermath, religious and ethical traditions played a major role in winning support not just for the U.S. and Iraqi peoples but of public opinion worldwide. Throughout Vaux demonstrates the wide gaps between religious rhetoric and the political-military action it has been called on to support.

Ethics and the Gulf War is not a typical ethical treatise; Vaux understands ethical reflection to encompass history, philosophy, psychology, ecology, theology, and eschatology. His book is a valuable contribution to the understanding of the Gulf War, and it is fascinating for scholars and laypersons coming to this subject from almost any area of interest.

Kenneth L. Vaux is professor of ethics in the program in Medical Humanities at the University of Illinois at Chicago.

Index

Bible References Index